Pow[illegible] for W[illegible]ndows VisiRef

Susan P. Stover

QUE

PowerPoint 4 for Windows VisiRef

Library of Congress Catalog No.: 94-66543

ISBN: 1-56529-862-4

96 95 94 6 5 4 3 2 1

Interpretation of the printing code: the rightmost double-digit number is the year of the book's printing; the rightmost single-digit number, the number of the book's printing. For example, a printing code of 94-1 shows that the first printing of the book occurred in 1994.

Screen reproductions in this book were created with Collage Plus from Inner Media, Inc., Hollis, NH.

Publisher: David P. Ewing

Associate Publisher: Corinne Walls

Publishing Director: Lisa A. Bucki

Managing Editor: Anne Owen

Product Marketing Manager: Greg Wiegand

Credits

Acquisitions Editor
Nancy Stevenson

Product Directors
Jim Minatel
Chris Nelson

Production Editor
Chris Nelson

Technical Editor
Lisa Lynch

Book Designer
Amy Peppler-Adams

Cover Designers
Dan Armstrong
Amy Peppler-Adams

Production Team
Stephen Adams
Claudia Bell
Anne Dickerson
Teresa Forrester
Joelynn Gifford
Bob LaRoche
Beth Lewis
Tim Montgomery
Nanci Sears Perry
Michael Thomas
Dennis Sheehan
Sue VandeWalle
Mary Beth Wakefield
Lillian Yates

Indexer
Charlotte Clapp

Composed in *Stone Serif* and *MCPdigital* by Que Corporation

About the Author

Susan Parker Stover has been writing documentation and training manuals for the last six years. During that time, she has written manuals for DacEasy, Inc., and the Texas Education Agency regional service centers. She is the author of Que's *Freelance Graphics for Windows QuickStart* and has assisted in the production of several other Que books on PowerPoint for Windows. Susan lives in Spicewood, Texas, with her husband, Scott, and her son, Parker.

Trademark Acknowledgments

Contents

How To Use This Book

Welcome to a revolutionary concept in quick references! Unlike traditional pocket references, which usually pack a lot of text on the page but few, if any, illustrations, the *VisiRef* series presents nearly all its "how-to" information *visually*. You'll find all the essential tasks here, color-coded and organized alphabetically by task category. Use the color-coded sections to quickly locate the task you need to find, follow the full-color screen shots to see each step in the process, and then complete the task yourself. If you're someone who prefers to learn or recall information by being *shown* how a task is accomplished, Que's *VisiRef* series is well matched to your needs. The *VisiRef* series is the perfect complement to today's graphical software. You don't have to read a lot of text to find the reference information you need.

Each page provides the following information:

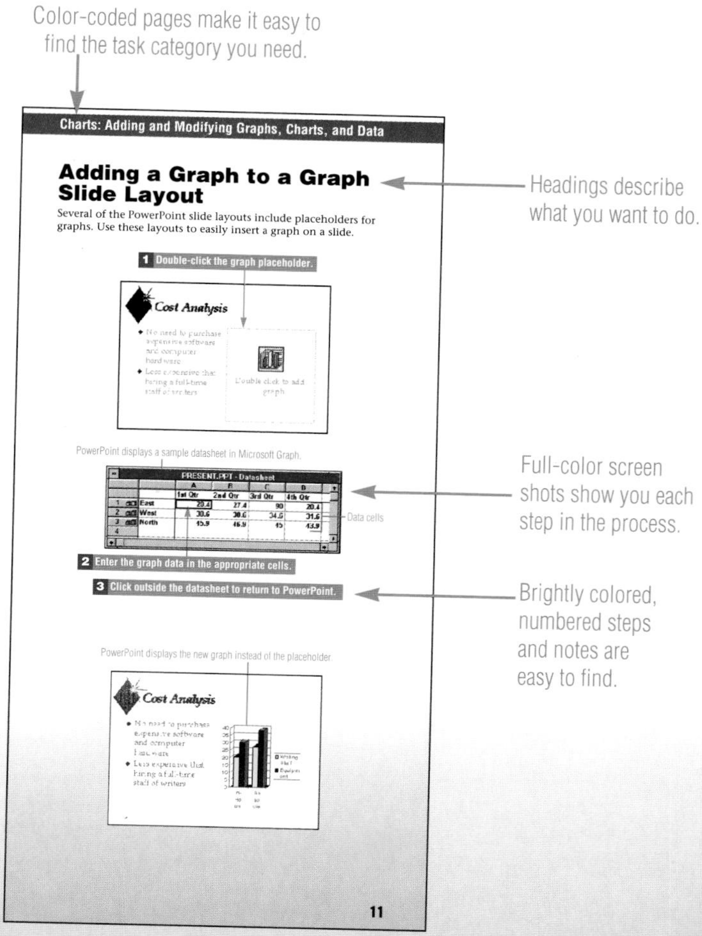
Color-coded pages make it easy to find the task category you need.
Charts: Adding and Modifying Graphs, Charts, and Data
Adding a Graph to a Graph Slide Layout
Several of the PowerPoint slide layouts include placeholders for graphs. Use these layouts to easily insert a graph on a slide.
1 Double-click the graph placeholder.
Cost Analysis
PowerPoint displays a sample datasheet in Microsoft Graph.
PRESENT.PPT - Datasheet
Data cells
2 Enter the graph data in the appropriate cells.
3 Click outside the datasheet to return to PowerPoint.
PowerPoint displays the new graph instead of the placeholder.
Cost Analysis
11
Headings describe what you want to do.
Full-color screen shots show you each step in the process.
Brightly colored, numbered steps and notes are easy to find.

UNDO

NEW

SLIDE VIEW

Starting PowerPoint

The first step to creating a winning presentation is to start PowerPoint for Windows.

1 Double-click the program group containing the PowerPoint icon.

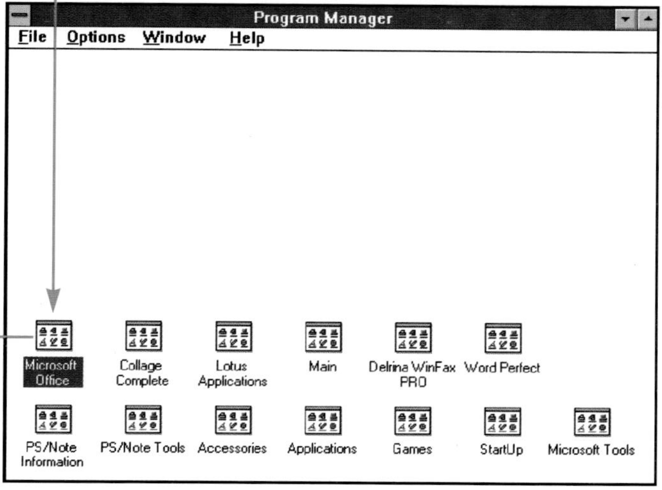

The default program is Microsoft Office.

2 Double-click the PowerPoint program icon.

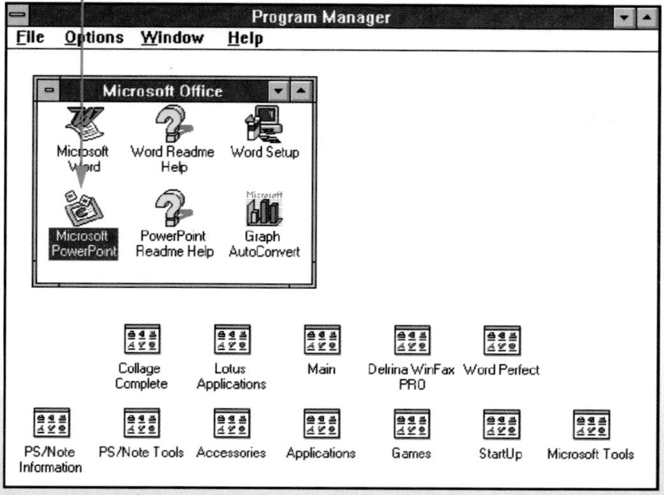

Opening a New Presentation

When you start PowerPoint for Windows, the startup dialog box appears. You can use this dialog box to start a new presentation file. You also can use the New File icon to start a new presentation.

To open a new file from the PowerPoint startup dialog box

1 Select a method for creating a presentation—use Template here.

2 Choose OK.

Lets you start without a background
Lets you select a predefined look
Helps you define the look and style
Helps you organize content

3 Select a presentation template. You can select a template directory here.

4 Choose Apply.

5 Select a layout.

6 Choose OK.

4

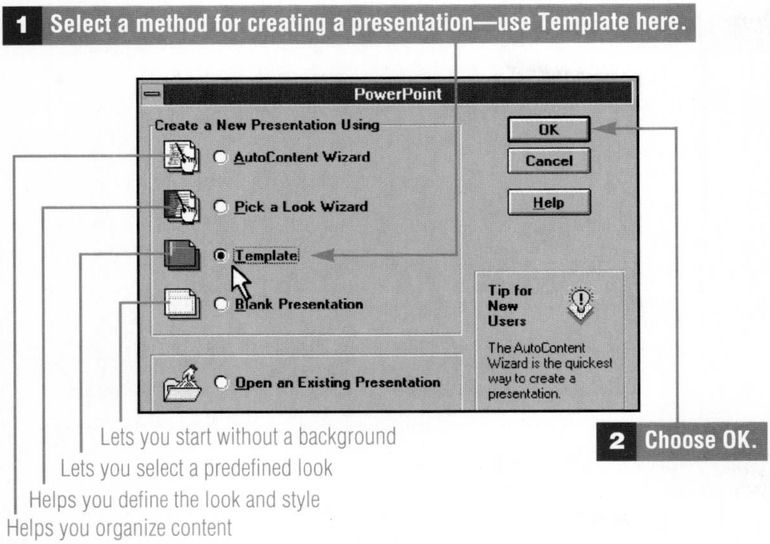

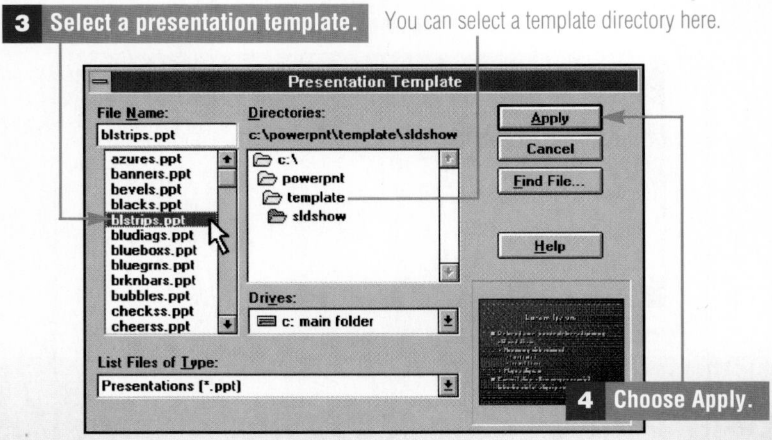

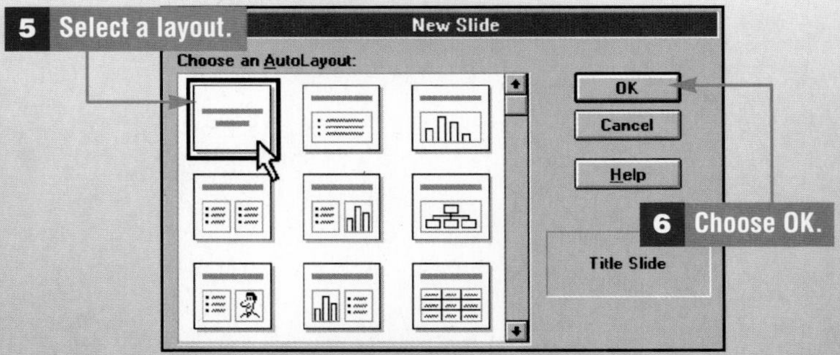

To open a new file using the New File button

1 Click the New File button.

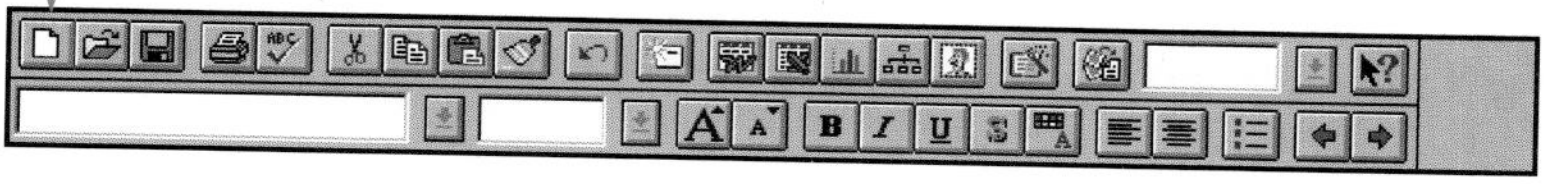

2 Select a method for creating a presentation—use Template here.

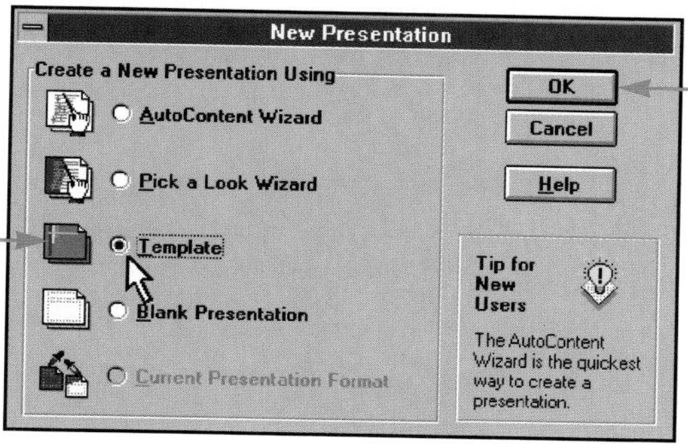

3 Choose OK.

4 Select a presentation template.

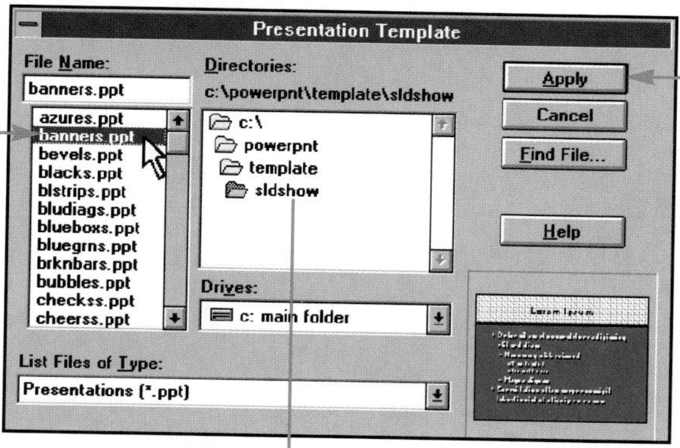

You can select a template directory here.

5 Choose Apply.

6 Select a layout.

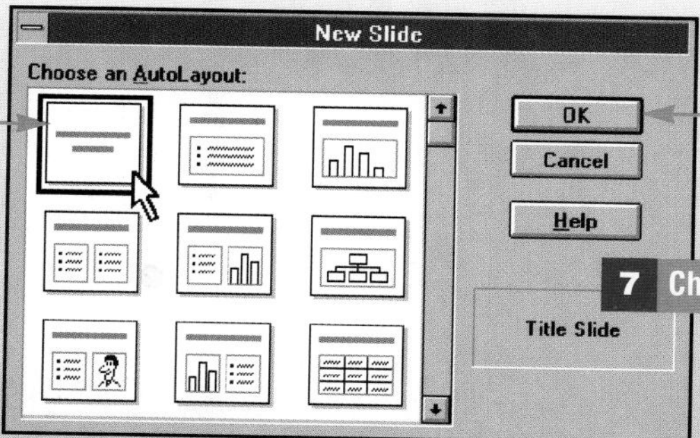

7 Choose OK.

Entering Text in Text Placeholders

Most of the slide layouts in PowerPoint provide you with predefined text areas. These text placeholders allow you to enter text quickly and easily on a slide without having to worry about placing and formatting the text.

1 Click the placeholder where you want to enter text.

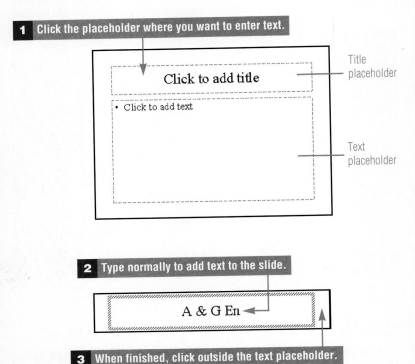

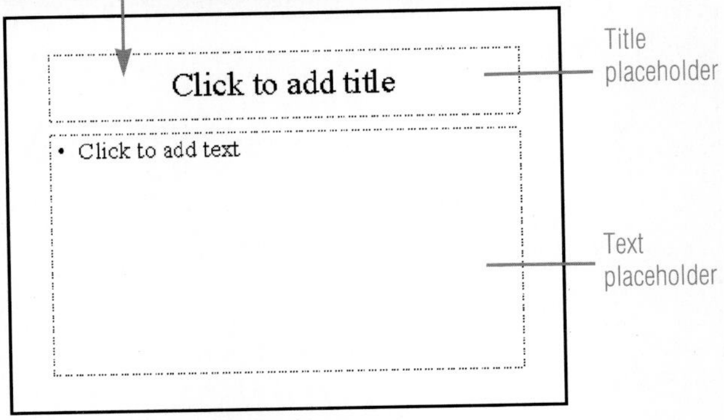

2 Type normally to add text to the slide.

3 When finished, click outside the text placeholder.

The text you typed replaces the placeholder prompt.

Undoing Mistakes

If you delete text by mistake, or make another change to your slide that you don't want, you can use the Undo feature to reverse your last action. Some actions, however, cannot be undone. The Undo feature works only when the last action is one that can be reversed.

1 Click the Undo button.

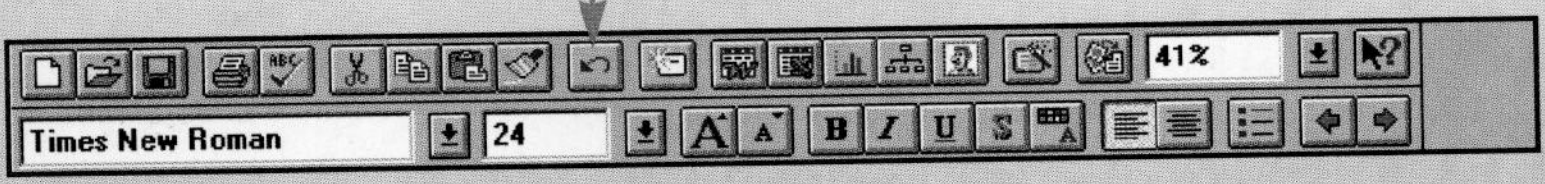

Moving among Slides

Once you create a presentation and begin adding new slides, you need to be able to navigate through the slides in your presentation. There are different methods for moving through the slides in your presentation.

1 Click and drag the scroll box to select the slide you want to view.

Current slide number

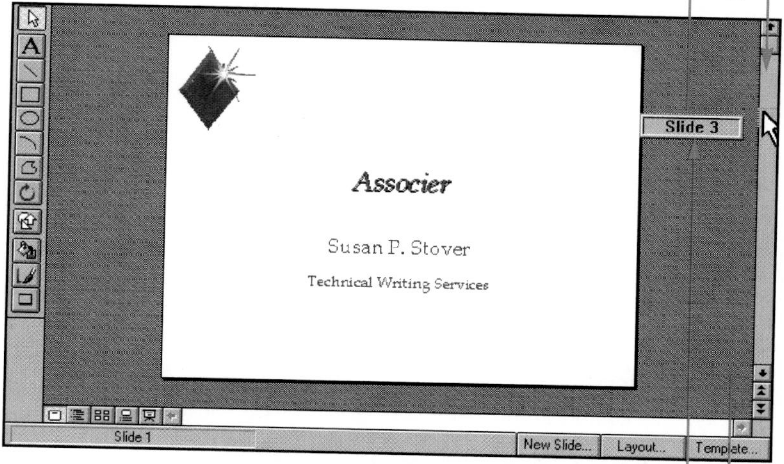

2 Release the mouse button at the desired slide.

You can click Previous Slide or Next Slide to display another slide.

Switching Viewing Options

The default view in PowerPoint is Slide view, in which you see one slide at a time. Other viewing options let you look at your presentation from different perspectives.

To switch to Outline view

Slide view

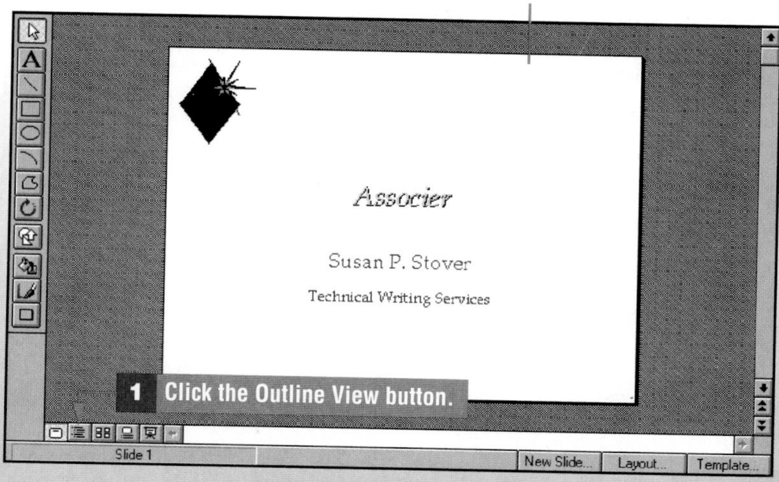

1 Click the Outline View button.

more ▶

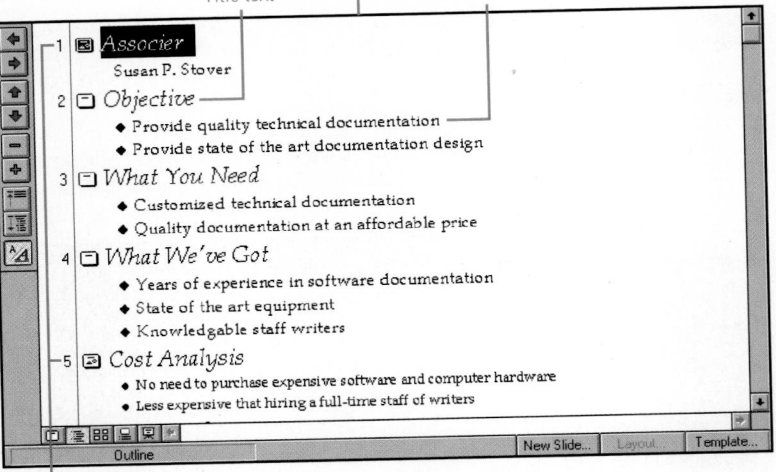

The text in the title and text placeholders appears in outline format.

To switch to Slide Sorter view

1 Click the Slide Sorter View button.

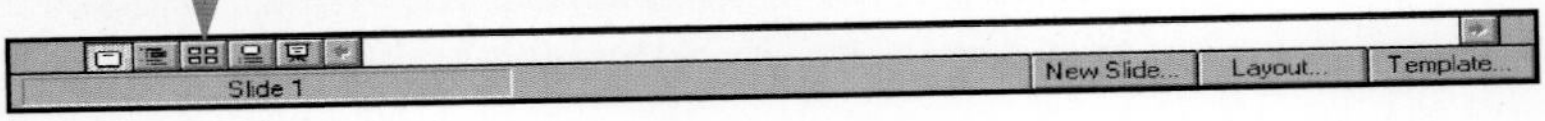

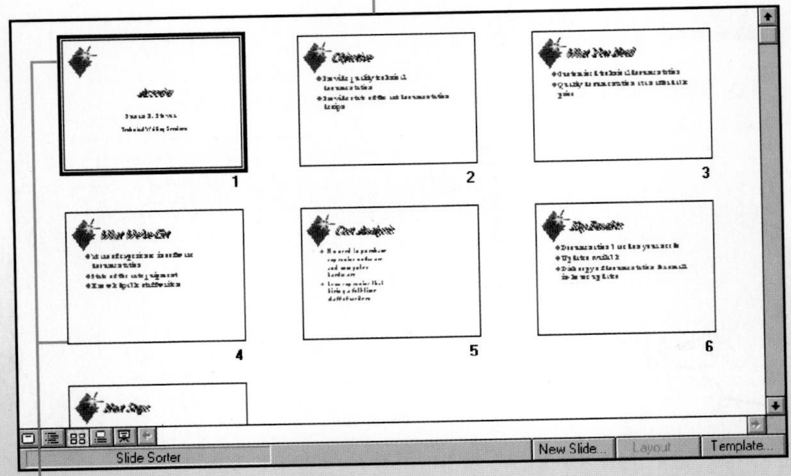

Miniatures of each slide appear in the PowerPoint window.

To switch to Notes Page view

1 Click the Notes Page View button.

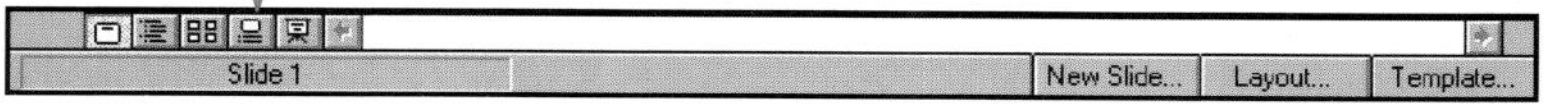

The current slide and the notes placeholder appear in the window.

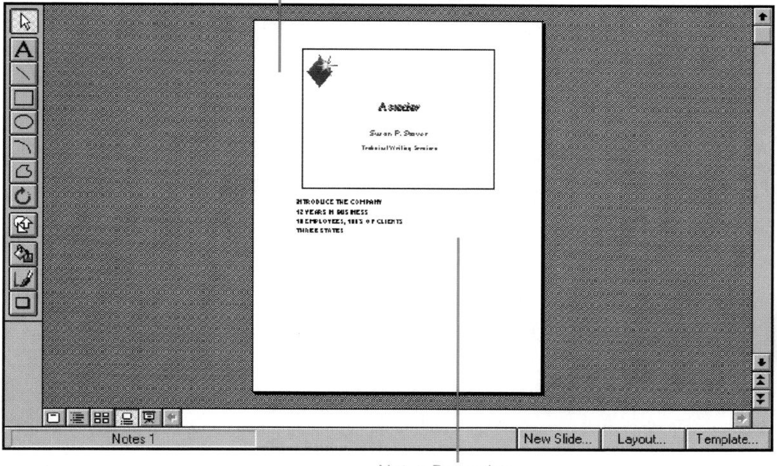

Notes Page view

To switch to Slide view from Outline or Slide Sorter view

1 Select the slide to display in Slide view.

The dark outline indicates the selected slide in Slide Sorter view.

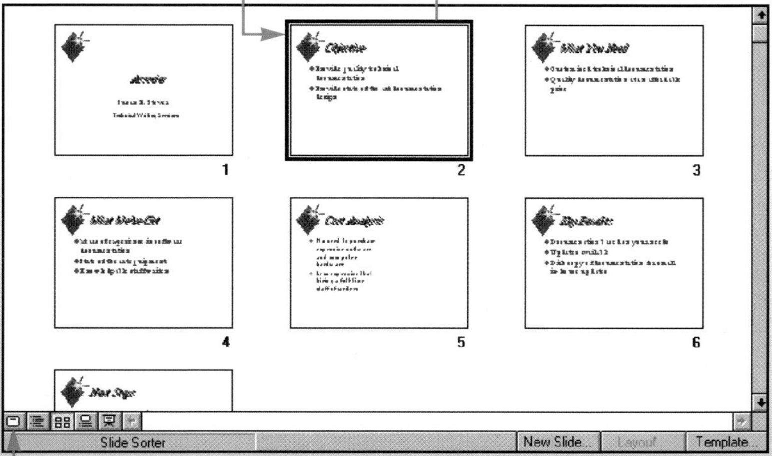

2 Click the Slide View button.

more ▶

The selected slide appears in Slide view.

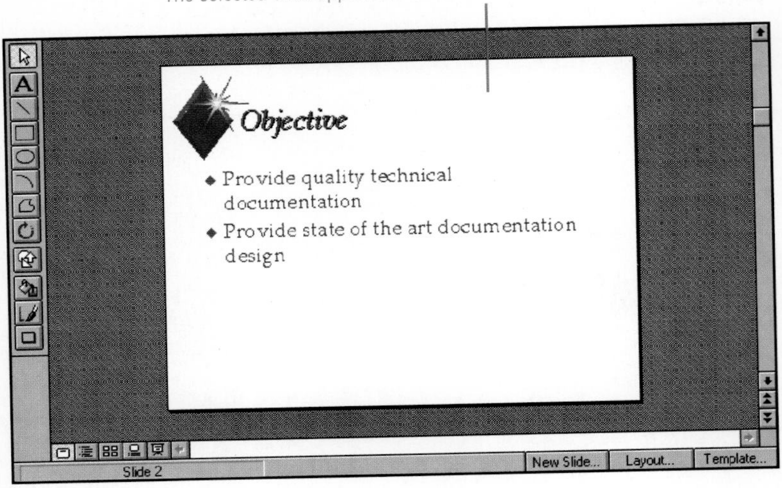

To switch to Slide view from Notes Page view

1 Click the Slide View button.

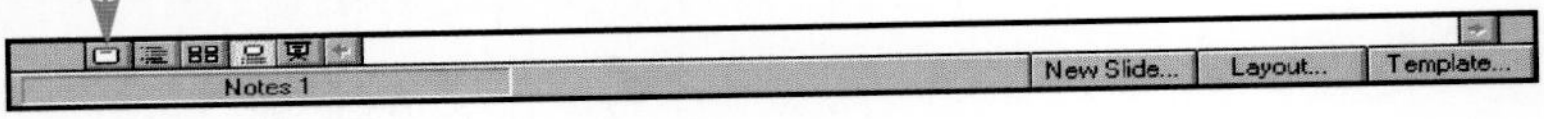

The current slide appears in Slide view.

Adding a Graph to a Graph Slide Layout

Several of the PowerPoint slide layouts include placeholders for graphs. Use these layouts to easily insert a graph on a slide.

1 Double-click the graph placeholder.

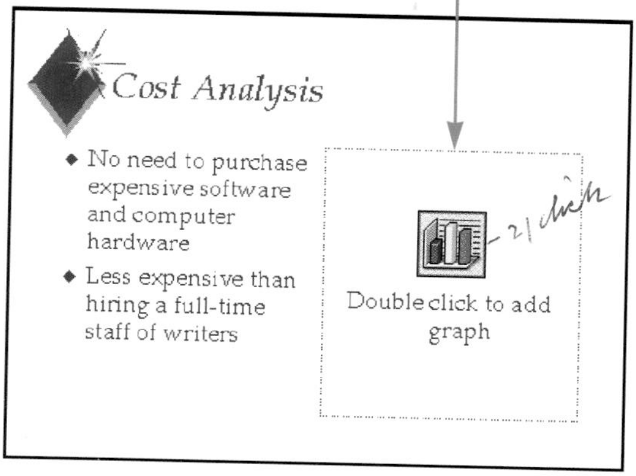

PowerPoint displays a sample datasheet in Microsoft Graph.

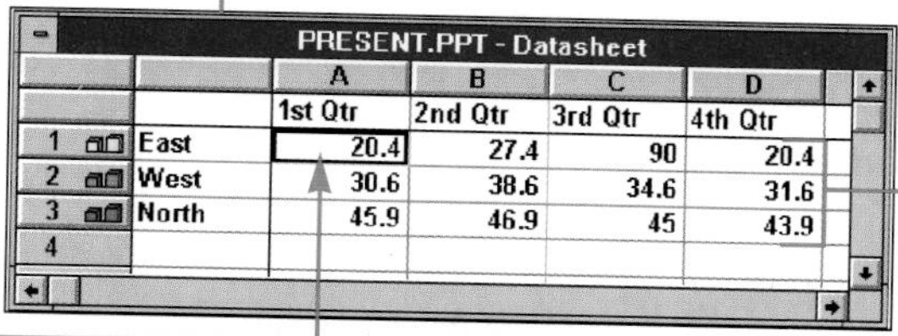
PRESENT.PPT - Datasheet
A B C D
1st Qtr 2nd Qtr 3rd Qtr 4th Qtr
1 East 20.4 27.4 90 20.4
2 West 30.6 38.6 34.6 31.6
3 North 45.9 46.9 45 43.9
4

Data cells

2 Enter the graph data in the appropriate cells.

3 Click outside the datasheet to return to PowerPoint.

PowerPoint displays the new graph instead of the placeholder.

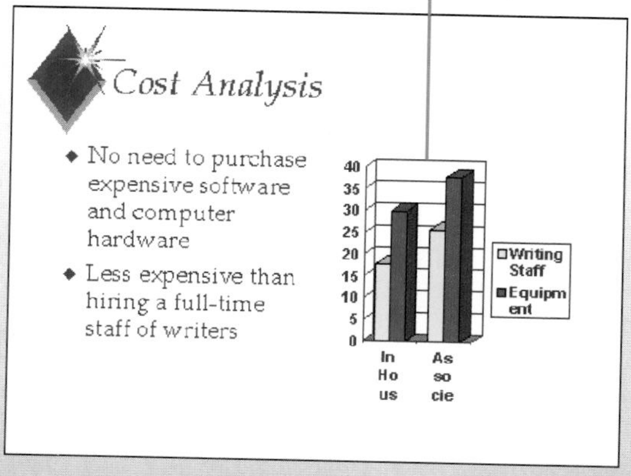

Adding a Graph to Any Slide

In addition to adding graphs to slides with placeholders, you can add a graph to any slide in your presentation. After you insert the graph, you can move it and size it as necessary.

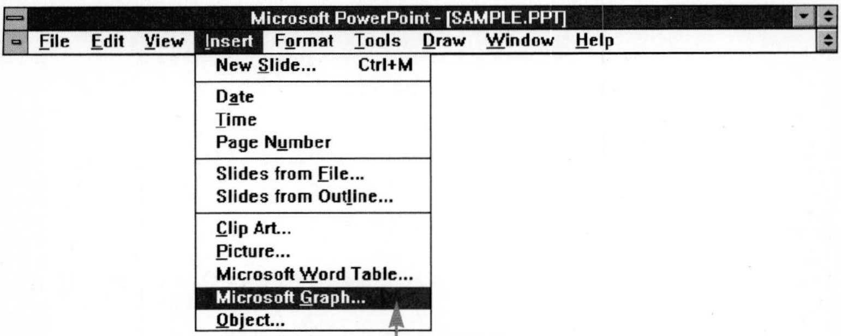

1 Choose Insert, Microsoft Graph.

2 Enter your graph data in the sample datasheet.

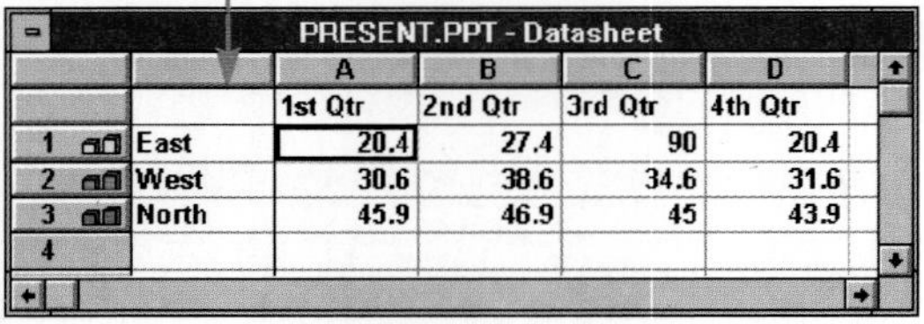

3 Click anywhere outside the datasheet to return to PowerPoint.

Entering Graph Data

When creating a graph, the datasheet window allows you to enter your data for the graph.

1 Click the cell where you want to enter data.

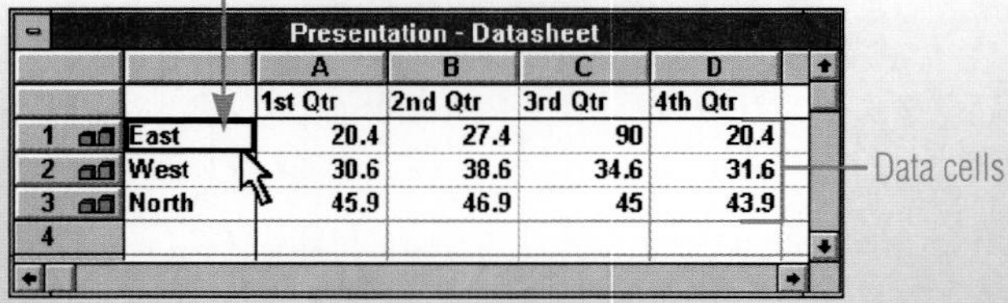

2 Type normally to enter data.

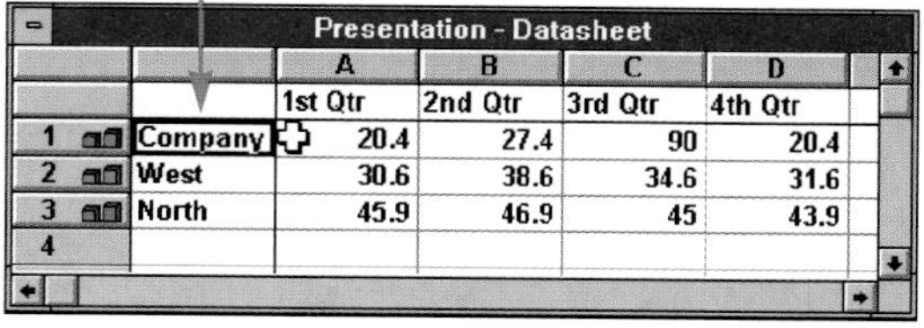

3 Click outside the datasheet to close the window.

Editing Graph Data

You can enter additional data or edit existing data for the graph at any time.

1 Double-click the graph.

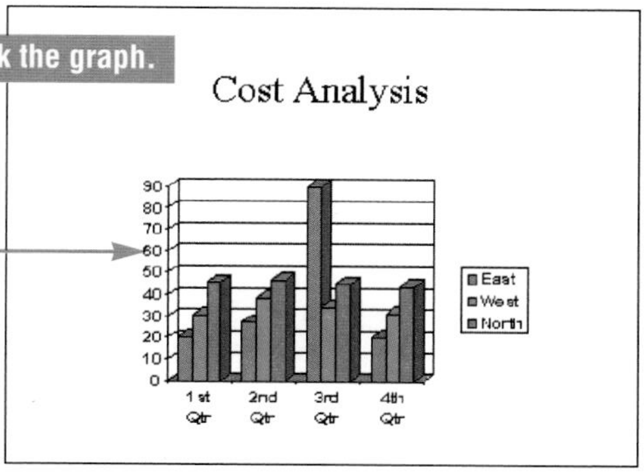

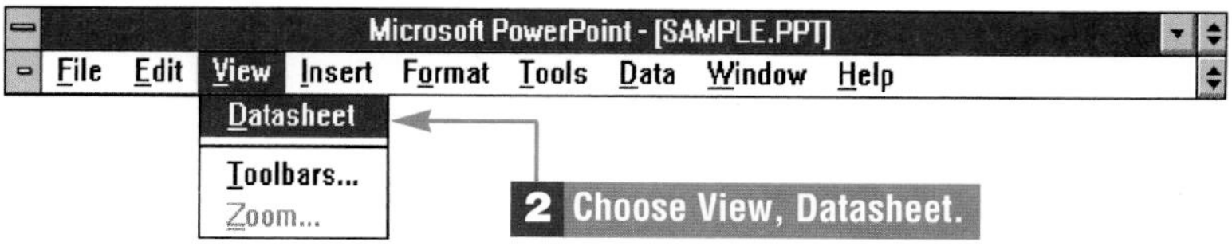

2 Choose View, Datasheet.

3 Click the cell to edit.

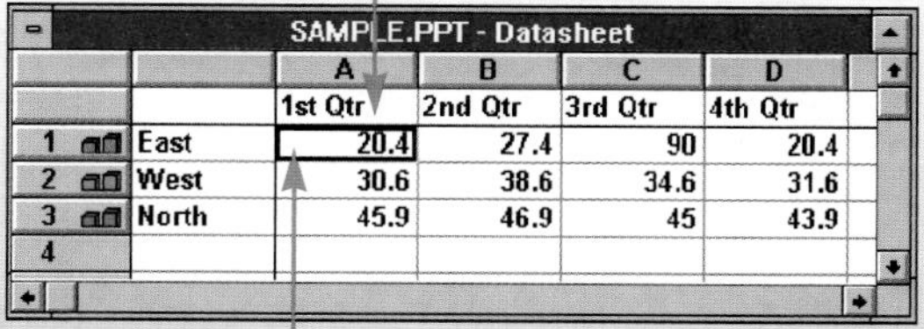

4 Type the graph data.

5 Click outside the datasheet to return to PowerPoint.

Selecting a New Graph Type

Once you insert a graph in a PowerPoint slide, you can change the graph type any time. This lets you look at your data presented in different ways and select the graph type that looks best.

1 Double-click the graph.

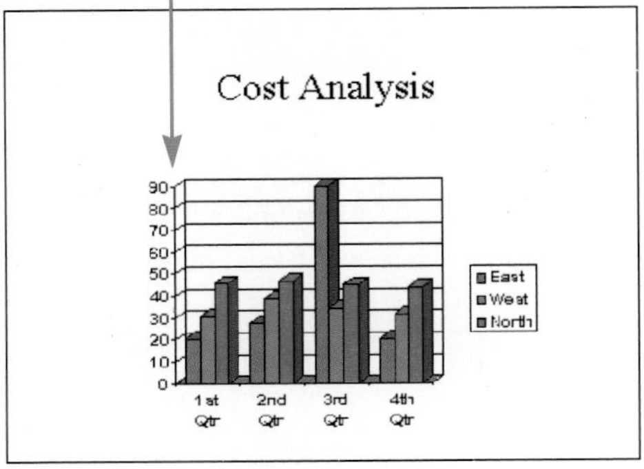

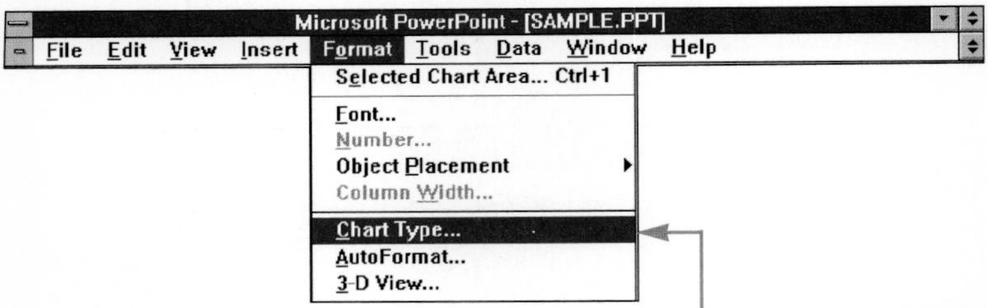

2 Choose Format, Chart Type.

3 Select the Chart Dimension.

4 Select the desired chart type.

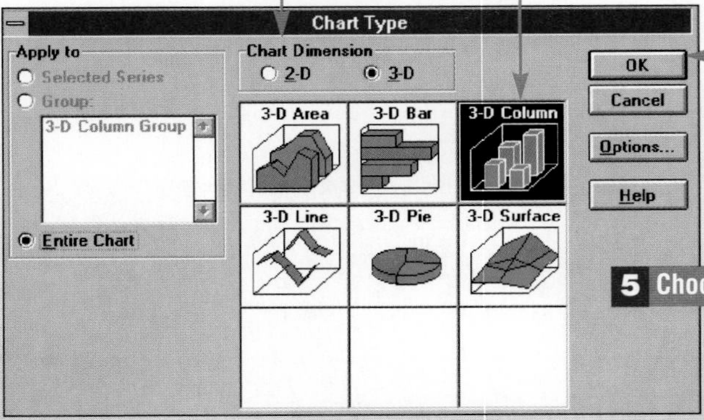

5 Choose OK.

Resizing a Graph

Once you create a graph on a presentation slide, you can size that graph to any dimension.

Use the left and right handles to change width.

Use the top and bottom handles to change height.

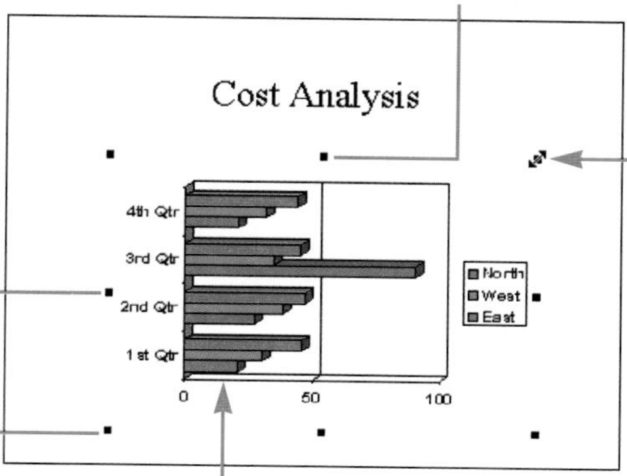

Use the corner handles to change height and width.

1 Select the graph to resize.

2 Position the mouse pointer on one of the handles.

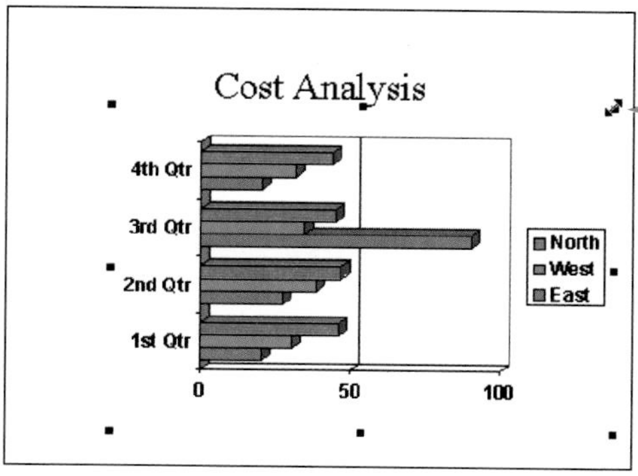

3 Click and drag the handle to resize the graph.

4 Release the mouse button.

Formatting Graphs

When you insert a graph on a slide, PowerPoint uses the default colors and graph format. You can make changes to the graph format and colors at any time.

To change the graph format

1 Double-click the graph.

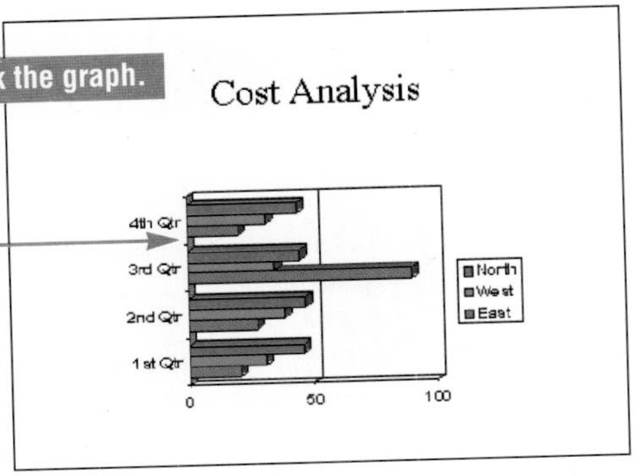

2 Choose Format.

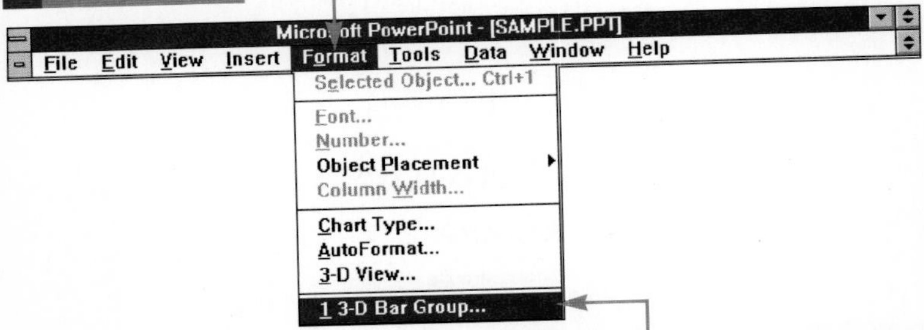

3 Choose the current chart format command at the bottom of the menu.

4 Click the Subtype tab.

Variations of the selected chart type

5 Select the Subtype of your choice.

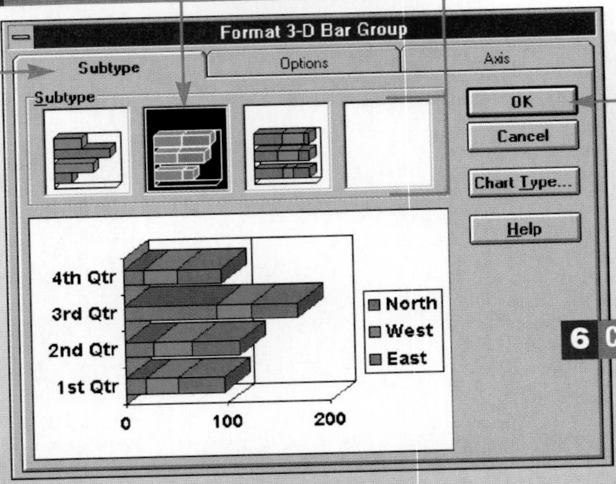

6 Choose OK.

To ch ge the color of a graph element

1 Double-click the graph.

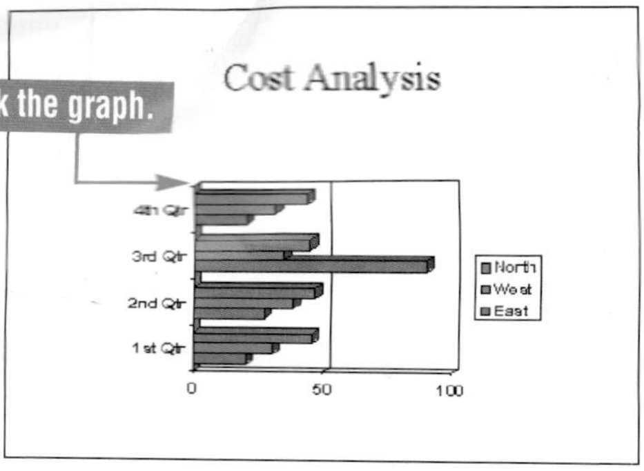

2 Double-click the graph element whose color you want to change.

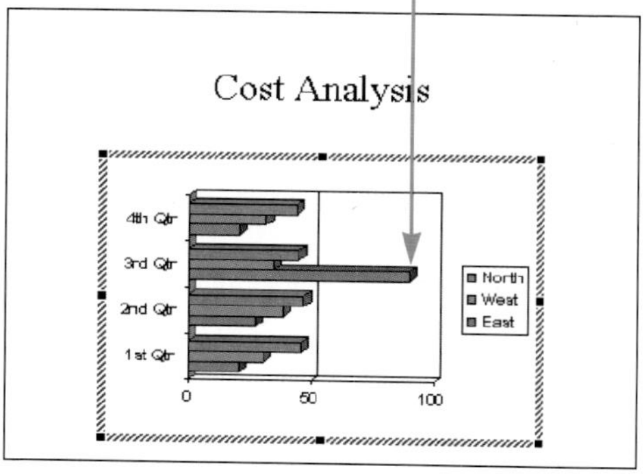

3 Click the Patterns tab if necessary.

4 Select the coloring options for the graph element.

Select Automatic to stay within a color scheme.

5 Choose OK.

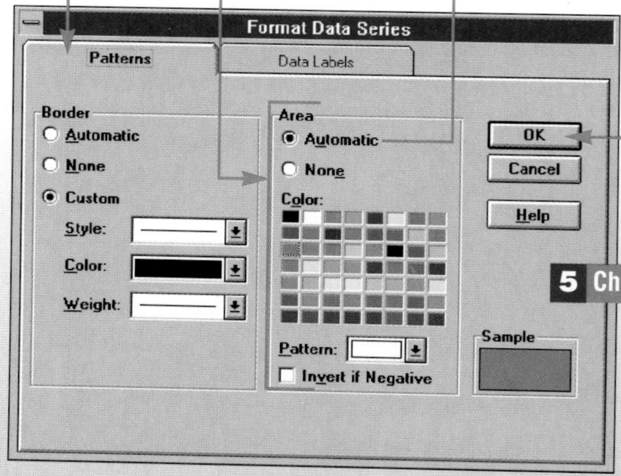

To change the format of any graph e... nt

1 Double-click the graph element to format—the legend here.

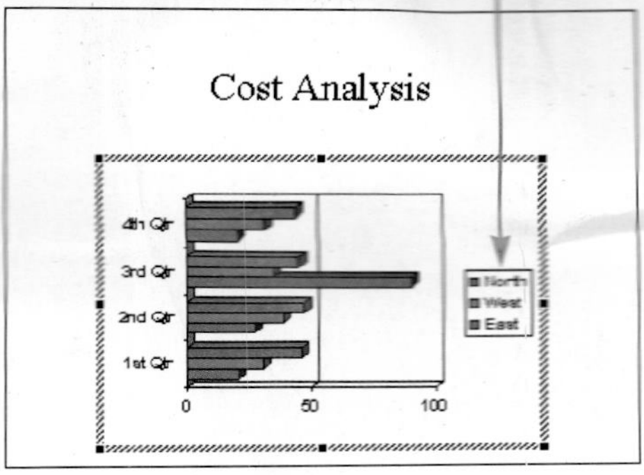

2 Click the tab for the desired format change.

Changes color and fills patterns | Changes text attributes | Changes positioning

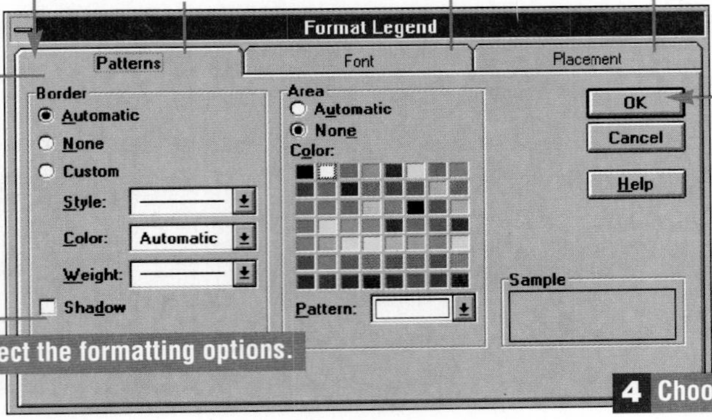

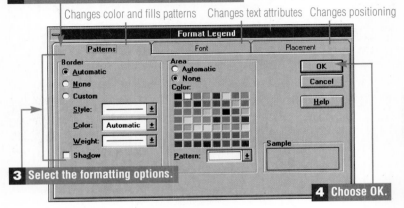

3 Select the formatting options.

4 Choose OK.

Deleting a Graph

You can select a graph on a slide and delete it. If you used a graph placeholder to create the graph, the placeholder replaces the deleted graph on the slide.

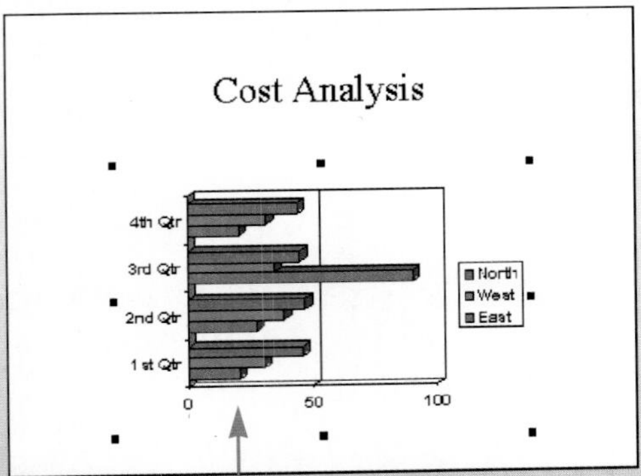

1 Select the graph to delete.

2 Press Delete.

Creating an Organization Chart

One of the chart types available in PowerPoint is an organization chart. You select the type of chart and enter the data; PowerPoint then draws the chart and fills in the blanks.

To add an organization chart to a slide

Click the Insert Organization Chart button to add a chart to any slide.

1 Double-click the chart placeholder.

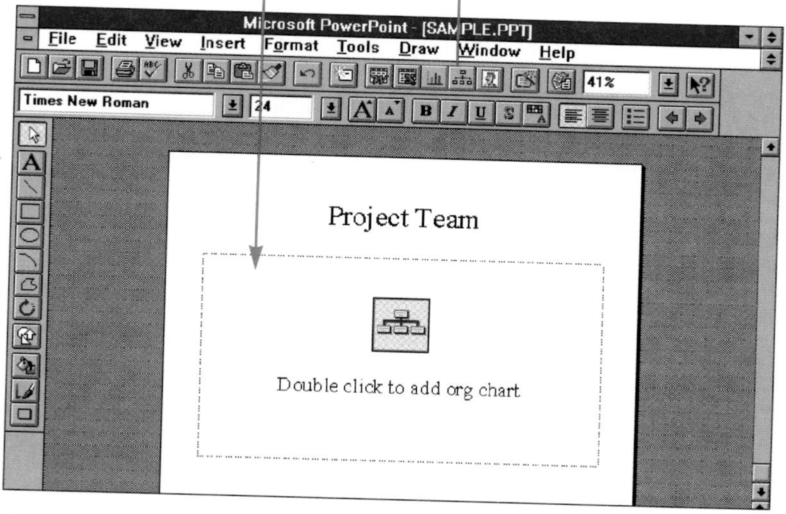

See "Adding a New Slide to a Presentation" to learn how to add a slide with a particular layout.

2 Click inside a box to enter chart data.

3 Type normally to enter text.

4 Press enter to add a second line of text.

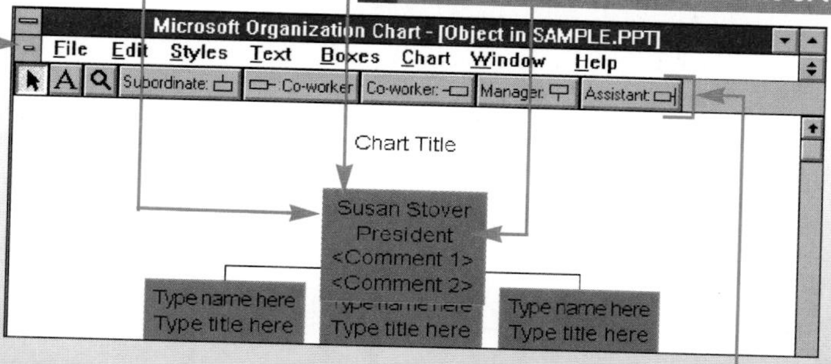

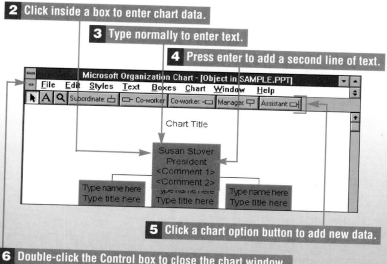

5 Click a chart option button to add new data.

6 Double-click the Control box to close the chart window.

more ▶

PowerPoint displays the organization chart in the slide.

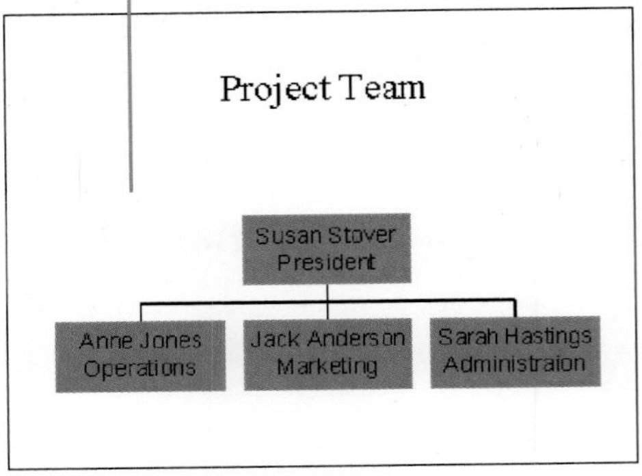

To edit an organization chart

1 Double-click the organization chart.

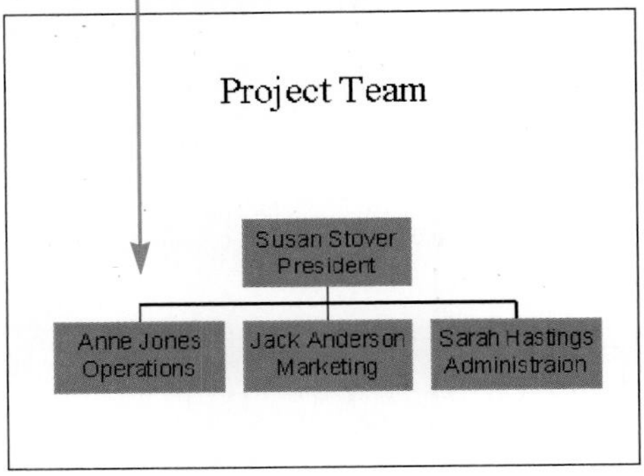

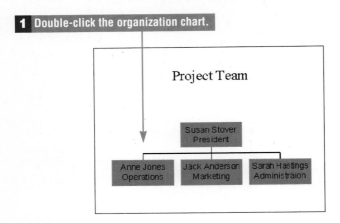

2 Select the box to edit.

3 Enter new data.

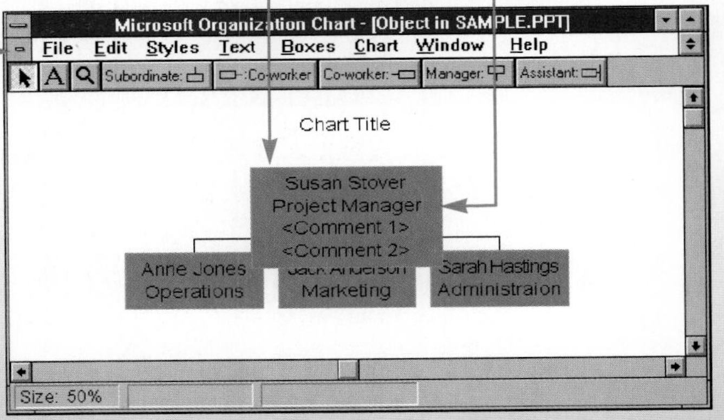

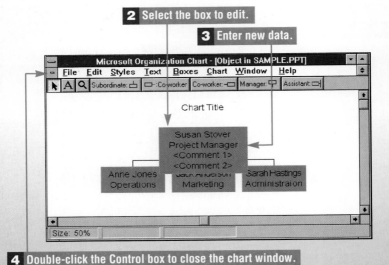

4 Double-click the Control box to close the chart window.

Creating Custom Toolbars

In addition to using the standard toolbars provided by PowerPoint, you can customize toolbars to display a select set of buttons.

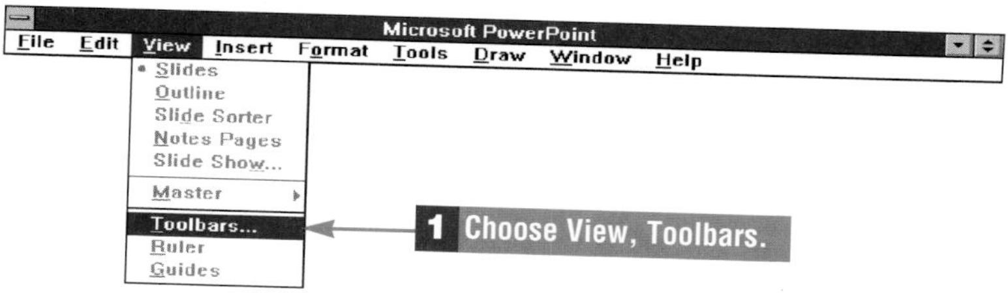

1 Choose View, Toolbars.

2 Select Custom.

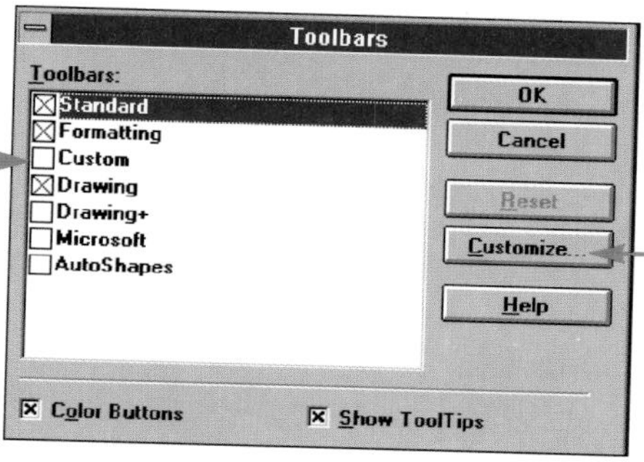

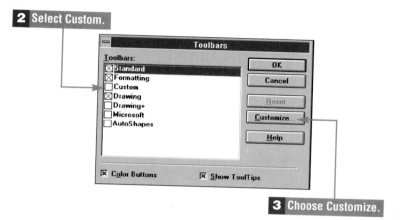

3 Choose Customize.

4 Select a button category.

5 Drag the desired button to one of the toolbars.

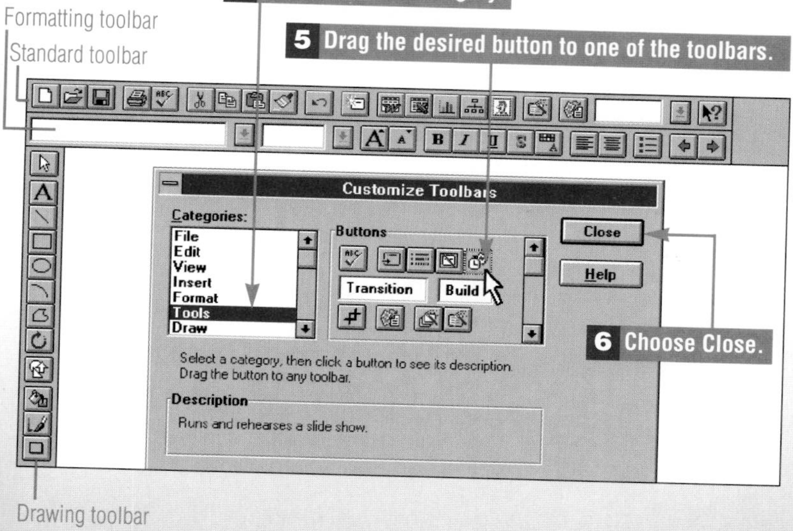

6 Choose Close.

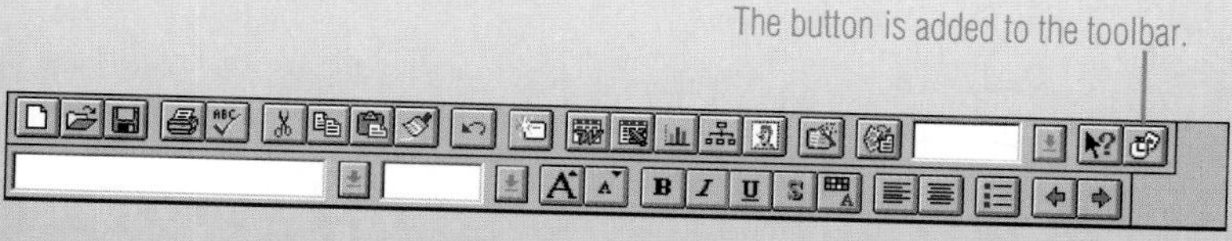

Displaying and Hiding Toolbars

You can choose to display or hide any PowerPoint toolbar at any time.

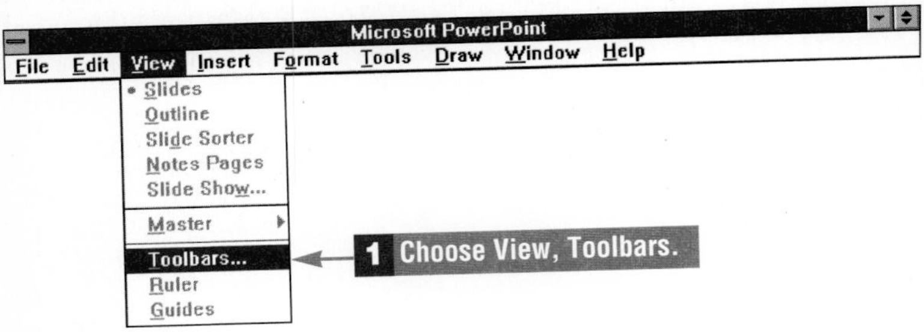

1 Choose View, Toolbars.

2 Select or deselect the toolbars to display or hide.

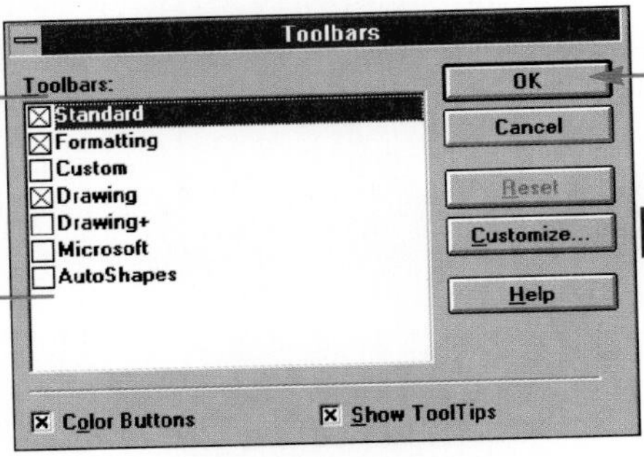

3 Choose OK.

Moving Toolbars

Depending on the toolbars you have displayed, you may need to change the location of one or more of the toolbars so you can see them.

1 Click an open area on the toolbar and hold down the mouse button.

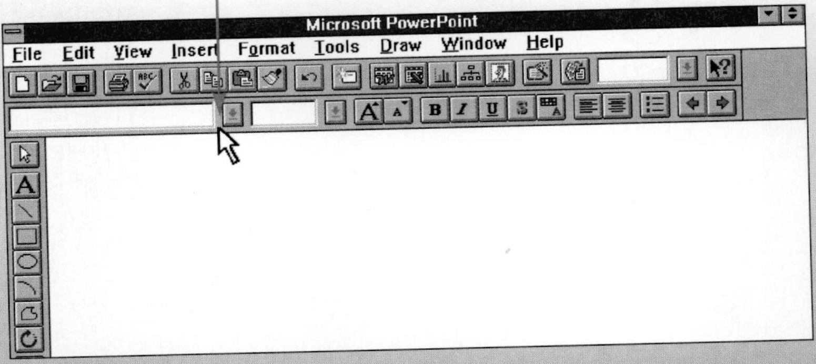

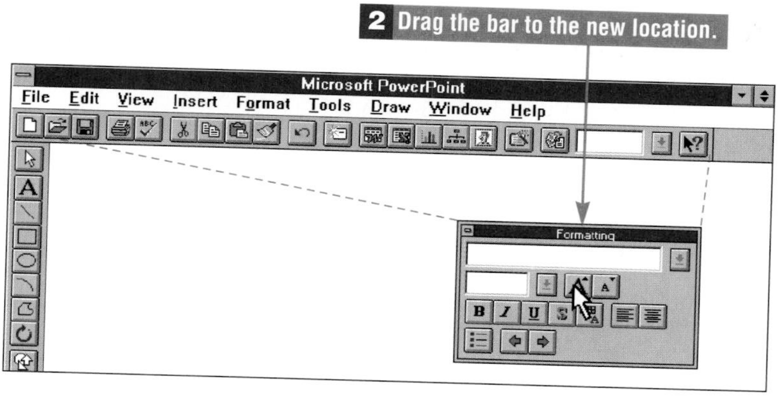

The outline that appears as you drag shows how the toolbar will fit in the current loaction.

Displaying Rulers

Rulers allow you to see the precise location of the cursor on-screen. Use the rulers when placing objects on a slide.

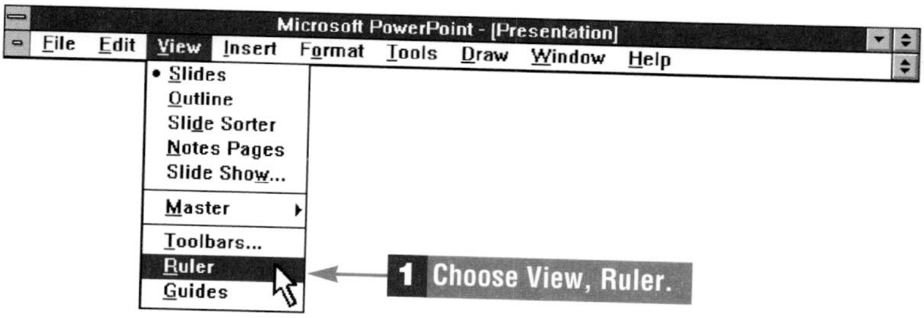

Rulers appear on the top and left of the slide window.

Displaying Guides

Guides allow for precise alignment. Use the guides to align objects on a slide. You can turn this option on or off at any time.

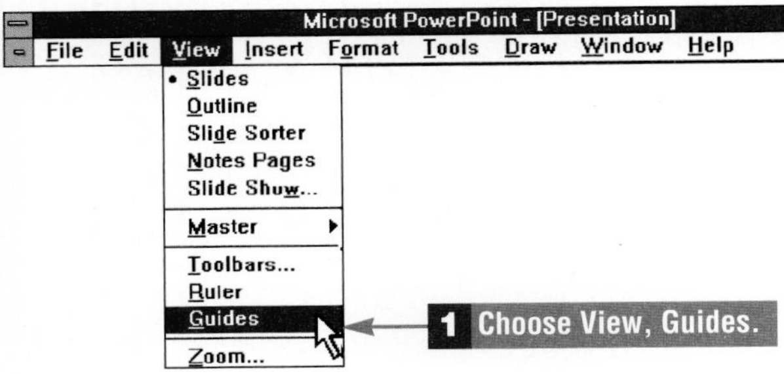

Guides display centered in the slide window.

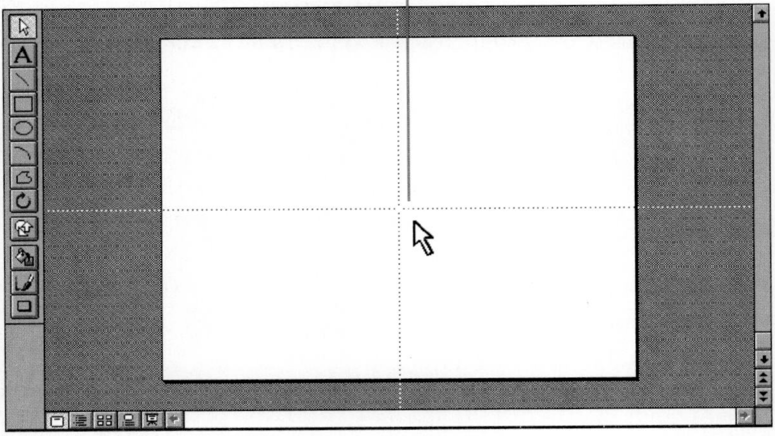

Setting User Options

PowerPoint allows you to determine how you use several features. You can change these selections at any time.

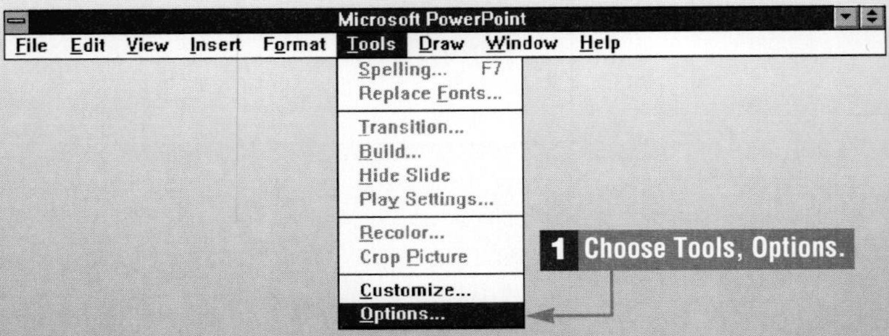

2 Select the desired options.

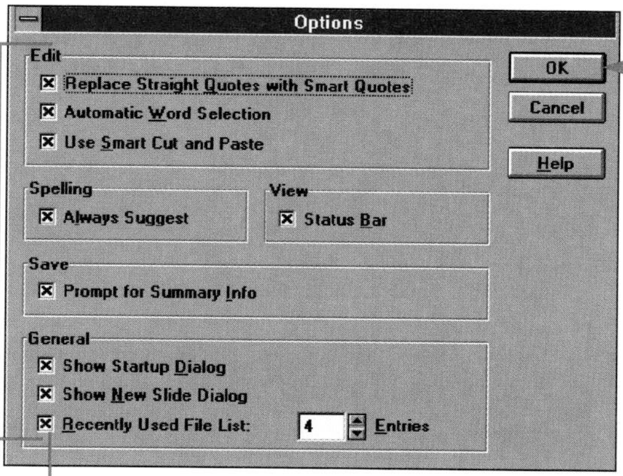

An × indicates the option is selected.

3 Choose OK.

Option	When On	When Off
Replace Straight Quotes with Smart Quotes	Curly quotes replace straight quotes.	Quotes appear as straight quotes.
Automatic Word Selection	Dragging selects a word at a time.	Dragging selects a character at a time.
Use Smart Cut and Paste	Automatically inserts spaces between words when you paste.	Does not add spacing when you paste.
Always Suggest	Displays a list of suggestions for a misspelled word.	Does not show suggested words unless you choose Suggest.
Status Bar	Displays the status bar at the bottom of the window.	Hides the status bar.
Prompt for Summary Info	Displays the summary information dialog box when you save a file.	Does not display the dialog box when you save a file.
Show Startup Dialog	Displays the Startup dialog box when you start PowerPoint.	Does not display the dialog box when you start PowerPoint.
Show New Slide Dialog	Displays the New Slide dialog box when you start PowerPoint.	Does not display the dialog box when you start PowerPoint.
Recently Used File List	Displays the most recently used files on the File menu.	Does not keep track of recently used files.

Opening an Existing File

To work on a file that you previously created and saved, you need to open the file.

1 Click the Open button.

2 Select the appropriate drive.

3 Select the appropriate directory.

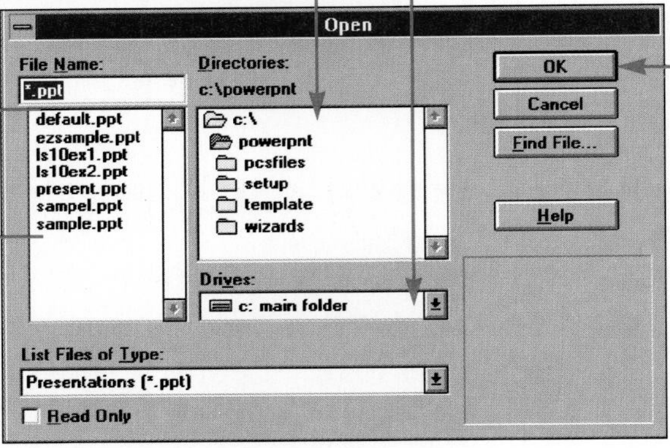

4 Select the file to open.

5 Choose OK.

Finding a File

PowerPoint provides you with a method for locating a file. Rather than scroll through directory after directory in search of that elusive file, you can use Find File to locate it in a few seconds.

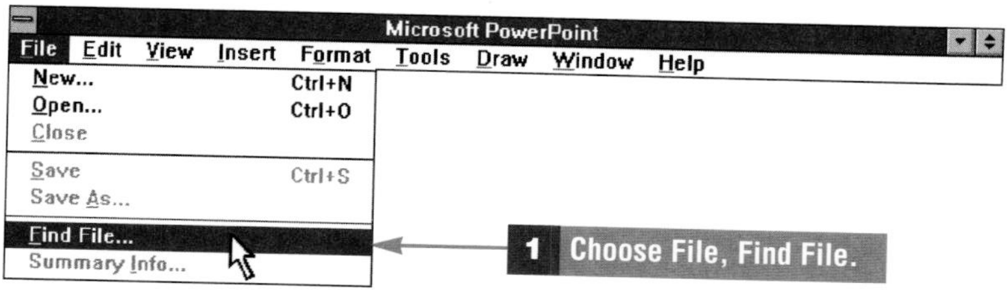

1 Choose File, Find File.

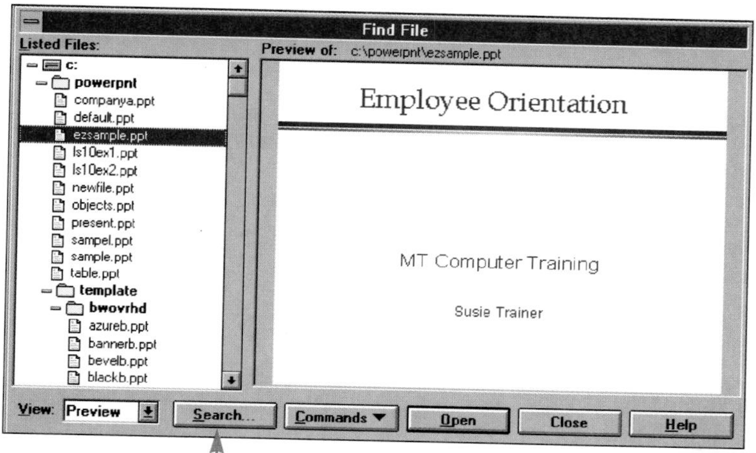

2 Choose Search.

The first time you use the Find File option, you do not see this window. The Search dialog box automatically opens.

3 Select the file name criteria.

4 Select the drive and directory.

5 Choose OK.

Saved Searches displays a list of previously defined and saved search criteria.

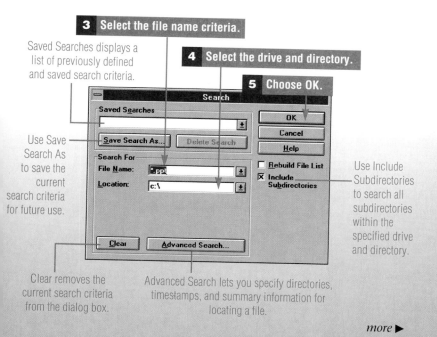

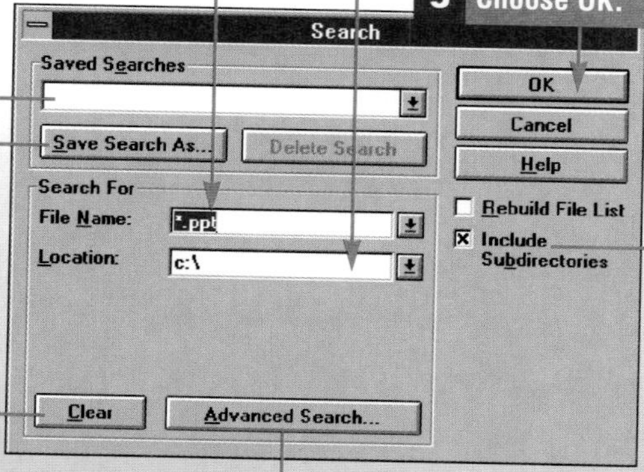

Use Save Search As to save the current search criteria for future use.

Use Include Subdirectories to search all subdirectories within the specified drive and directory.

Clear removes the current search criteria from the dialog box.

Advanced Search lets you specify directories, timestamps, and summary information for locating a file.

more ▶

6 Select the desired file from the list of selected files.

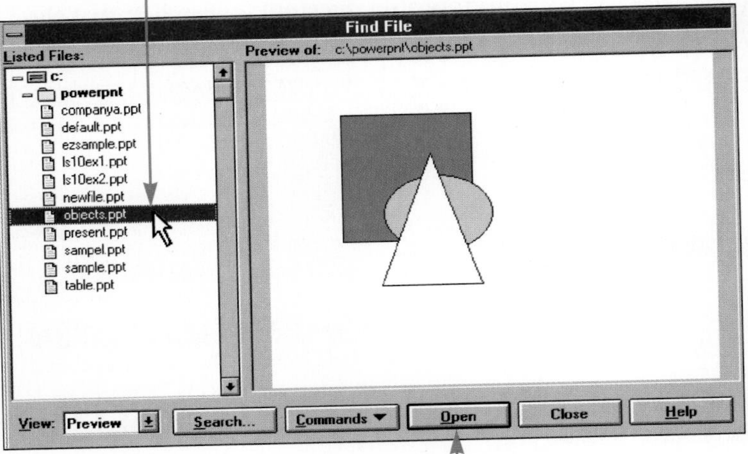

7 Choose Open.

Navigating Directories

You can use the Open, Save, or other dialog box to select a directory and view a list of files in that directory.

1 Click the Open button (or another command with file selection).

2 Double click the directory you want to view.

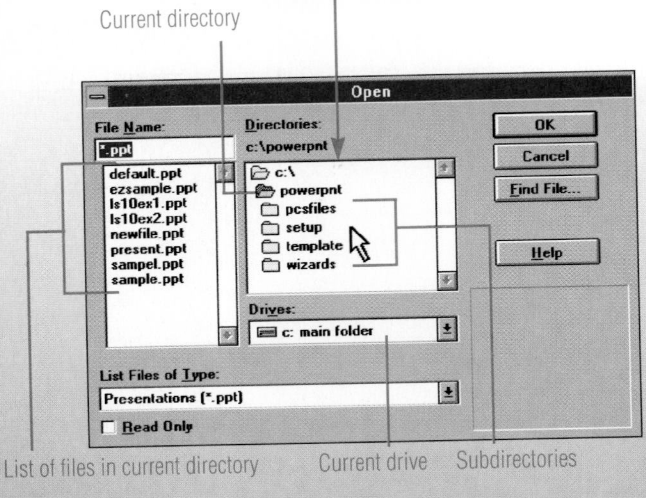

Saving a File for the First Time

While you are working on a presentation, the file's contents are temporarily stored in your computer's memory. To protect your work or store it for later use, you must save the file to your hard drive or on a floppy disk.

1 Click the Save button.

2 Enter the file name.

3 Select the drive.

4 Select the directory.

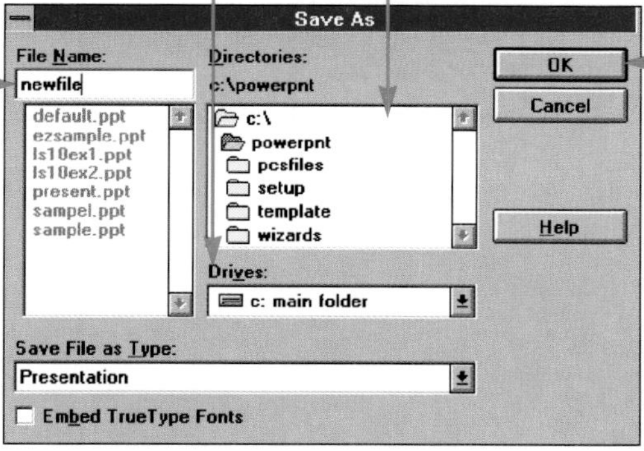

5 Choose OK.

6 Entering summary information is optional.

7 Choose OK.

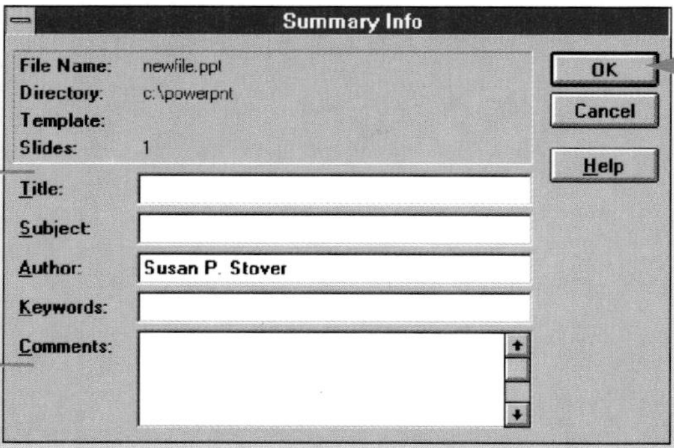

Saving an Existing File

Each time you make changes to a file, you must save the file in order to make these changes permanent.

To save the file with the same name

1 Click the Save button.

To save a file with a different name or file type, or to a different drive or directory

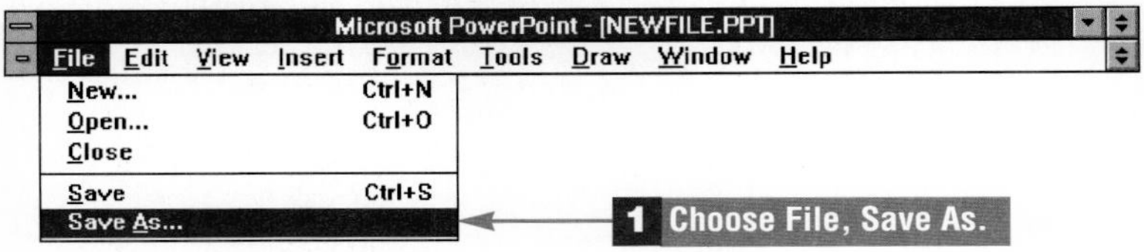

1 Choose File, Save As.

2 Enter the file name.

3 Select the drive.

4 Select the directory.

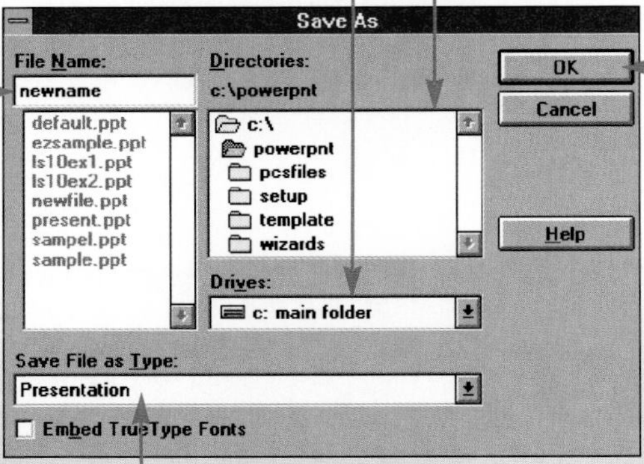

5 Select the file type.

6 Choose OK.

Closing a File

After you finish working with a file, you can close the file to remove it from the PowerPoint window.

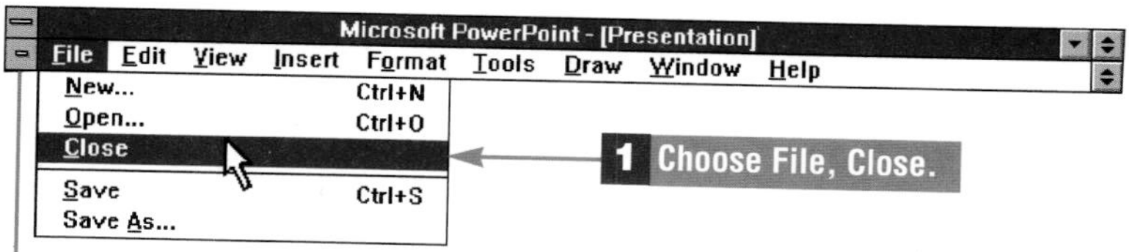

1 Choose File, Close.

You also can double-click the Control box to close the file.

2 Choose Yes to save your work.

Choose Cancel to return to the document.

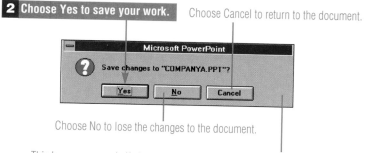

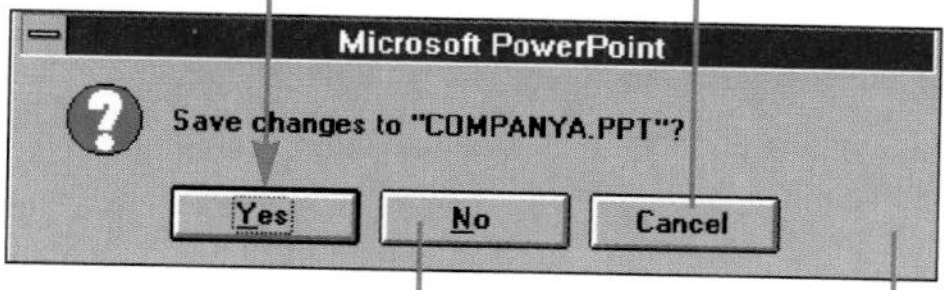

Choose No to lose the changes to the document.

This box appears only if changes have been made since the last save.

Adding a Clip Art Image to a Clip Art Slide Layout

Several PowerPoint slide layouts include placeholders for clip art images. Use these placeholders to add graphic images to your slides.

1 Double-click the clip art placeholder.

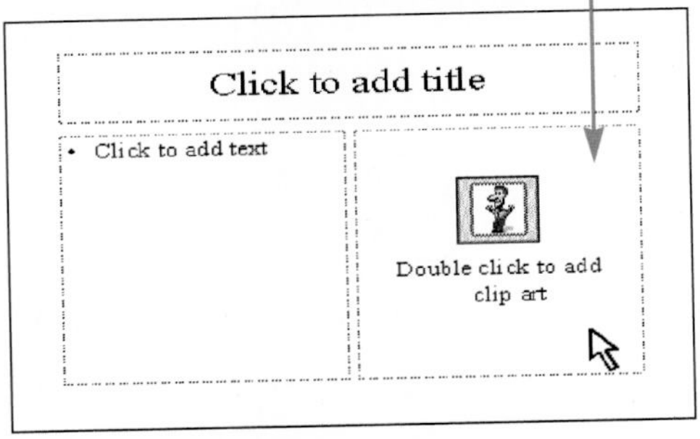

See "Adding a New Slide to a Presentation" to learn how to add a slide with a particular layout.

2 Select the clip art category.

3 Select the clip art image to add to the slide.

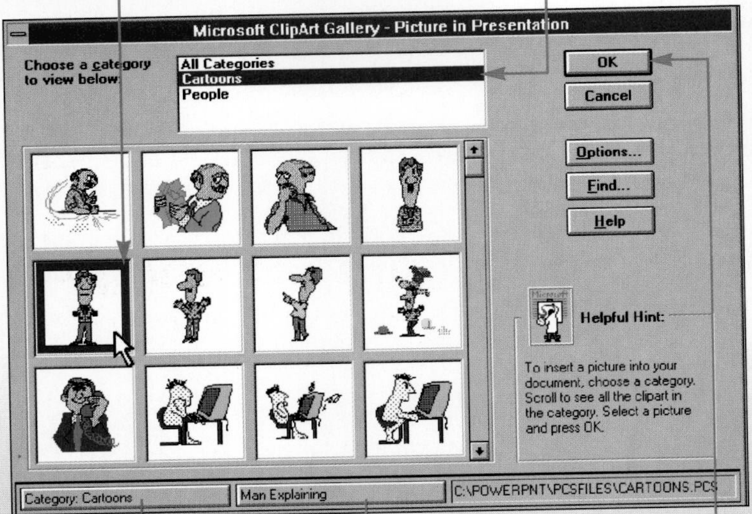

Current category

Current clip art image

4 Choose OK.

Adding Clip Art to Any Slide

In addition to using the slide layouts with clip art placeholders, you also can add a clip art image to any other slide in your presentation.

1 Click the Insert clip art button.

2 Select the clip art category.

3 Select the clip art image.

4 Choose OK.

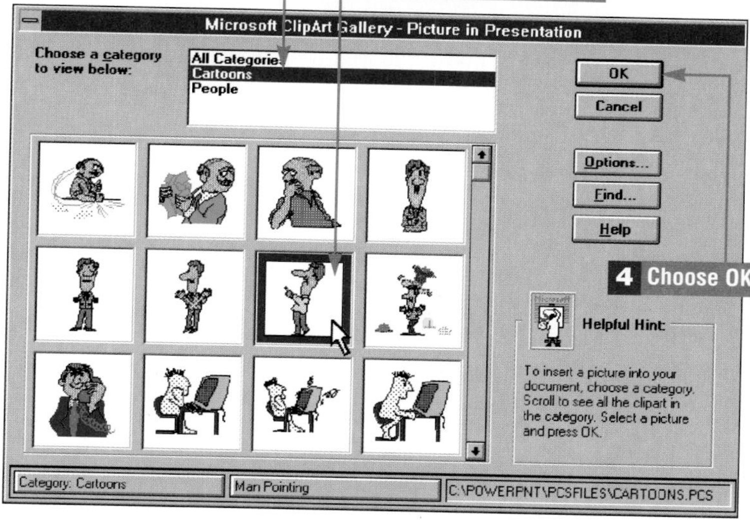

Replacing a Clip Art Image

You can change the current clip art image on a slide at any time.

1 Double-click the clip art image.

more ▶

2 Select the clip art category.

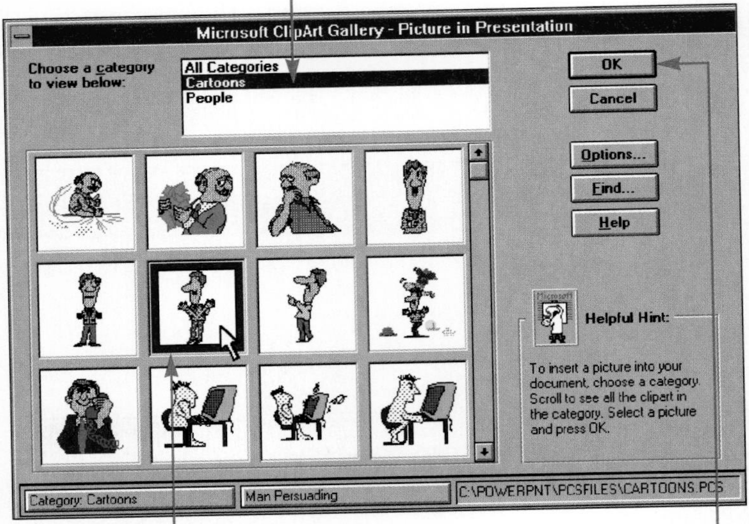

3 Select the new clip art image.

4 Choose OK.

Deleting a Clip Art Image

You can remove a clip art image from a slide by selecting and deleting the object. If the image was in a placeholder, the placeholder prompt returns.

1 Click the clip art image once to select it.

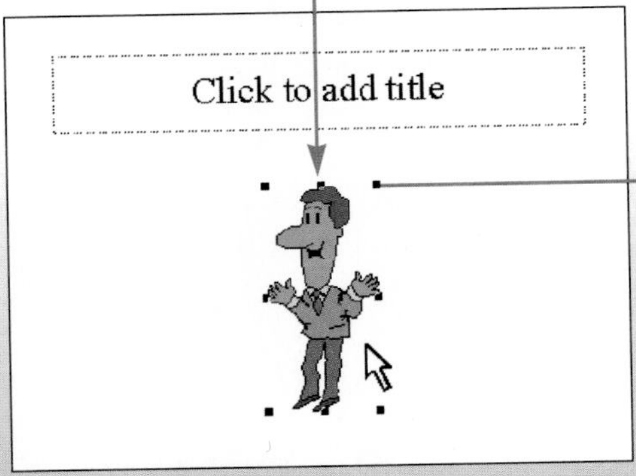

Handles indicate that the object is selected.

2 Press Delete.

Adding an Image to the ClipArt Gallery

In addition to the clip art images provided by PowerPoint, you can add other images to the gallery.

1 Click the Insert Clip Art button.

41%
Times New Roman
24

2 Choose Options.

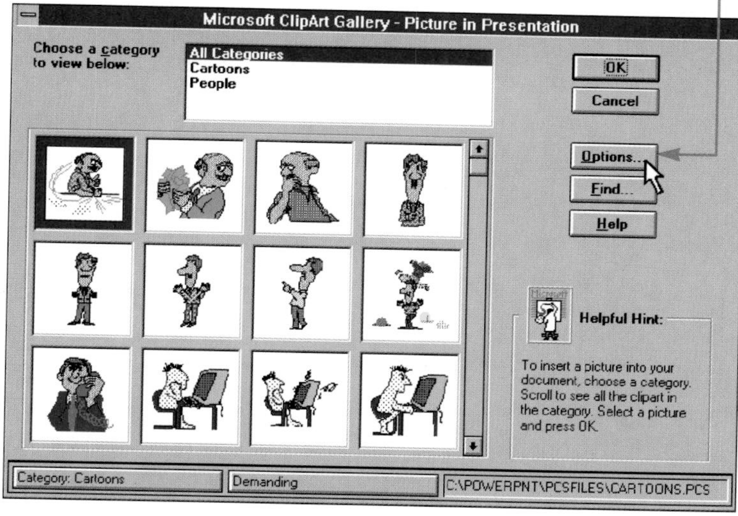
Microsoft ClipArt Gallery - Picture in Presentation
Choose a category to view below:
All Categories
Cartoons
People
OK
Cancel
Options...
Find...
Help
Helpful Hint:
To insert a picture into your document, choose a category. Scroll to see all the clipart in the category. Select a picture and press OK.
Category: Cartoons
Demanding
C:\POWERPNT\PCSFILES\CARTOONS.PCS

3 Choose Add.

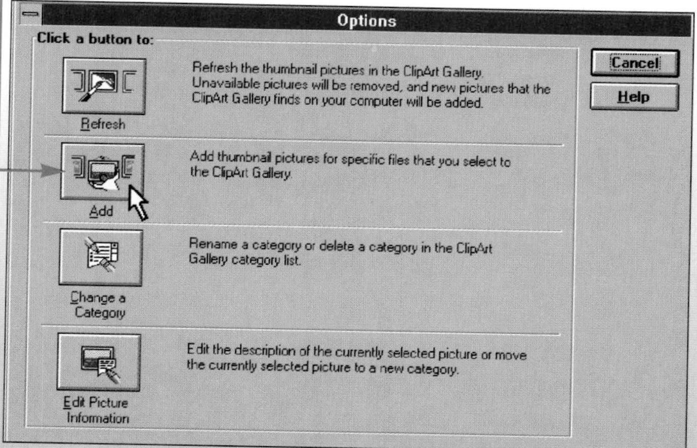
Options
Click a button to:
Refresh
Refresh the thumbnail pictures in the ClipArt Gallery. Unavailable pictures will be removed, and new pictures that the ClipArt Gallery finds on your computer will be added.
Add
Add thumbnail pictures for specific files that you select to the ClipArt Gallery.
Change a Category
Rename a category or delete a category in the ClipArt Gallery category list.
Edit Picture Information
Edit the description of the currently selected picture or move the currently selected picture to a new category.
Cancel
Help

more ▶

4 Select the drive.

5 Select the directory.

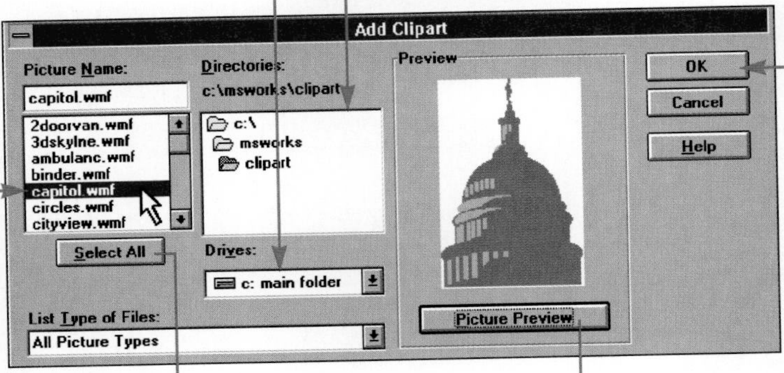

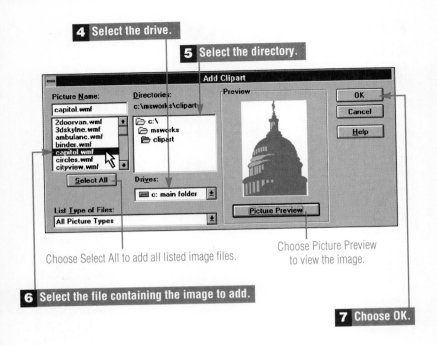

Choose Select All to add all listed image files.

Choose Picture Preview to view the image.

6 Select the file containing the image to add.

7 Choose OK.

8 Select the category.

Choose Don't Add to close the dialog box without adding the image to the gallery.

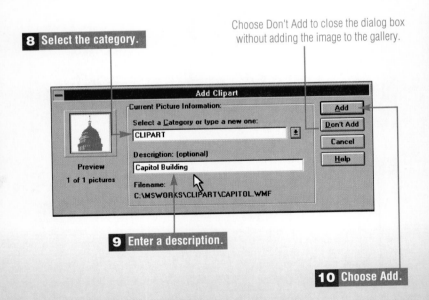

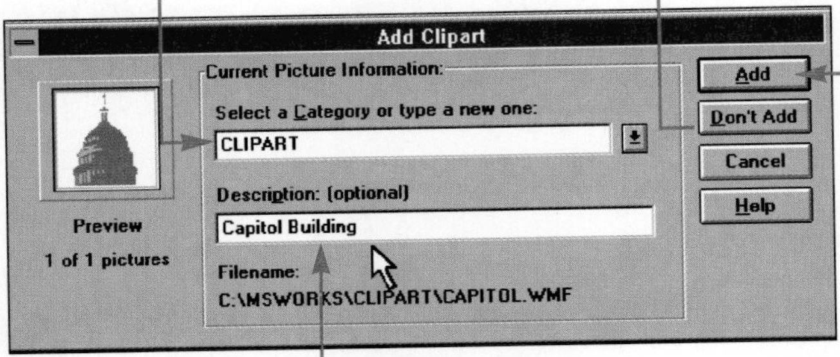

9 Enter a description.

10 Choose Add.

Recoloring a Clip Art Image

Once you include a clip art image on a slide in your presentation, you can change any of the colors in the image. These changes affect the image only in the presentation.

1 Select the image to recolor.

2 Choose Tools, Recolor.

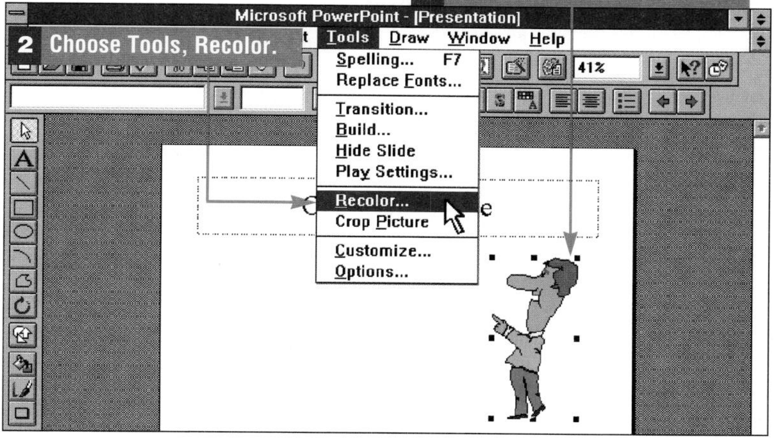

3 Select the original image color.

4 Select the new color.

Use Preview to look at the color changes before closing the dialog box.

5 Choose OK.

Changes all colors in the picture

Changes fill and background colors only, without changing line color

The image's colors are changed.

Inserting a Picture in a Slide

In addition to images in the ClipArt Gallery, you can insert other pictures in your slide. PowerPoint accepts such an image provided that the picture is in a recognizable format.

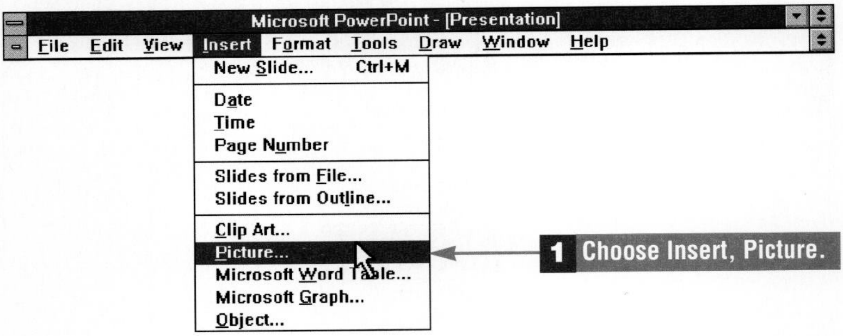

1 Choose Insert, Picture.

2 Select the drive.

3 Select the directory.

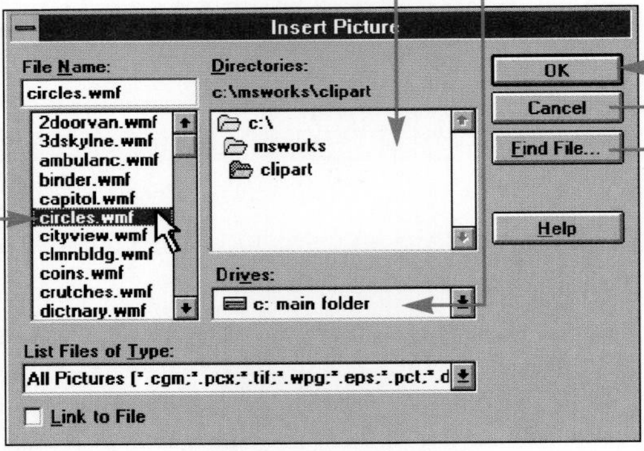

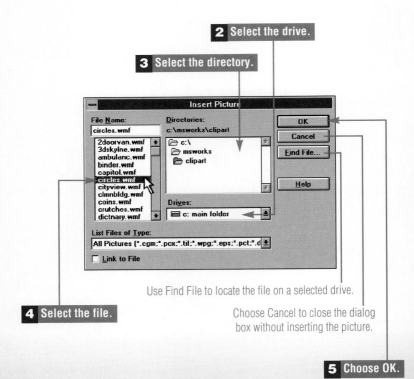

Use Find File to locate the file on a selected drive.

4 Select the file.

Choose Cancel to close the dialog box without inserting the picture.

5 Choose OK.

Drawing Objects

The Drawing toolbar includes tools that let you create and manipulate various objects, such as lines, rectangles, and arcs. The toolbar also has tools for creating freeform objects and predefined AutoShapes.

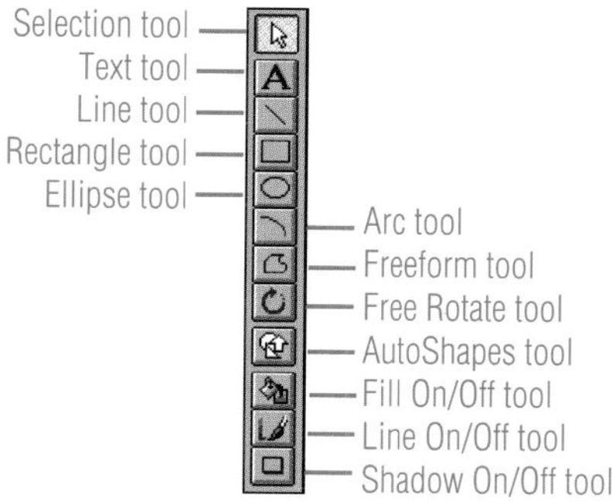
Selection tool
Text tool
Line tool
Rectangle tool
Ellipse tool
Arc tool
Freeform tool
Free Rotate tool
AutoShapes tool
Fill On/Off tool
Line On/Off tool
Shadow On/Off tool

To draw lines

1 Click the Line tool.

2 Click where you want to start the line.

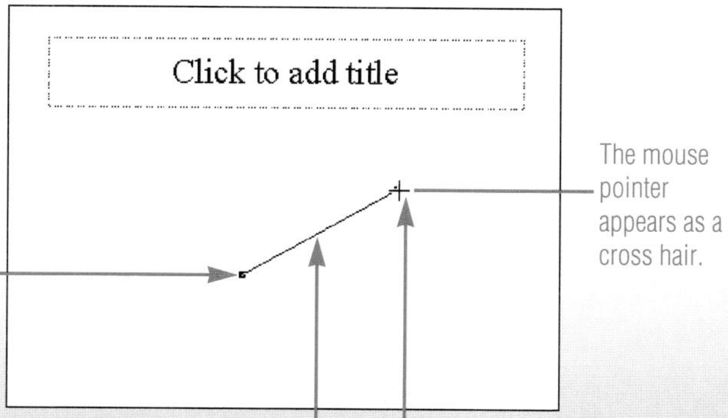
Click to add title
The mouse pointer appears as a cross hair.

3 Drag the pointer to draw the line.

4 Release where you want to end the line.

To draw arcs

1 Click the Arc tool.

2 Click where you want to begin the arc.

3 Drag the pointer to draw the arc.

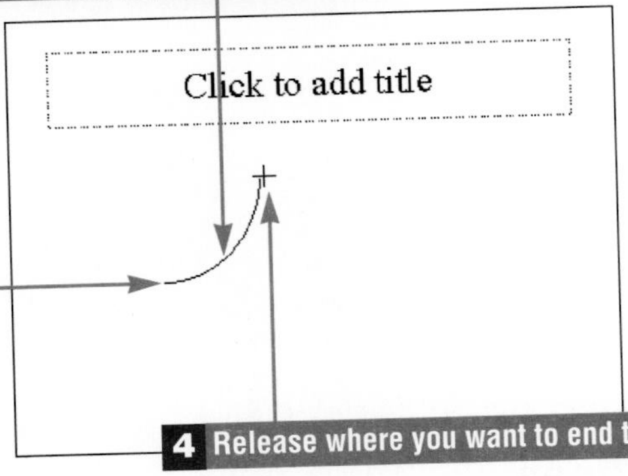

4 Release where you want to end the arc.

Hold the Ctrl key to center the arc on the starting point.
Hold the Shift key to draw a quarter circle.
Hold the Shift and Ctrl keys to draw a quarter circle centered on the starting point.

To draw freeforms

1 Click the Freeform tool.

2 Click the beginning point of the polygon.

3 Click the next point of the polygon.

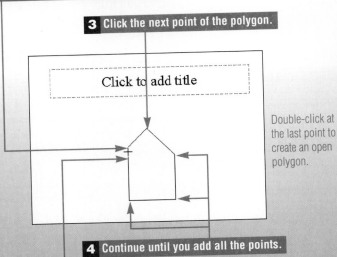

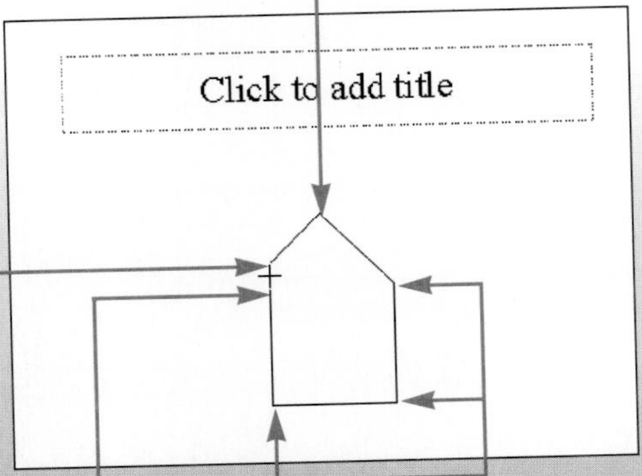

Double-click at the last point to create an open polygon.

4 Continue until you add all the points.

5 Click next to the first point to close the polygon.

To use AutoShapes

1 Click the AutoShape tool.

2 Select the shape to draw.

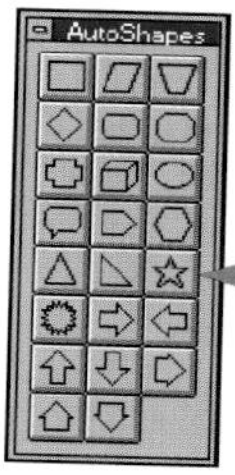

3 Click where you want to begin the shape.

Hold the Shift key while drawing to draw a regular shape.

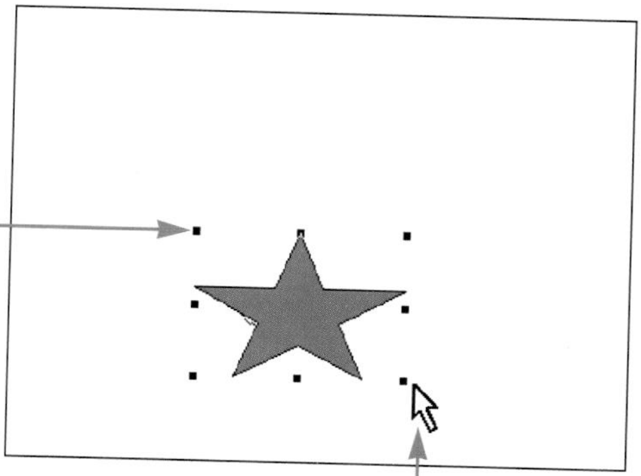

4 Drag the pointer to draw the shape.

5 Release when you complete the shape.

Searching for a Help Topic

PowerPoint lets you look for information about a specific topic by entering a key word to identify the topic. PowerPoint displays the topics related to the key word, and you select the Help information you want to review.

1 Choose Help, Search for Help on...

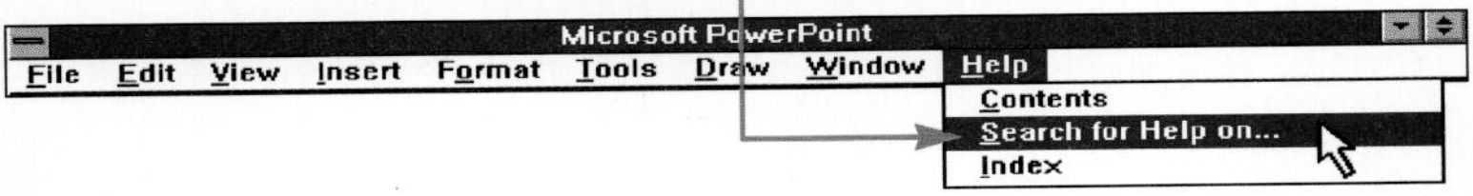

2 Type a keyword for the topic search.

3 Choose Show Topics.

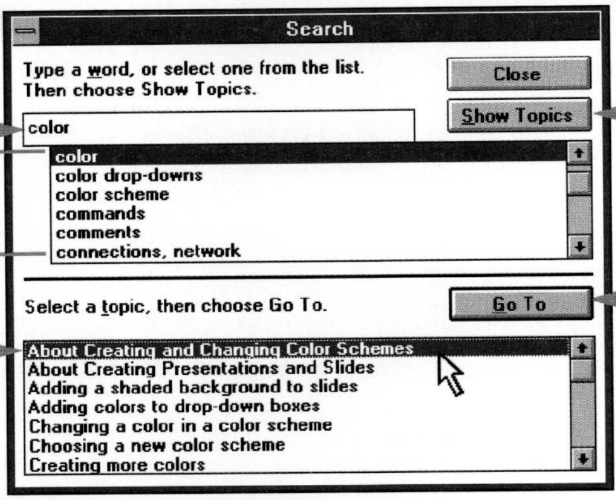

4 Select the topic to view.

You also can select a keyword from the list.

5 Choose Go To.

Using the Help Index

The PowerPoint Help Index provides an alphabetical listing of topics. You can scroll through the entire list, or jump to topics beginning with a specific letter.

1 Choose Help, Index.

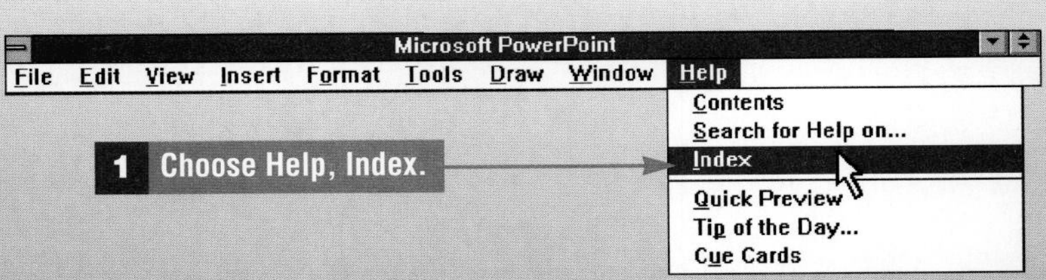

2 Click the first letter of the topic.

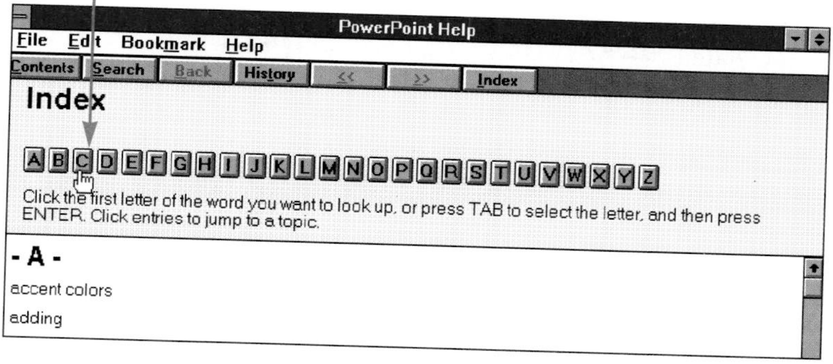

3 Click the topic to view.

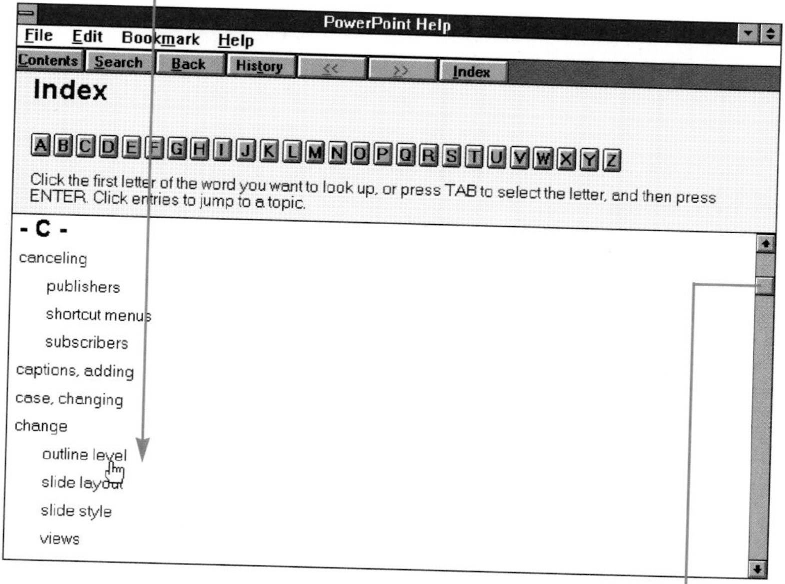

Use the scroll bar to see additional topics.

What the Help Buttons Mean

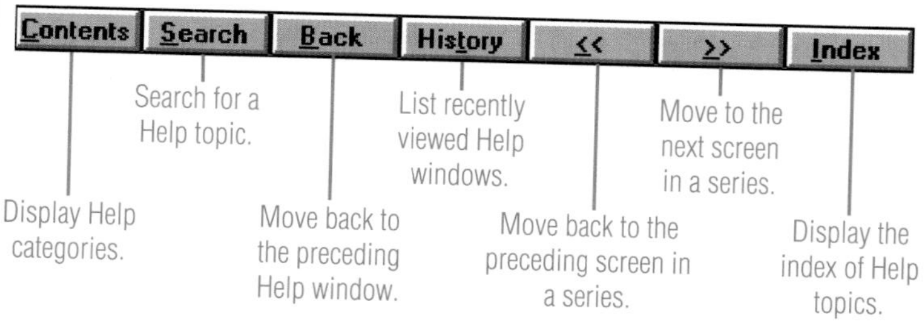
Contents
Search
Back
History
<<
>>
Index
Search for a Help topic.
List recently viewed Help windows.
Move to the next screen in a series.
Display Help categories.
Move back to the preceding Help window.
Move back to the preceding screen in a series.
Display the index of Help topics.

Using the Help Contents

The PowerPoint Help Contents is actually a table of contents organized by tasks. Select the appropriate chapter, and then continue to
make more specific selections until you find the information you
need.

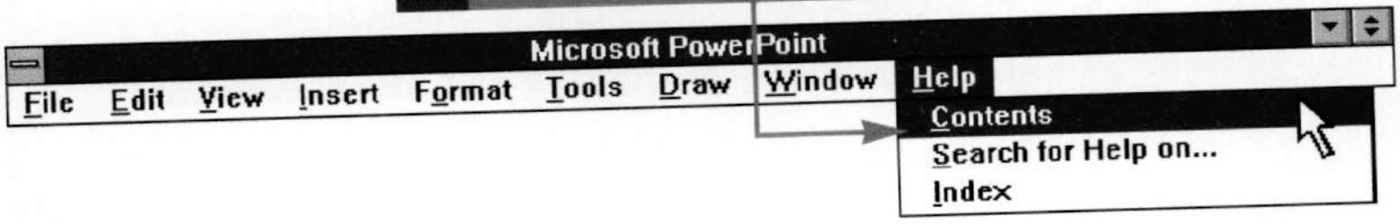

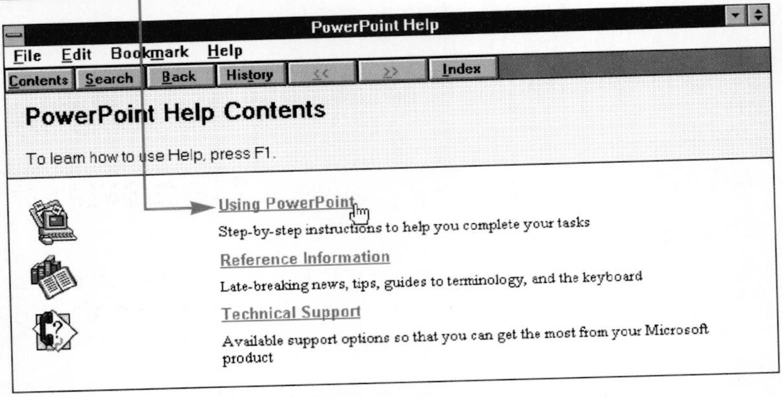

Clicking any underlined topic moves you to that topic.

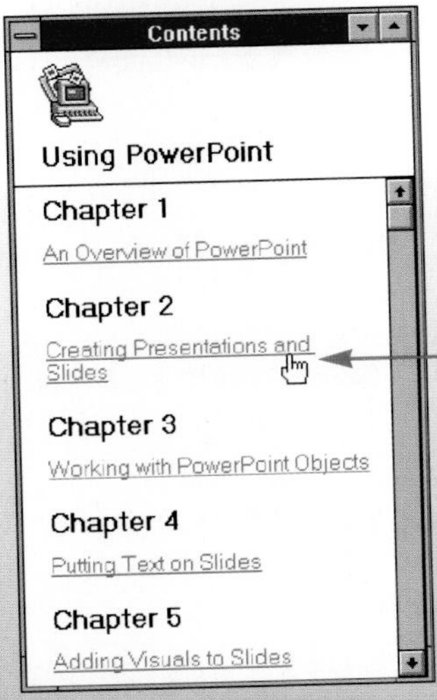

4 Click an underlined term to display Help information.

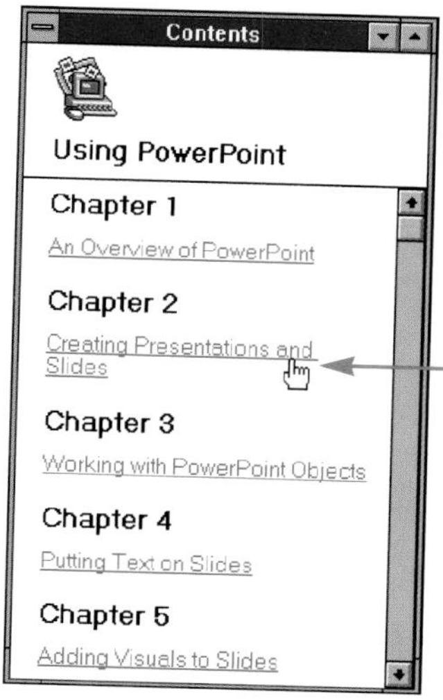

Displaying Context-Sensitive Help

When working with a dialog box, you can display Help information about the feature you are using without having to search through Help topics.

To display Help from a dialog box

1 Choose the Help button.

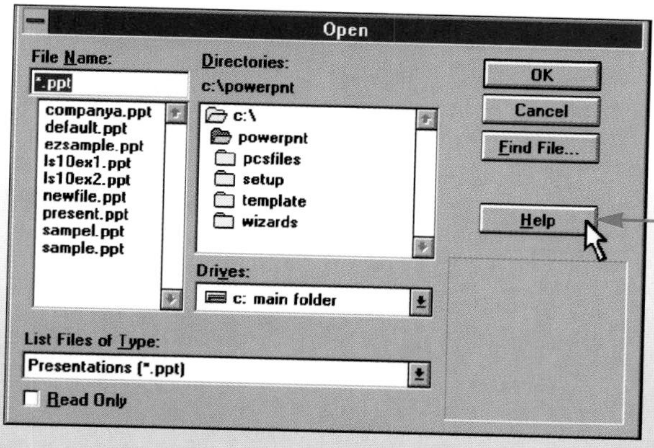

You also can press F1 to display context-sensitive Help information.

To display Help for on-screen elements

1 Click the Help button.

2 Click the screen element, menu option, or button.

The pointer includes a question mark when in Help mode.

The Help screen for the element will display.

Running the Quick Preview

PowerPoint suggests that you run the Quick Preview the first time you start PowerPoint. You also can run the Quick Preview any time you want to review.

1 Choose Help, Quick Preview.

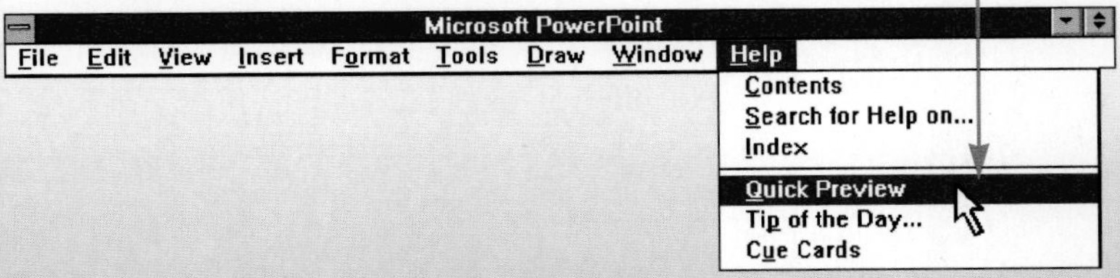

2 Choose Click to Start.

3 Use Back and Next to move through the Quick Preview screens.

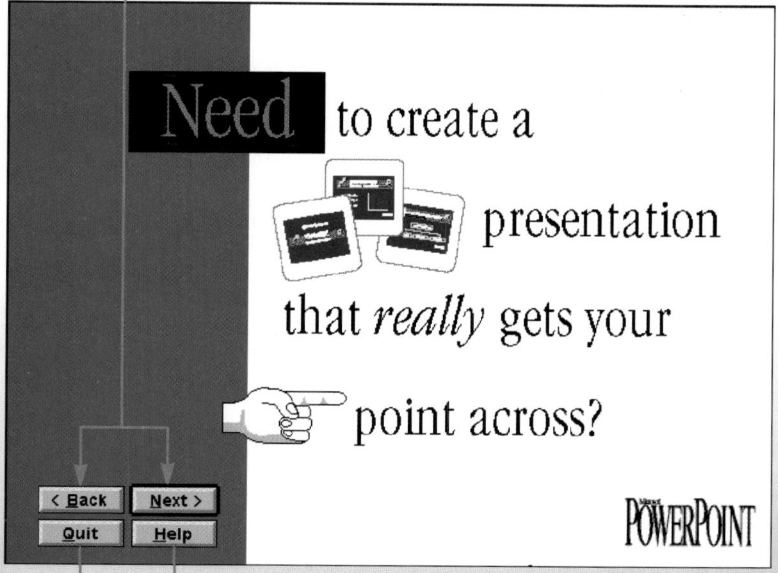

Clicking Help displays instructions for using the Quick Preview controls.

Clicking Quit ends the Quick Preview.

Displaying the Tip of the Day

PowerPoint provides you with helpful information about available features. You can view this information in the Tip of the Day format.

To view the Tip of the Day at startup

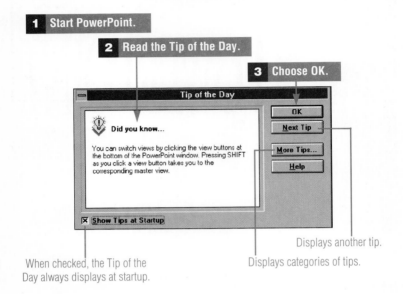

1 Start PowerPoint.

2 Read the Tip of the Day.

3 Choose OK.

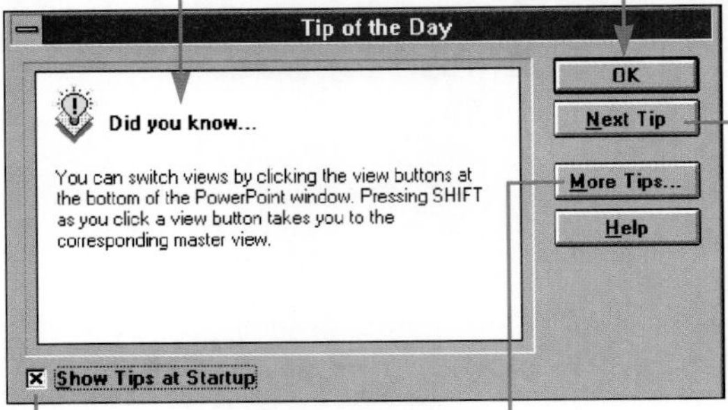
Tip of the Day
Did you know...
You can switch views by clicking the view buttons at the bottom of the PowerPoint window. Pressing SHIFT as you click a view button takes you to the corresponding master view.
OK
Next Tip
More Tips...
Help
Show Tips at Startup

Displays another tip.

When checked, the Tip of the Day always displays at startup.

Displays categories of tips.

To display the Tip of the Day at any time

1 Choose Help, Tip of the Day.

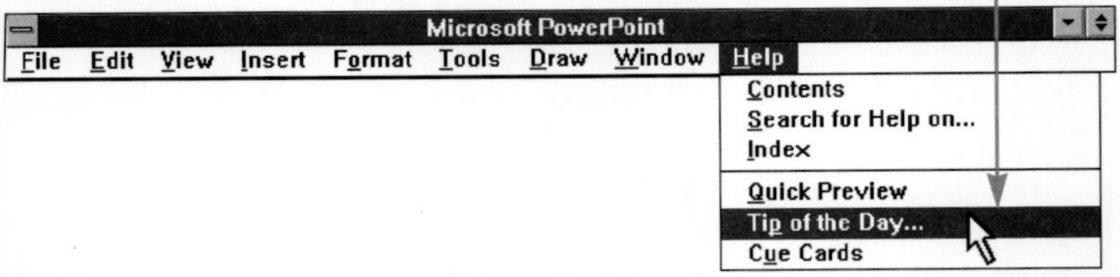
Microsoft PowerPoint
File Edit View Insert Format Tools Draw Window Help
Contents
Search for Help on...
Index
Quick Preview
Tip of the Day...
Cue Cards

2 Read the Tip of the Day.

3 Choose OK.

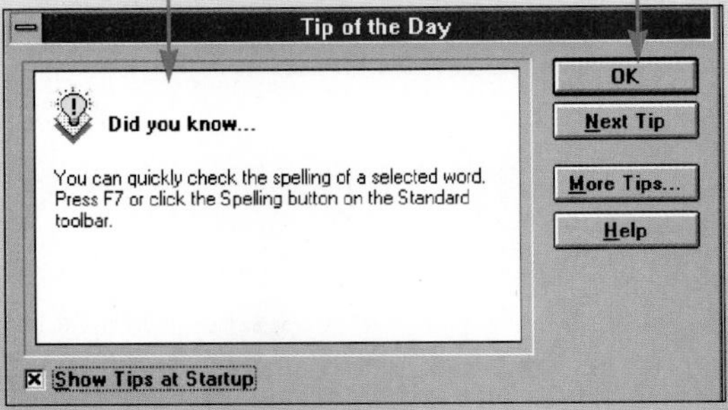
Tip of the Day
Did you know...
You can quickly check the spelling of a selected word. Press F7 or click the Spelling button on the Standard toolbar.
OK
Next Tip
More Tips...
Help
Show Tips at Startup

Displaying Cue Cards

The Cue Card feature provides you with a step-by-step checklist for completing a task in PowerPoint. The Cue Card remains on-screen as you perform the task.

1 Choose Help, Cue Cards.

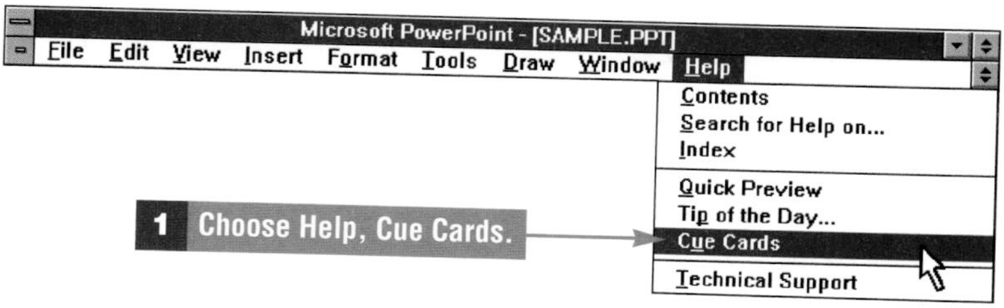
Microsoft PowerPoint - [SAMPLE.PPT]
File Edit View Insert Format Tools Draw Window Help
Contents
Search for Help on...
Index
Quick Preview
Tip of the Day...
Cue Cards
Technical Support

2 Click the Cue Card topic.

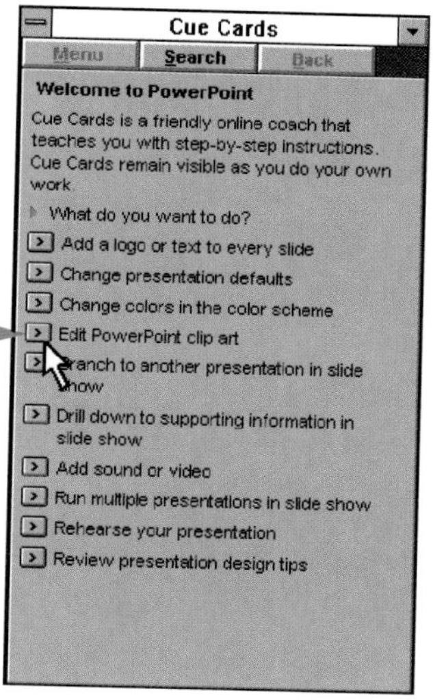
Cue Cards
Menu
Search
Back
Welcome to PowerPoint
Cue Cards is a friendly online coach that teaches you with step-by-step instructions. Cue Cards remain visible as you do your own work.
What do you want to do?
Add a logo or text to every slide
Change presentation defaults
Change colors in the color scheme
Edit PowerPoint clip art
Drill down to supporting information in slide show
Add sound or video
Run multiple presentations in slide show
Rehearse your presentation
Review presentation design tips

For some topics, you need to choose among subtopics that appear on a second Cue Card.

3 When you complete the task, close the Cue Card window.

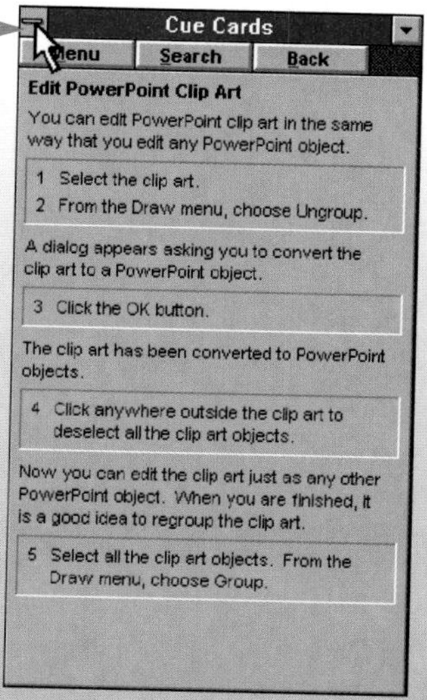
Cue Cards
Search
Back
Edit PowerPoint Clip Art
You can edit PowerPoint clip art in the same way that you edit any PowerPoint object.
1 Select the clip art.
2 From the Draw menu, choose Ungroup.
A dialog appears asking you to convert the clip art to a PowerPoint object.
3 Click the OK button.
The clip art has been converted to PowerPoint objects.
4 Click anywhere outside the clip art to deselect all the clip art objects.
Now you can edit the clip art just as any other PowerPoint object. When you are finished, it is a good idea to regroup the clip art.
5 Select all the clip art objects. From the Draw menu, choose Group.

Displaying ToolTips

The ToolTips feature displays the name of a button when you position the mouse pointer on that button. You can turn this feature on or off at any time.

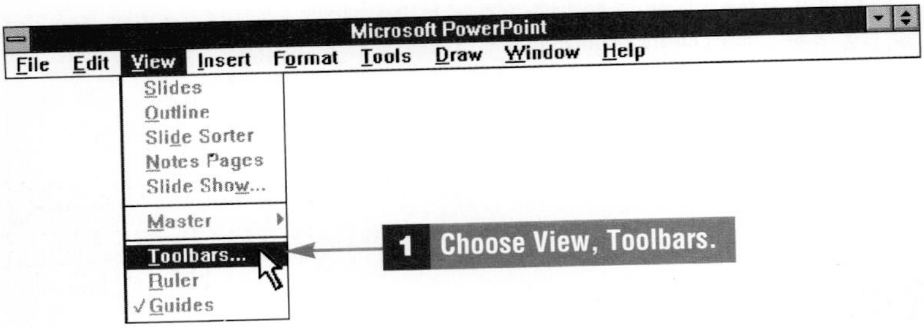

1 Choose View, Toolbars.

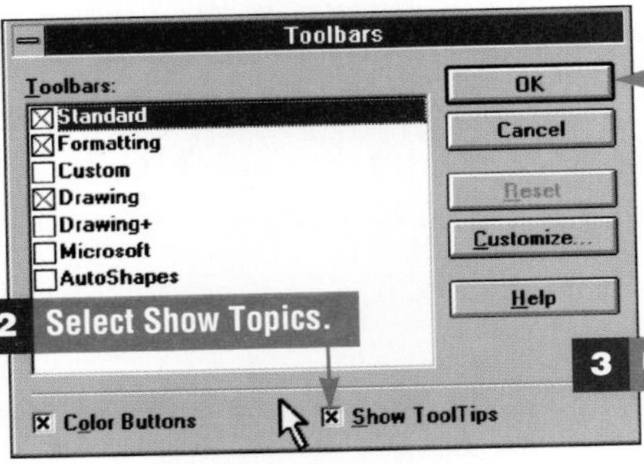

2 Select Show Topics.

3 Choose OK.

4 Position the mouse pointer on a button.

The ToolTip box displays the name of the button.

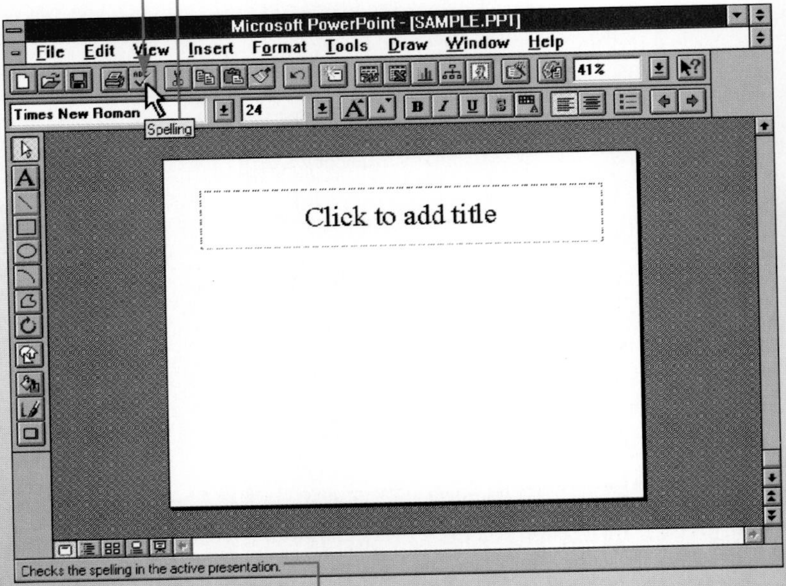

The status bar displays a description of the button.

Grouping Objects

You can group two or more objects together so that they act as a single object on a PowerPoint slide.

1 Select the first object in the group.

2 Hold the Shift key and select the additional objects.

3 Choose Draw, Group.

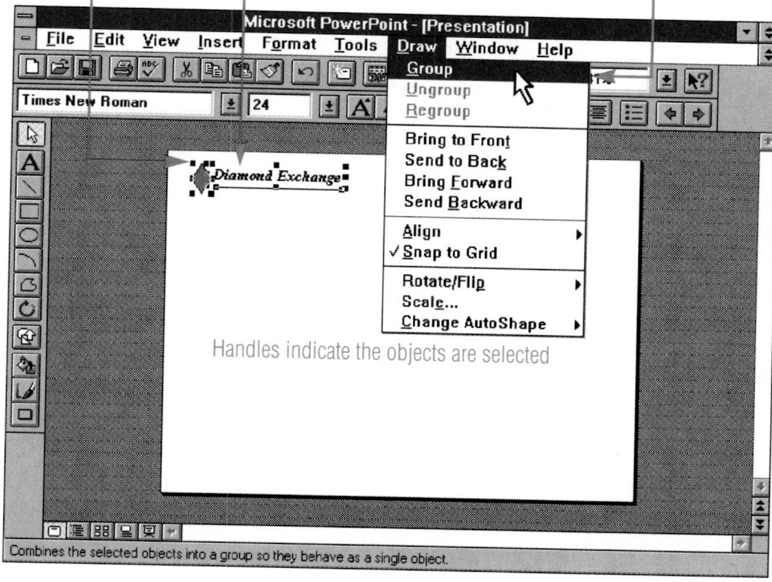

Handles indicate the objects are selected

Separate handles for the individual objects are replaced with a single set of handles around the object group.

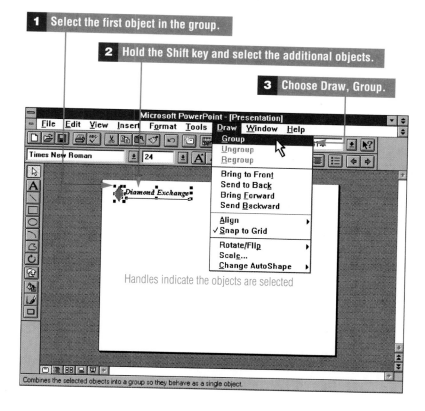

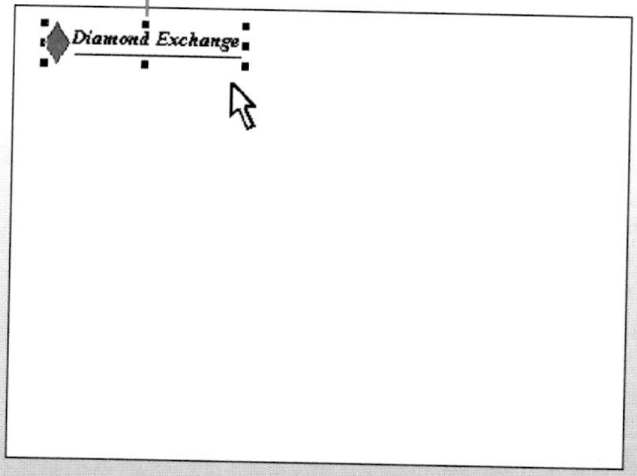

Sizing Objects

When you add objects to a slide in PowerPoint, the objects are not always the size you need. You can change the size and shape of any object on a PowerPoint slide.

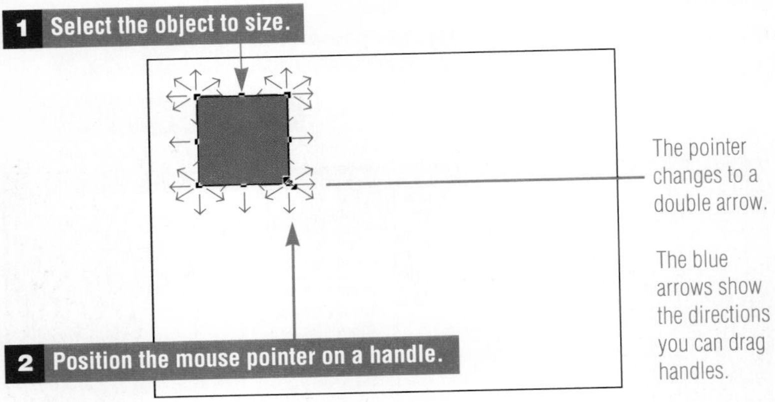
1 Select the object to size.
2 Position the mouse pointer on a handle.
The pointer changes to a double arrow.
The blue arrows show the directions you can drag handles.

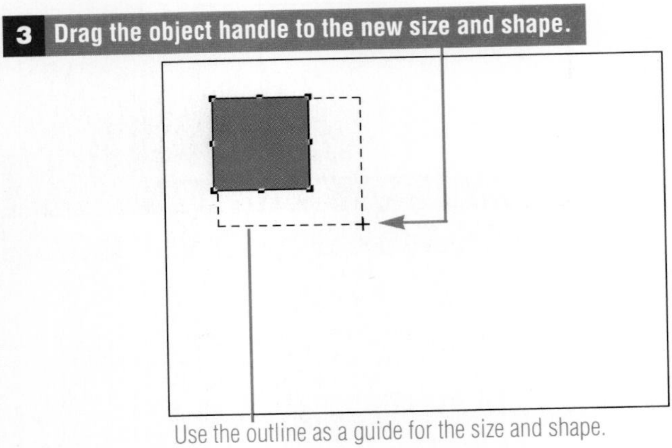
3 Drag the object handle to the new size and shape.
Use the outline as a guide for the size and shape.

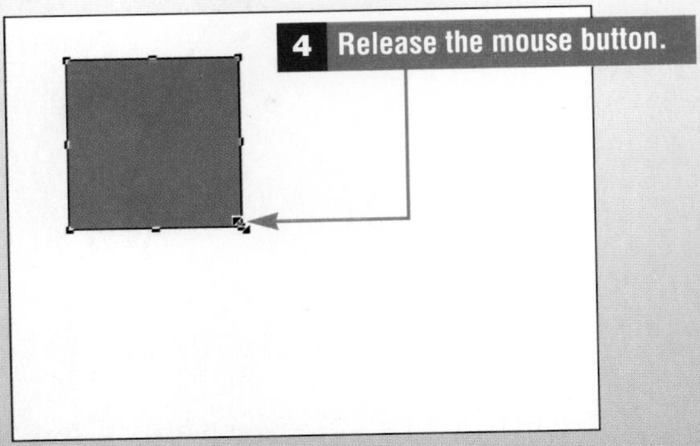
4 Release the mouse button.

Scaling an Object

You can use the Scale feature to change the size of an object without losing its shape. This feature resizes the entire object proportionately.

1 Select the object to scale.

2 Choose Draw, Scale.

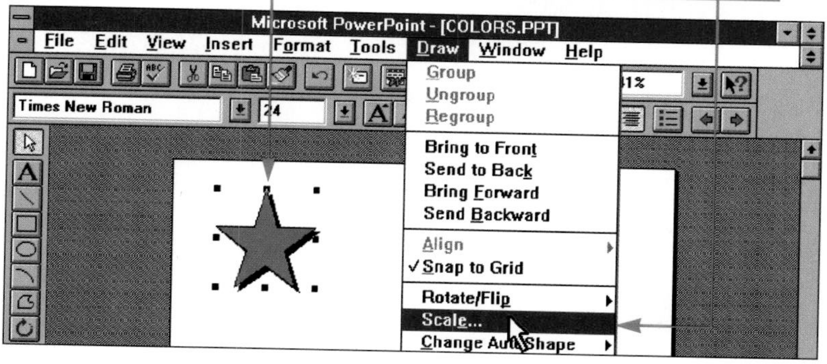

3 Set the scale percentage.

4 Choose OK.

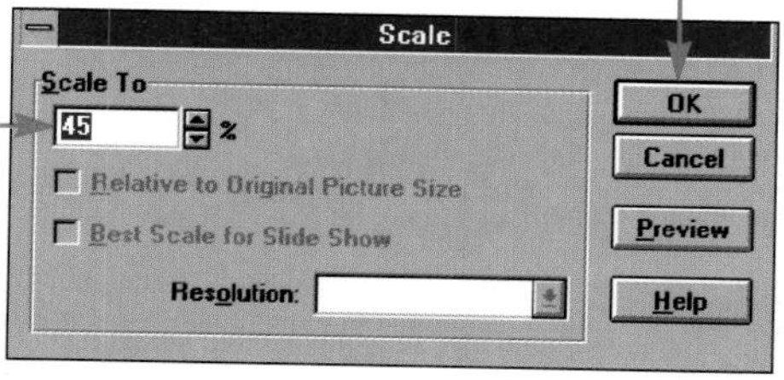

The scaled object appears on the slide.

Moving Objects

You can reposition objects on your presentation slides to change the look of your slide.

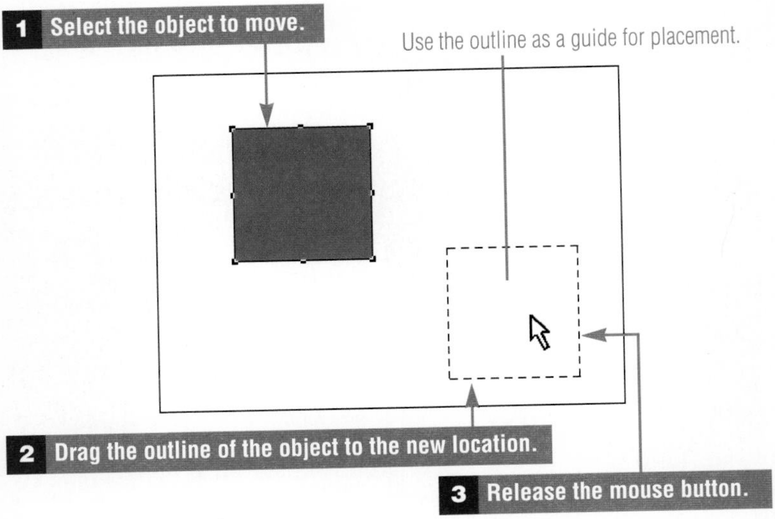
1 Select the object to move.
Use the outline as a guide for placement.
2 Drag the outline of the object to the new location.
3 Release the mouse button.

Stacking Objects

As you add objects to a slide, the objects sometimes overlap. You can change the order in which these objects overlap.

To move an object to the front

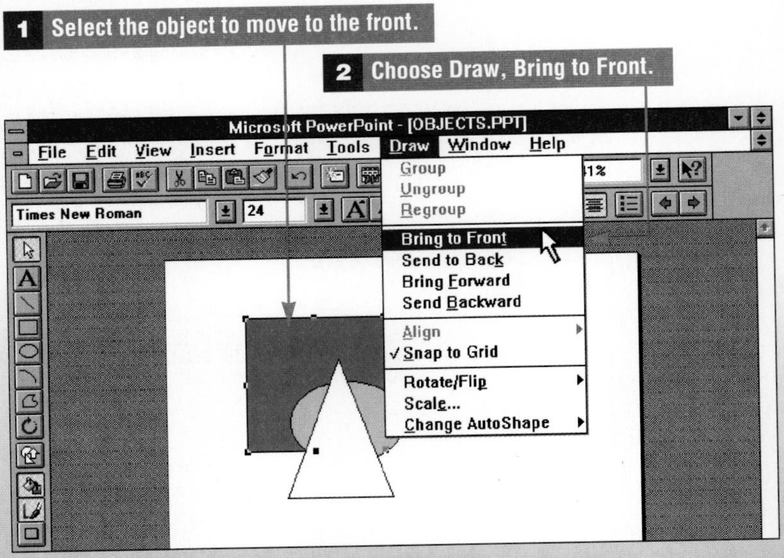

To move an object to the back

1 Select the object to move to the back.

2 Choose Draw, Send to Back.

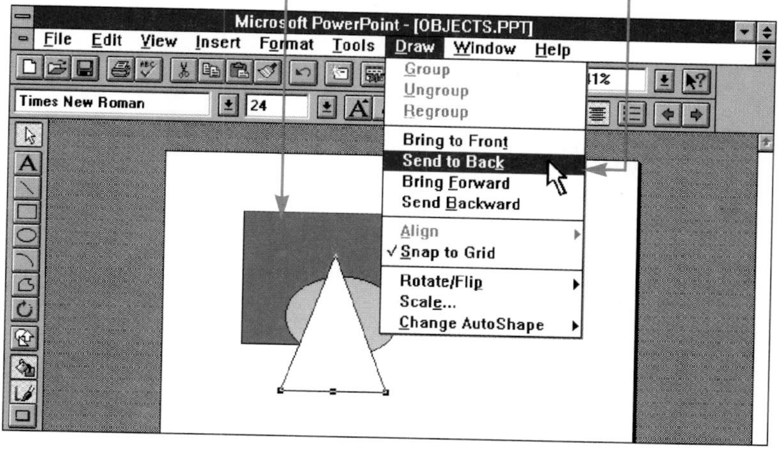

To move an object forward one level

1 Select the object to move.

2 Choose Draw, Bring Forward.

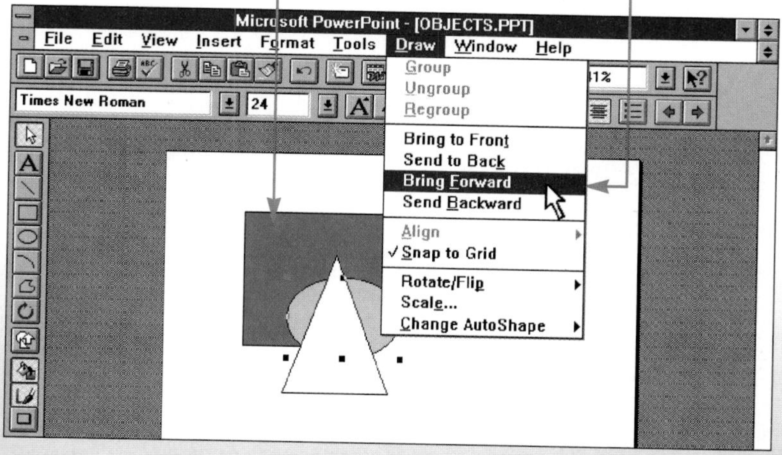

To move an object back one level

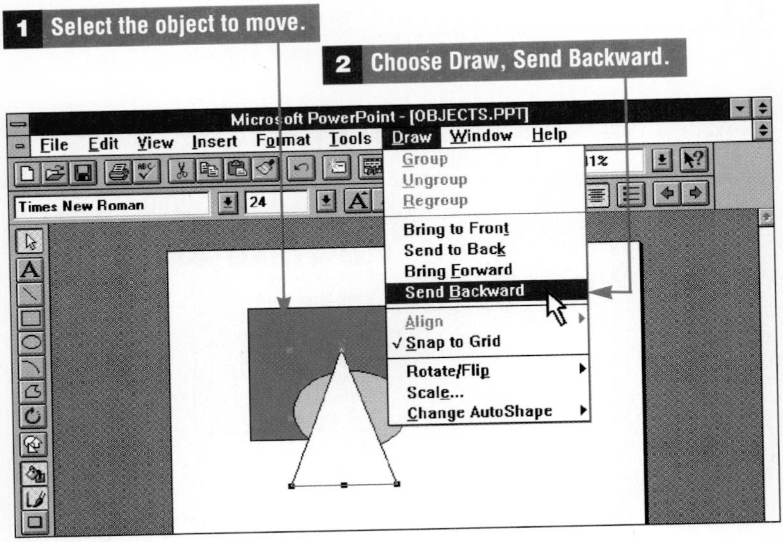

Rotating Objects

To change the look of an object, you can rotate the object around its center. You can rotate any single object or group provided the object does not include an imported picture.

To rotate an object 90 degrees

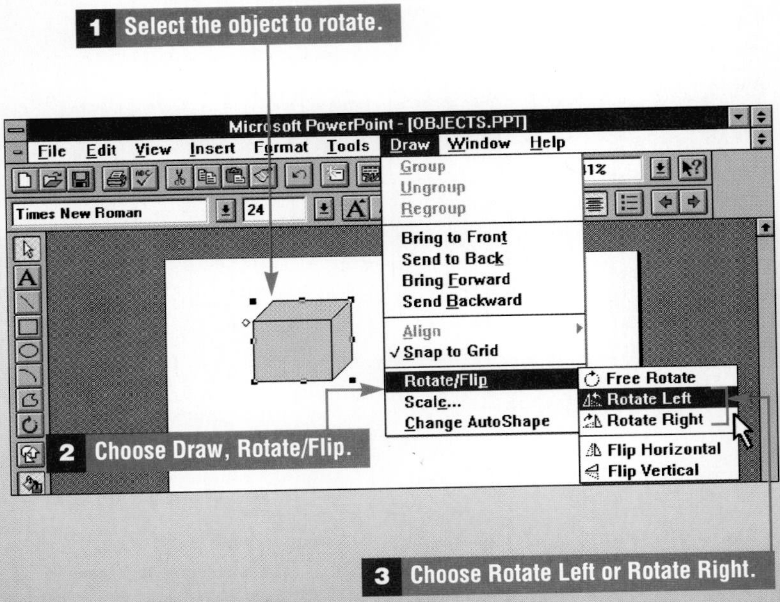

To rotate an object any angle

1 Select the object to rotate.

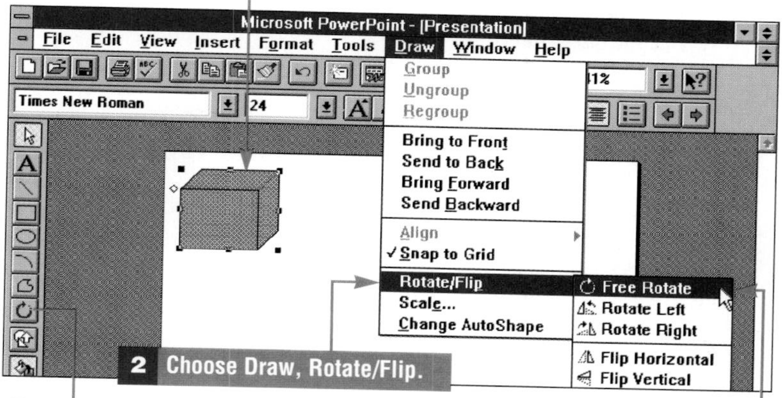

2 Choose Draw, Rotate/Flip.

You also can click the Free Rotate tool.

3 Choose Free Rotate.

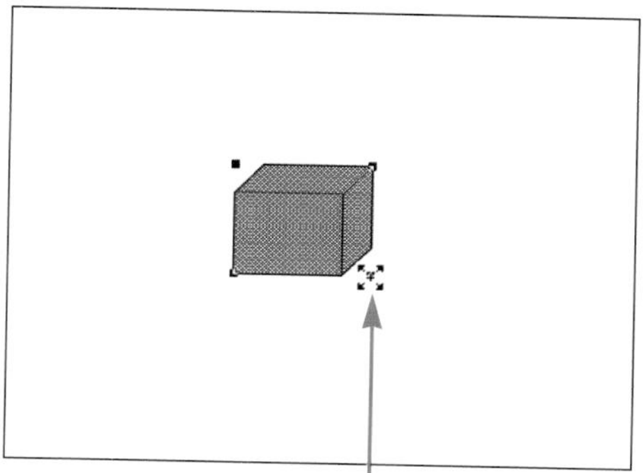

4 Position the pointer on a handle.

5 Drag the handle to rotate the object.

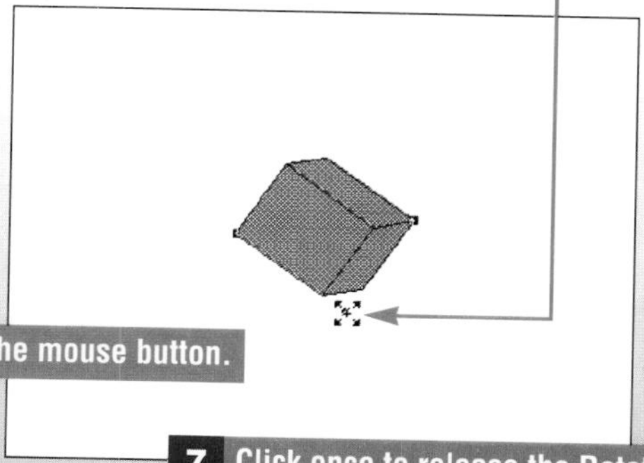

6 Release the mouse button.

7 Click once to release the Rotate command.

Flipping Objects

You can switch the orientation of an object horizontally or vertically using the PowerPoint Flip feature.

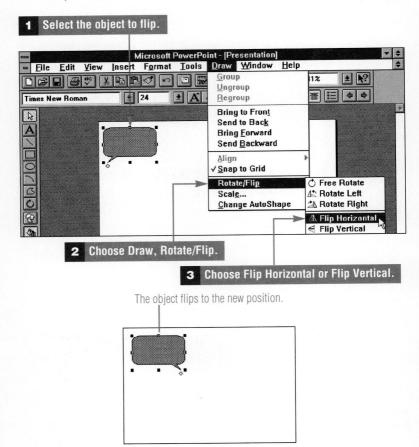

1 Select the object to flip.

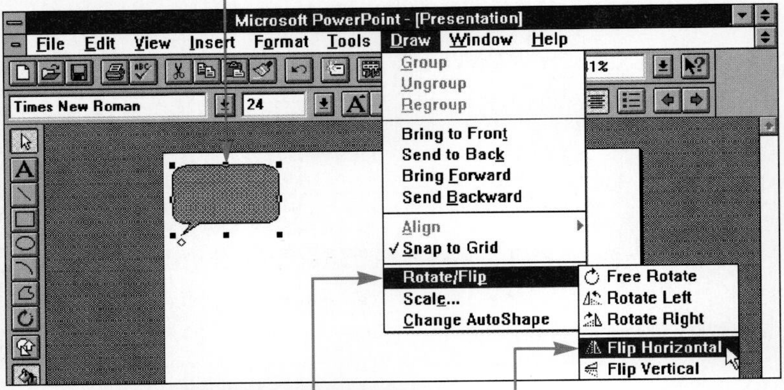

2 Choose Draw, Rotate/Flip.

3 Choose Flip Horizontal or Flip Vertical.

The object flips to the new position.

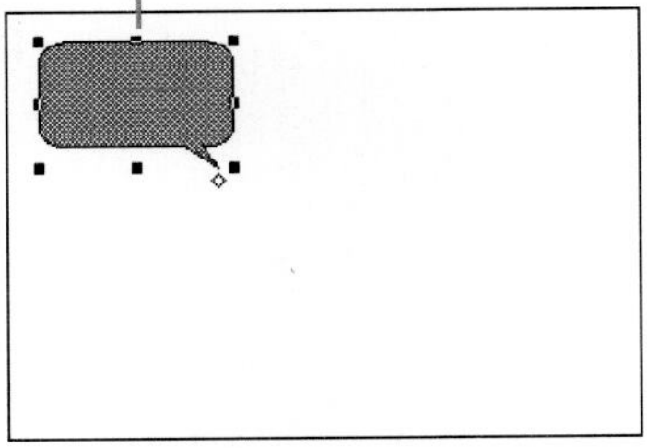

Attaching Text to a Drawn Object

You can add text to any closed object. When you add text, it becomes part of the object.

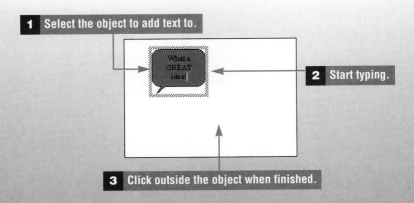

1 Select the object to add text to.

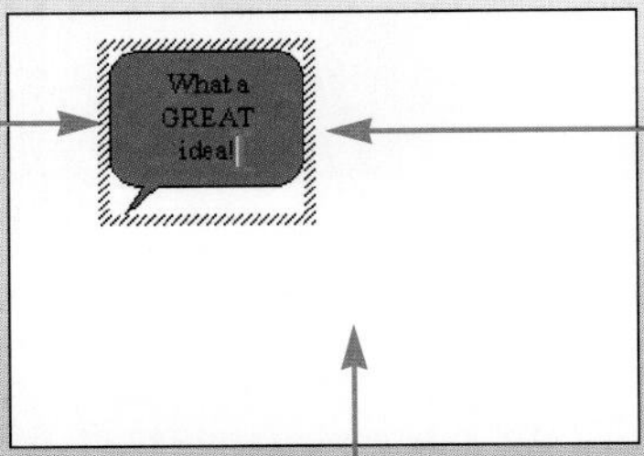

2 Start typing.

3 Click outside the object when finished.

Anchoring Text

Once you add text to an object, use the Text Anchor option to position the text within the object. You also can designate that the object automatically adjust its size to fit the text exactly.

1 Select the object in which to anchor text.

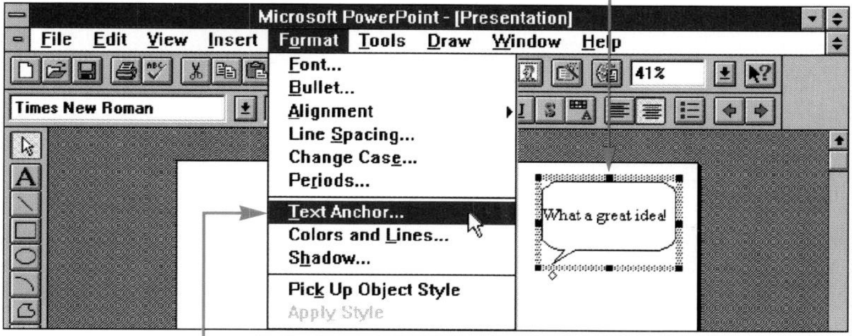

2 Choose Format, Text Anchor.

3 Select the anchor point for the text.

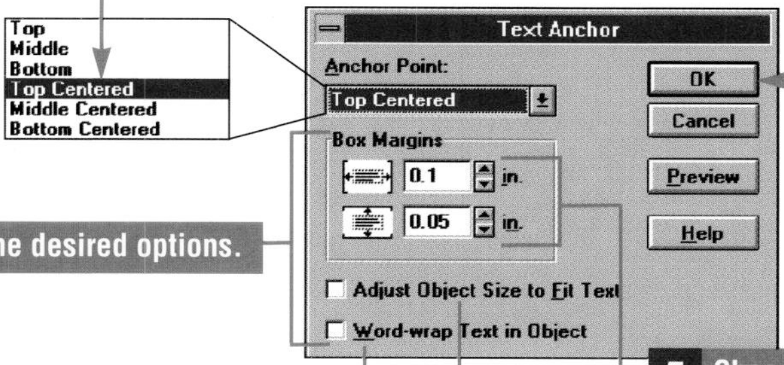

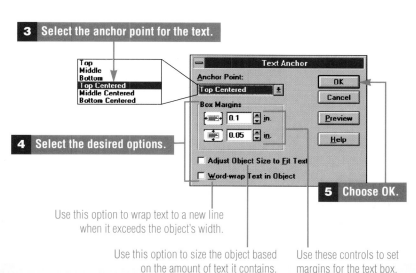

4 Select the desired options.

5 Choose OK.

Use this option to wrap text to a new line when it exceeds the object's width.

Use this option to size the object based on the amount of text it contains.

Use these controls to set margins for the text box.

The text is anchored to the selected point.

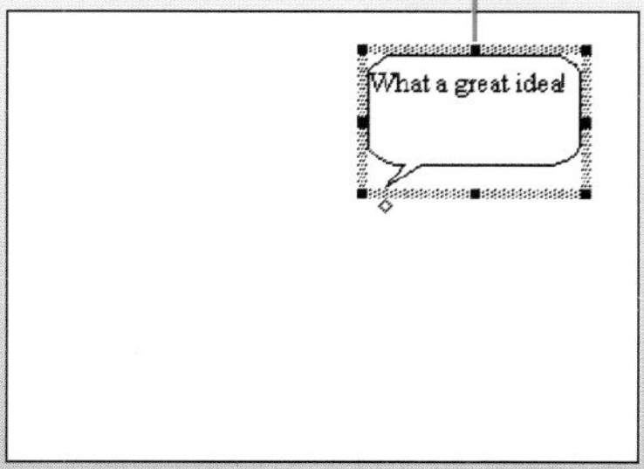

Adding Default Shadows and Fills

PowerPoint has default settings for shadows and fill colors that allow you to add a shadow or fill color to an object by selecting the appropriate drawing tool.

To add a default shadow

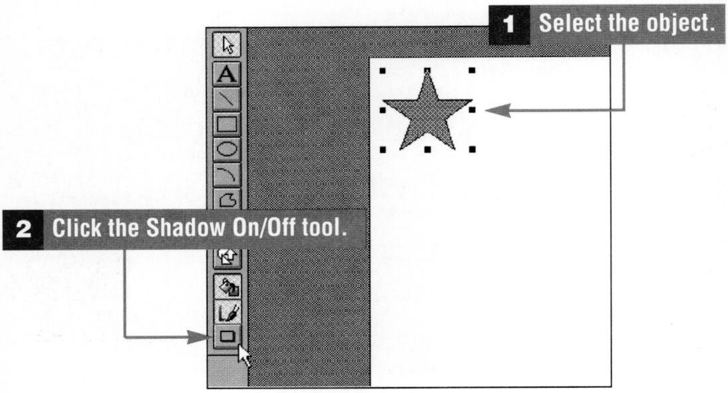

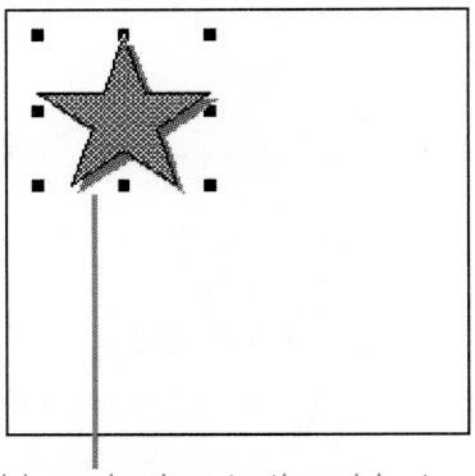

PowerPoint adds a shadow to the object.

To add a default fill color

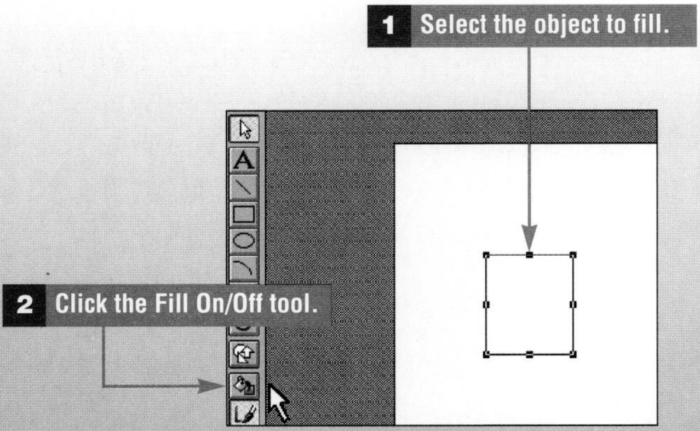

1 Select the object to fill.
2 Click the Fill On/Off tool.

Changing Default Fills, Lines, and Shadows

You can change PowerPoint's default fills, lines, and shadows, and then make your changes the new defaults.

1 Select an object.

2 Choose Format, Colors and Lines.

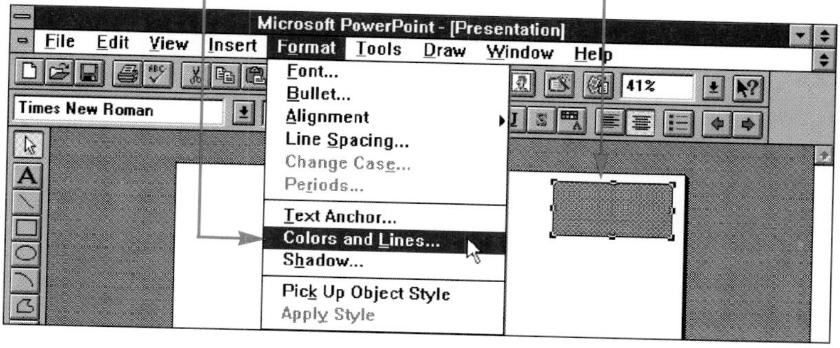

3 Select the fill color.

4 Select the line color.

5 Select the line style.

6 Choose OK.

7 Choose Format, Shadow.

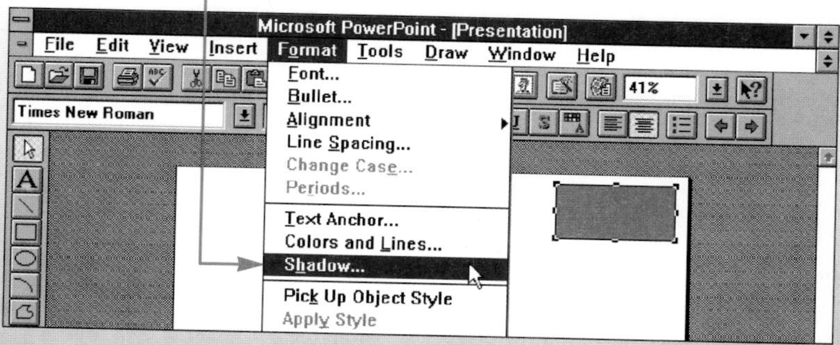

more ▶

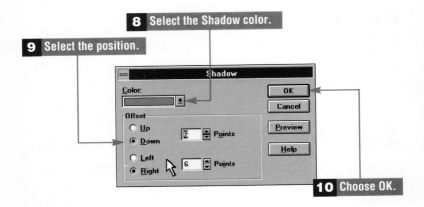

8 Select the Shadow color.

9 Select the position.

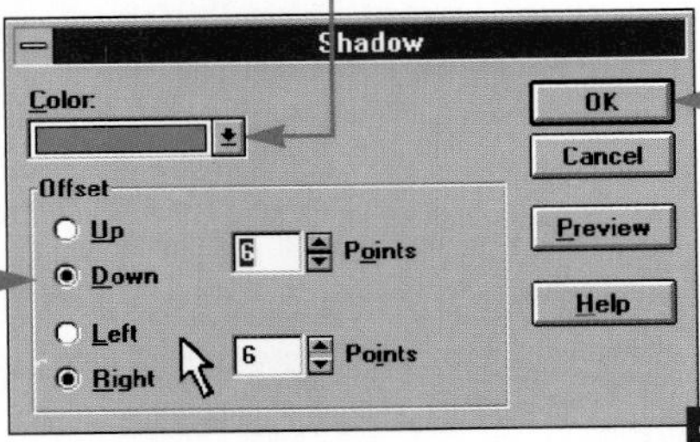

10 Choose OK.

11 Choose Format, Pick Up Object Style.

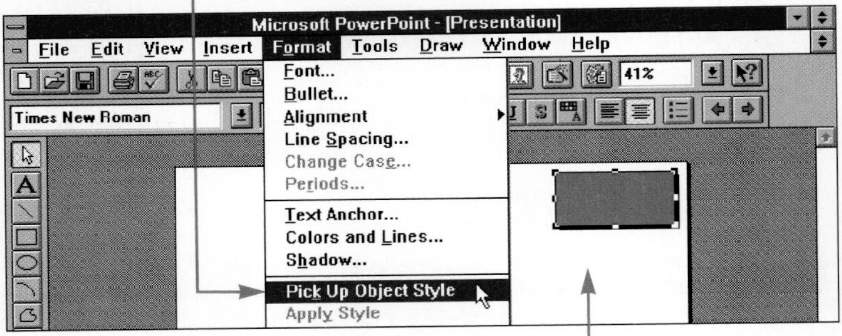

12 Click outside the object to deselect it.

13 Choose Format, Apply to Object Defaults.

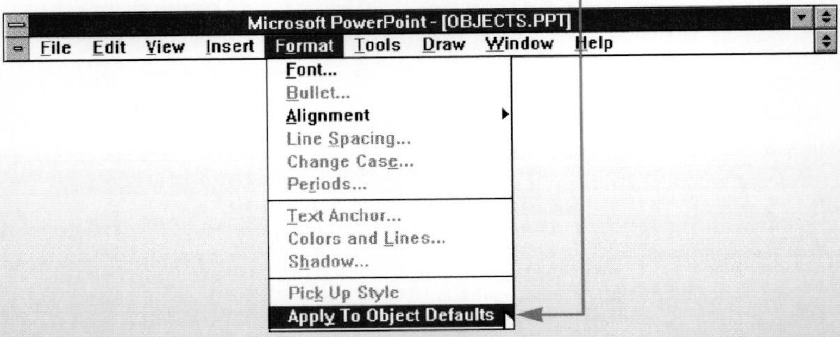

Painting Formats

You can use the Format Painter feature to copy the attributes of one object to another object.

1 Select the object to copy the attributes from.

2 Click the Format Painter button.

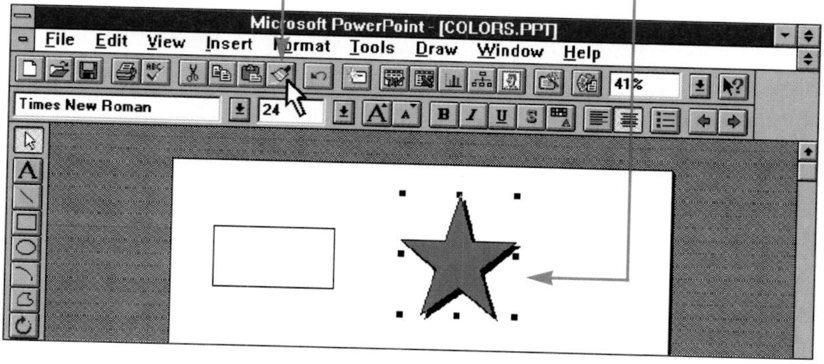

3 Select the object to apply the attributes to.

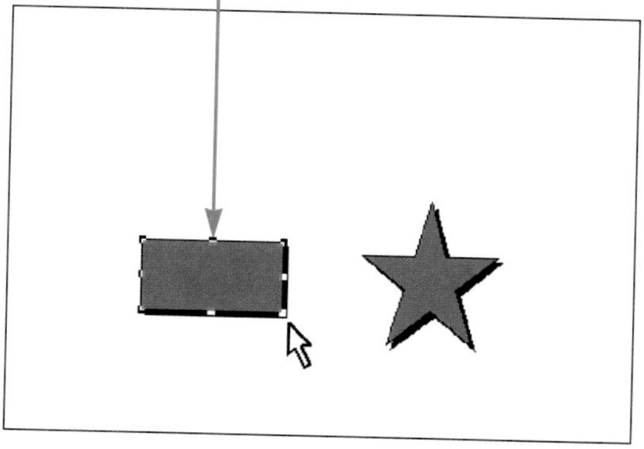

Entering Text

With the PowerPoint Outline feature, you enter the text in an outline form and PowerPoint automatically inserts the text on presentation slides.

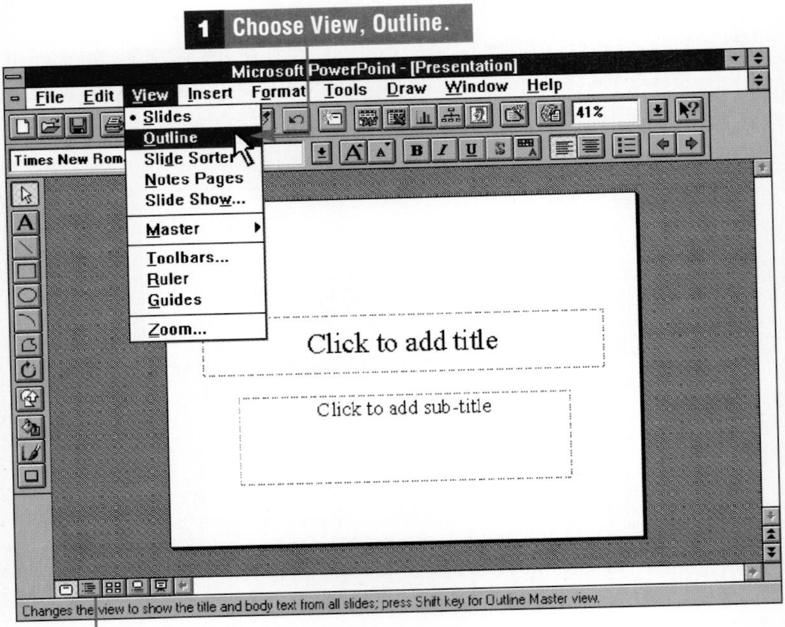

You can click the Outline View button to change quickly to Outline view.

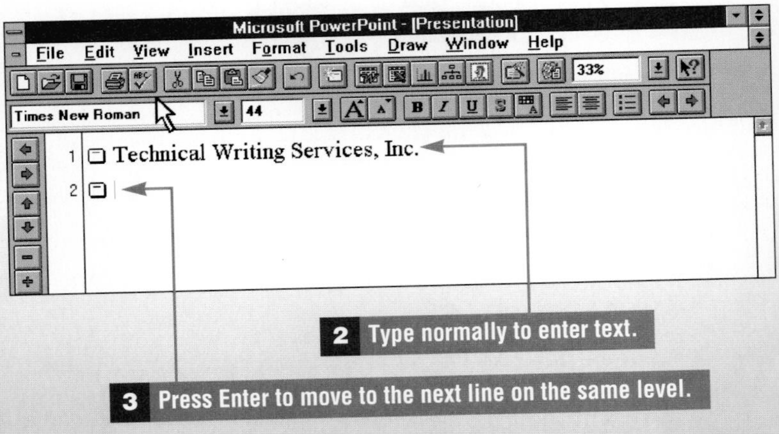

Step 3 creates a new slide when you're working at the first level.

Moving Entries

As you work and revise your outline, you can move entries rather than delete and type new text.

1 Click to the left of the entry to select the entire line.

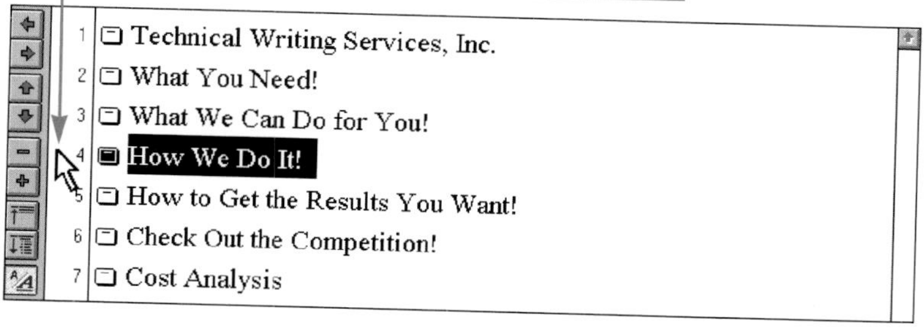
1 Technical Writing Services, Inc.
2 What You Need!
3 What We Can Do for You!
4 How We Do It!
5 How to Get the Results You Want!
6 Check Out the Competition!
7 Cost Analysis

2 Place the pointer on the slide icon and hold down the mouse button.

Click Move Up or Move Down to move the entry up or down one line at a time.

3 Drag to the desired location.

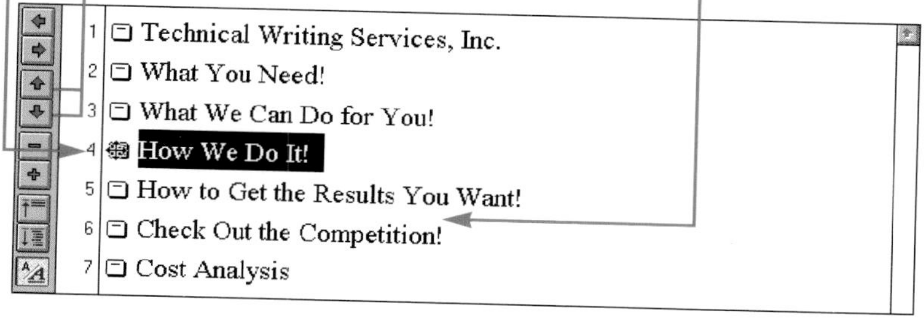
1 Technical Writing Services, Inc.
2 What You Need!
3 What We Can Do for You!
4 How We Do It!
5 How to Get the Results You Want!
6 Check Out the Competition!
7 Cost Analysis

As you drag, the pointer becomes a two-headed arrow and a horizontal line indicates your current position.

4 Release the mouse button.

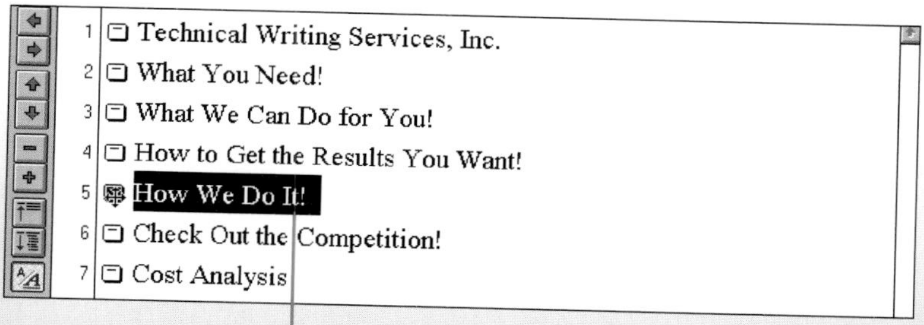
1 Technical Writing Services, Inc.
2 What You Need!
3 What We Can Do for You!
4 How to Get the Results You Want!
5 How We Do It!
6 Check Out the Competition!
7 Cost Analysis

The entry moves to the new location.

Demoting and Promoting Entries

You can change the levels of outline entries by using the Demote or Promote button to move entries down or up one or more levels.

To demote an entry

1 Select the entry to demote.

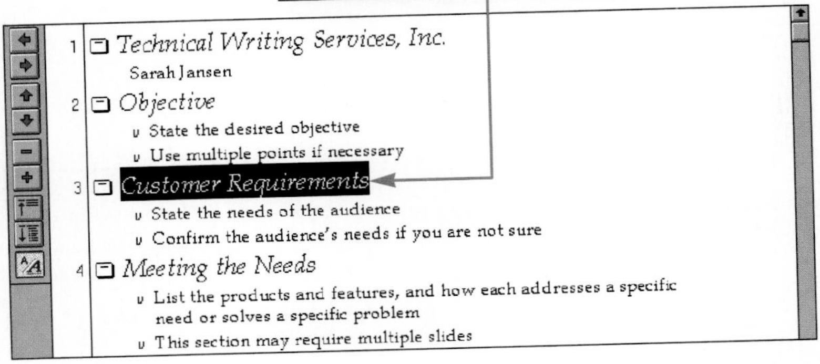
1 Technical Writing Services, Inc.
Sarah Jansen
2 Objective
State the desired objective
Use multiple points if necessary
3 Customer Requirements
State the needs of the audience
Confirm the audience's needs if you are not sure
4 Meeting the Needs
List the products and features, and how each addresses a specific need or solves a specific problem
This section may require multiple slides

2 Click the Demote button.

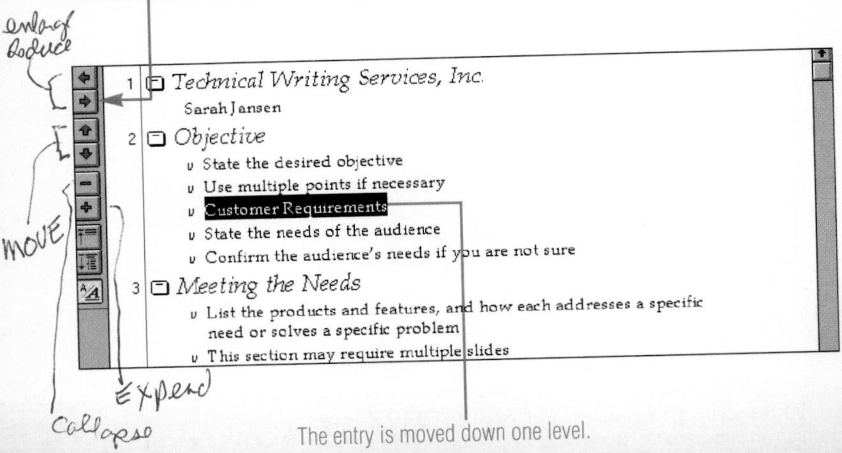
1 Technical Writing Services, Inc.
Sarah Jansen
2 Objective
State the desired objective
Use multiple points if necessary
Customer Requirements
State the needs of the audience
Confirm the audience's needs if you are not sure
3 Meeting the Needs
List the products and features, and how each addresses a specific need or solves a specific problem
This section may require multiple slides
enlarge
Reduce
MOVE
Expend
Collapse

The entry is moved down one level.

To promote an entry

1 Select the entry to promote.

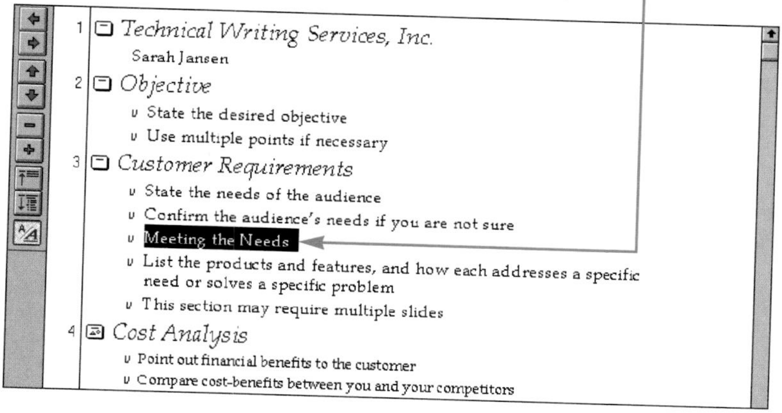
1 Technical Writing Services, Inc.
Sarah Jansen
2 Objective
State the desired objective
Use multiple points if necessary
3 Customer Requirements
State the needs of the audience
Confirm the audience's needs if you are not sure
Meeting the Needs
List the products and features, and how each addresses a specific need or solves a specific problem
This section may require multiple slides
4 Cost Analysis
Point out financial benefits to the customer
Compare cost-benefits between you and your competitors

2 Click the Promote button.

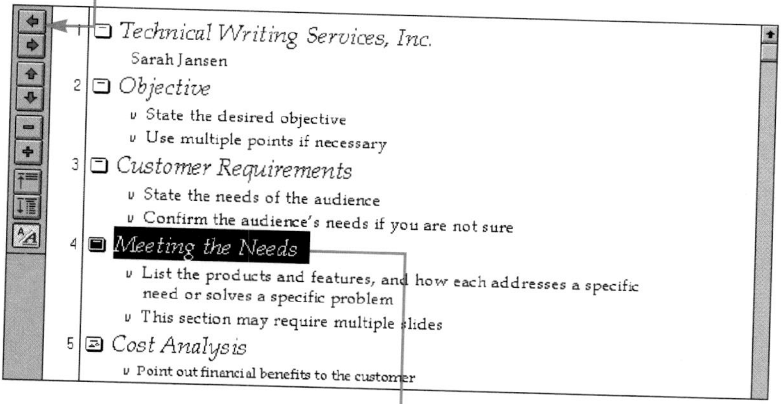
1 Technical Writing Services, Inc.
Sarah Jansen
2 Objective
State the desired objective
Use multiple points if necessary
3 Customer Requirements
State the needs of the audience
Confirm the audience's needs if you are not sure
4 Meeting the Needs
List the products and features, and how each addresses a specific need or solves a specific problem
This section may require multiple slides
5 Cost Analysis
Point out financial benefits to the customer

The entry is moved up one level.

Expanding and Collapsing Outline Sections

You may not always want to view the entire outline. You can expand any section of the outline to see all the levels, or you can collapse it to view only the title text.

To expand an outline section

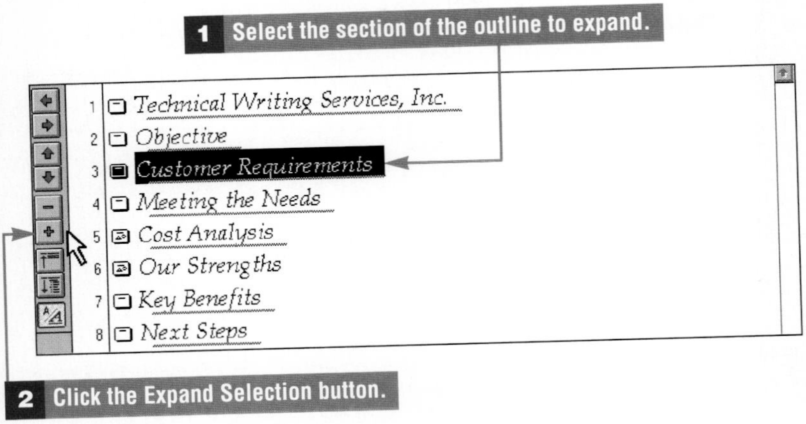
1 Select the section of the outline to expand.
1 Technical Writing Services, Inc.
2 Objective
3 Customer Requirements
4 Meeting the Needs
5 Cost Analysis
6 Our Strengths
7 Key Benefits
8 Next Steps
2 Click the Expand Selection button.

Titles with collapsed sublevels are indicated by underlines.

To collapse an outline section

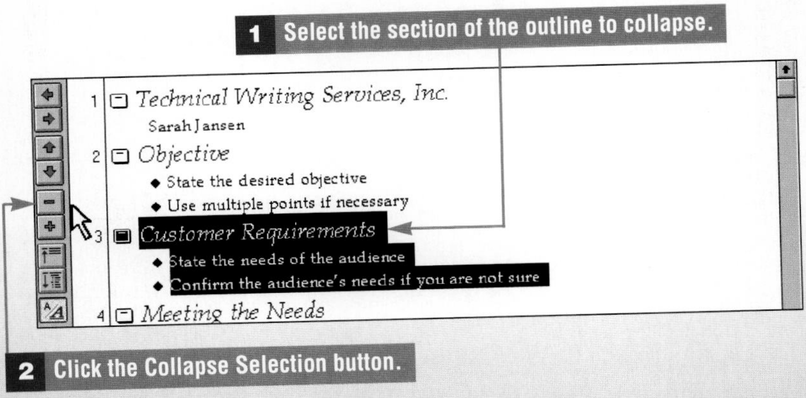
1 Select the section of the outline to collapse.
1 Technical Writing Services, Inc.
Sarah Jansen
2 Objective
State the desired objective
Use multiple points if necessary
3 Customer Requirements
State the needs of the audience
Confirm the audience's needs if you are not sure
4 Meeting the Needs
2 Click the Collapse Selection button.

Showing All or Part of the Outline

You can display the outline with all the outline text, or with title text only. The Show All and Show Titles buttons let you expand or collapse the entire outline with a single action.

To show the entire outline

1 Click the Show All button.

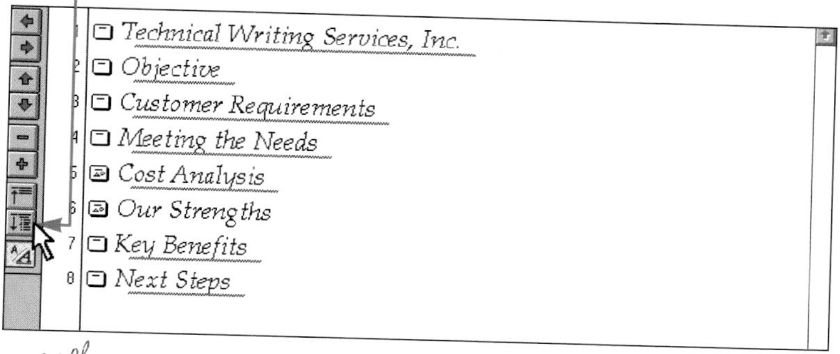
1 Technical Writing Services, Inc.
2 Objective
3 Customer Requirements
4 Meeting the Needs
5 Cost Analysis
6 Our Strengths
7 Key Benefits
8 Next Steps

Titles with collapsed sublevels are indicated by underlines.

To show the title text only

1 Click the Show Titles button.

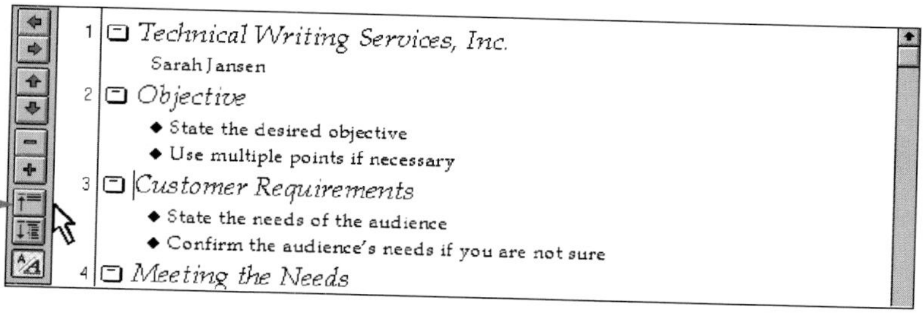
1 Technical Writing Services, Inc.
Sarah Jansen
2 Objective
◆ State the desired objective
◆ Use multiple points if necessary
3 Customer Requirements
◆ State the needs of the audience
◆ Confirm the audience's needs if you are not sure
4 Meeting the Needs

Making Global Formatting Changes in Outline View

Rather than format the text on each slide individually, you can select the entire outline and make global formatting changes at once.

1 Press Ctrl+A to select the entire outline.

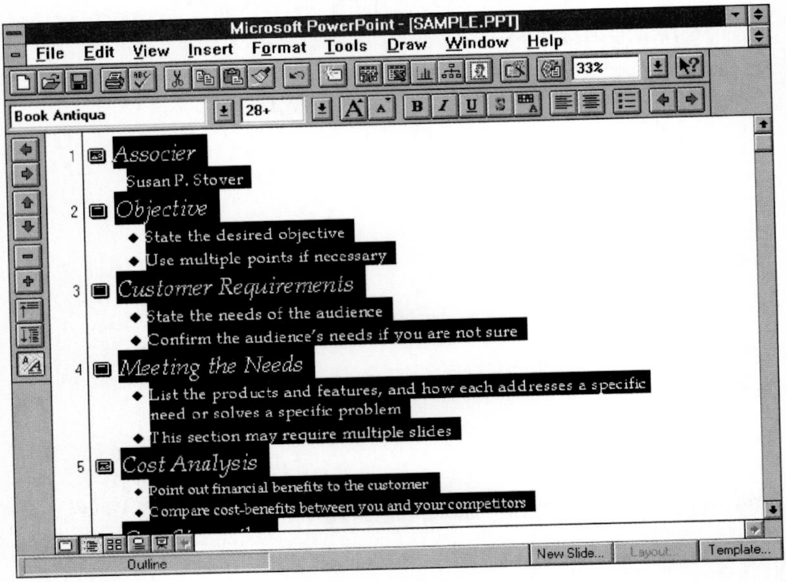
Microsoft PowerPoint - [SAMPLE.PPT]
File Edit View Insert Format Tools Draw Window Help
33%
Book Antiqua
28+
1 Associer
Susan P. Stover
2 Objective
State the desired objective
Use multiple points if necessary
3 Customer Requirements
State the needs of the audience
Confirm the audience's needs if you are not sure
4 Meeting the Needs
List the products and features, and how each addresses a specific need or solves a specific problem
This section may require multiple slides
5 Cost Analysis
Point out financial benefits to the customer
Compare cost-benefits between you and your competitors
Outline
New Slide...
Layout
Template...

2 Choose Format, Font.

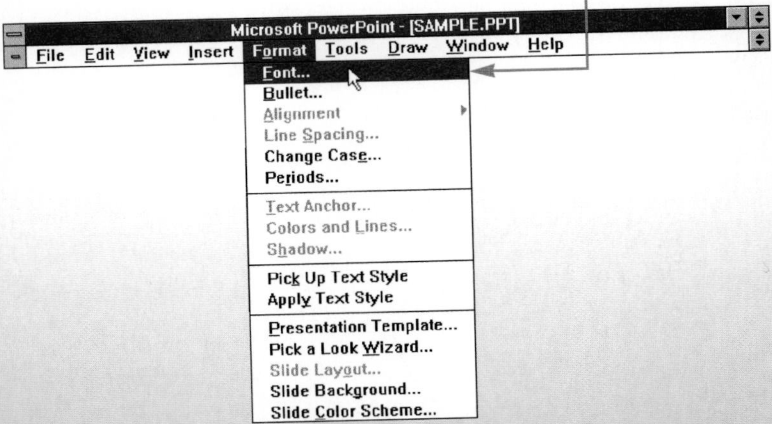
Microsoft PowerPoint - [SAMPLE.PPT]
File Edit View Insert Format Tools Draw Window Help
Font...
Bullet...
Alignment
Line Spacing...
Change Case...
Periods...
Text Anchor...
Colors and Lines...
Shadow...
Pick Up Text Style
Apply Text Style
Presentation Template...
Pick a Look Wizard...
Slide Layout...
Slide Background...
Slide Color Scheme...

You also can choose other formatting options from this menu.

3 Select the font.

4 Select the font style.

5 Select the font size.

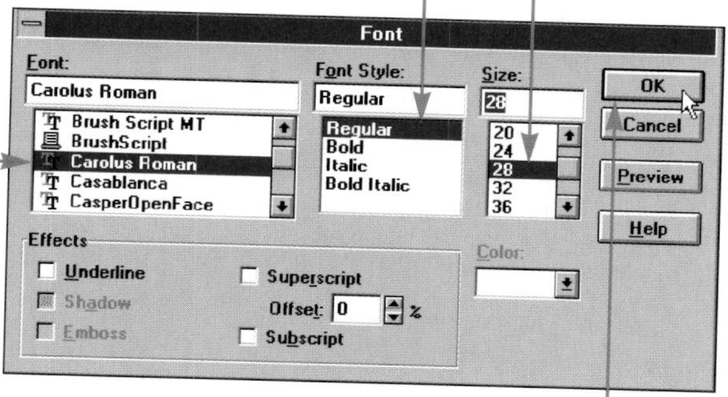
Font
Font:
Carolus Roman
Brush Script MT
BrushScript
Carolus Roman
Casablanca
CasperOpenFace
Font Style:
Regular
Regular
Bold
Italic
Bold Italic
Size:
28
20
24
28
32
36
OK
Cancel
Preview
Help
Effects
Underline
Shadow
Emboss
Superscript
Offset: 0 %
Subscript
Color:

6 Choose OK.

The formatting changes are applied to the entire presentation.

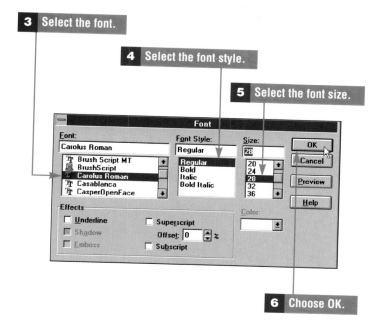

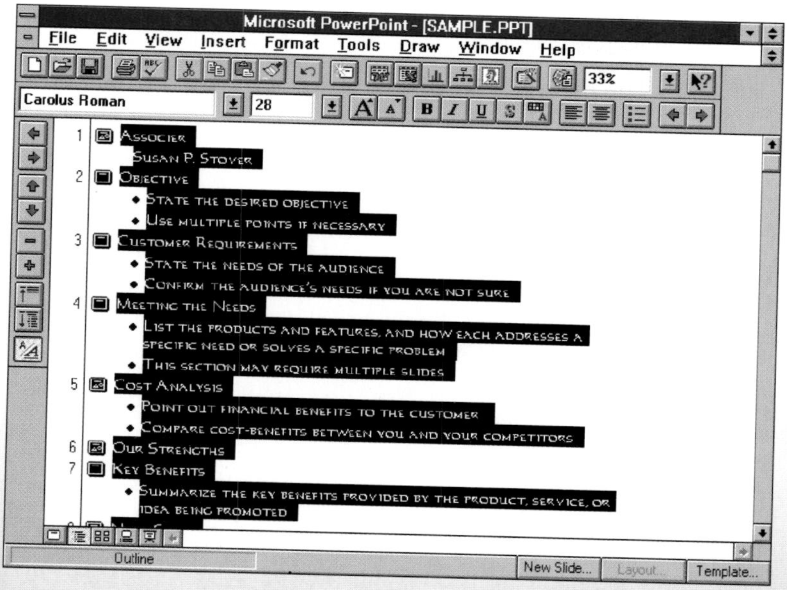
Microsoft PowerPoint - [SAMPLE.PPT]
File Edit View Insert Format Tools Draw Window Help
33%
Carolus Roman
28
Associer
Susan P. Stover
Objective
State the desired objective
Use multiple points if necessary
Customer Requirements
State the needs of the audience
Confirm the audience's needs if you are not sure
Meeting the Needs
List the products and features, and how each addresses a specific need or solves a specific problem
This section may require multiple slides
Cost Analysis
Point out financial benefits to the customer
Compare cost-benefits between you and your competitors
Our Strengths
Key Benefits
Summarize the key benefits provided by the product, service, or idea being promoted
Outline
New Slide...
Layout...
Template...

Using the AutoContent Wizard

The PowerPoint AutoContent Wizard provides you with guidelines for the content of your presentation. You select the type of presentation and enter some basic information, and PowerPoint does the rest.

1 Click the New button.

2 Select AutoContent Wizard.

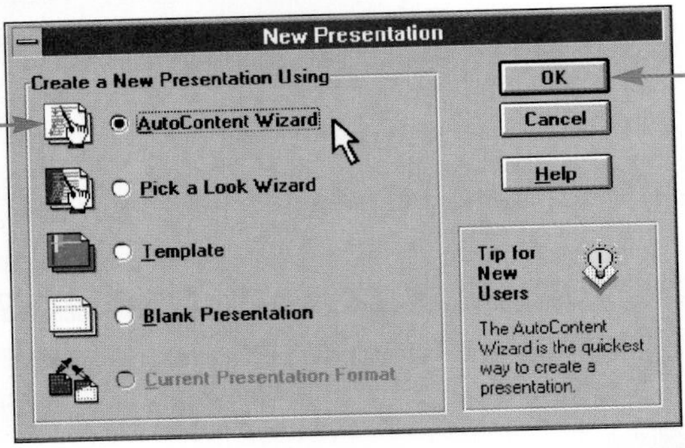

3 Choose OK.

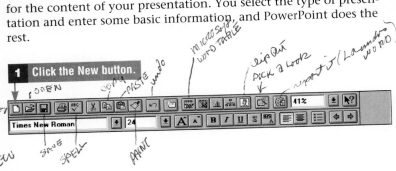

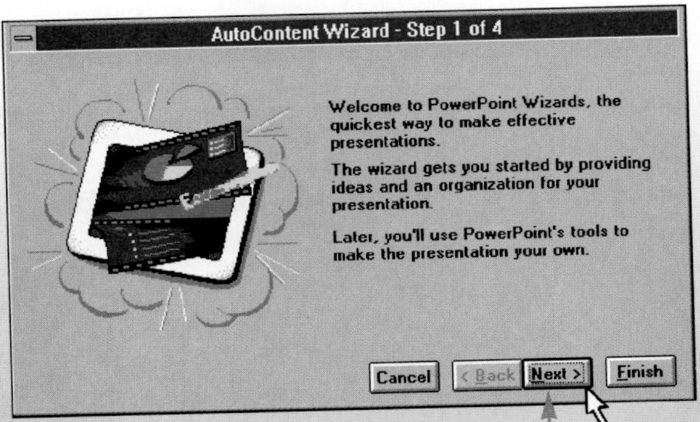

4 Choose Next.

5 Enter the title of your presentation.

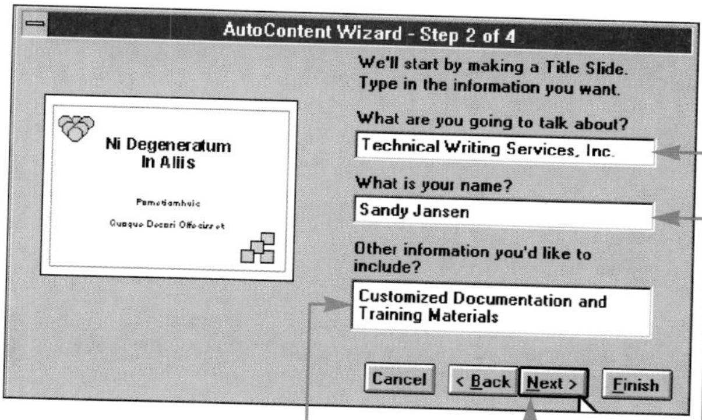
AutoContent Wizard - Step 2 of 4
We'll start by making a Title Slide.
Type in the information you want.
What are you going to talk about?
Technical Writing Services, Inc.
What is your name?
Sandy Jansen
Other information you'd like to include?
Customized Documentation and Training Materials
Ni Degeneratum In Aliis
Cancel
< Back
Next >
Finish

6 Enter your name.

7 Enter a subtitle.

8 Choose Next.

9 Select the type of presentation.

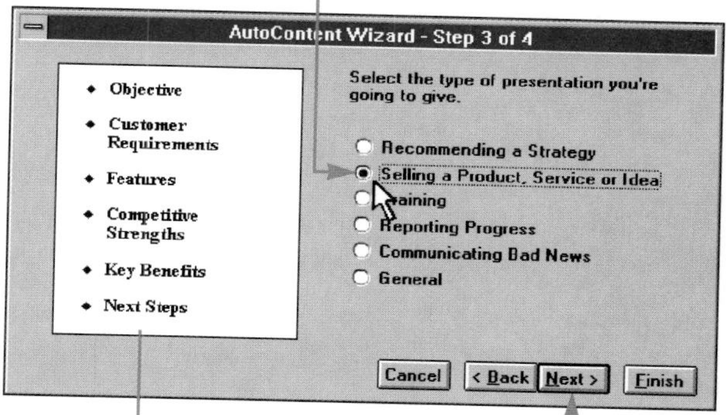
AutoContent Wizard - Step 3 of 4
Objective
Customer Requirements
Features
Competitive Strengths
Key Benefits
Next Steps
Select the type of presentation you're going to give.
Recommending a Strategy
Selling a Product, Service or Idea
Reporting Progress
Communicating Bad News
General
Cancel
< Back
Next >
Finish

Basic outline for the presentation type

10 Choose Next.

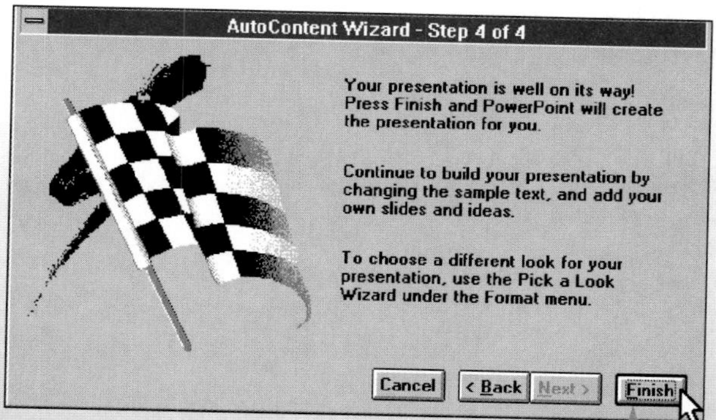
AutoContent Wizard - Step 4 of 4
Your presentation is well on its way! Press Finish and PowerPoint will create the presentation for you.
Continue to build your presentation by changing the sample text, and add your own slides and ideas.
To choose a different look for your presentation, use the Pick a Look Wizard under the Format menu.
Cancel
< Back
Next >
Finish

11 Choose Finish.

Selecting a New Template

You can change the look of your presentation by selecting a new presentation template. The new template provides a different background and layout using the same data.

1 Choose Format, Presentation Template.

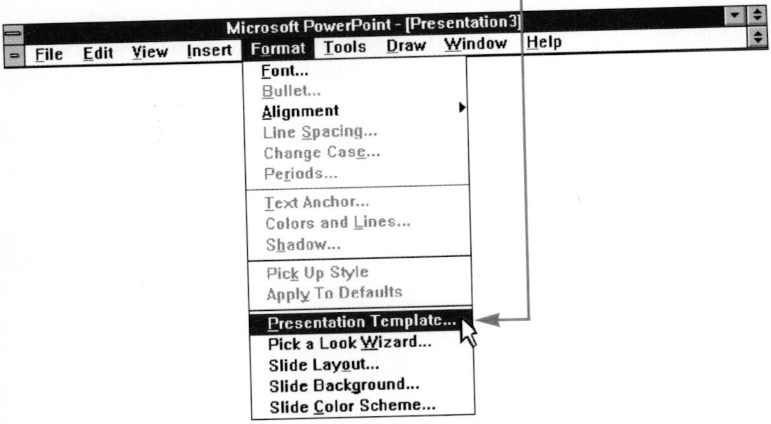

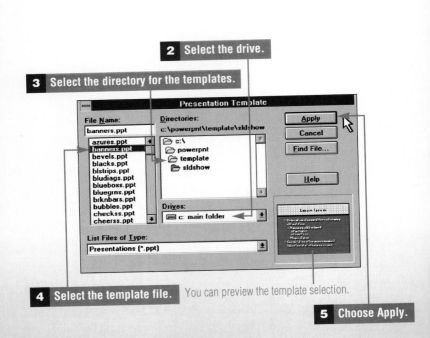

2 Select the drive.

3 Select the directory for the templates.

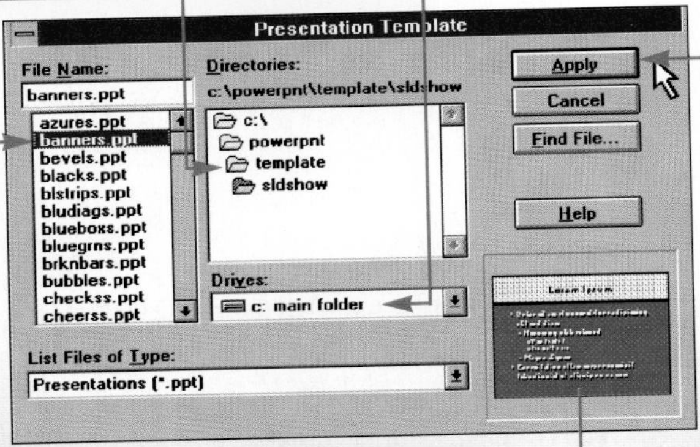

4 Select the template file.

You can preview the template selection.

5 Choose Apply.

Selecting a New Color Scheme

PowerPoint provides you with predefined color schemes that are comprised of select groups of complementary colors. You can select any of these schemes to change the colors used to display your slides. You can apply the scheme to the current slide or to all the slides in your presentation.

1 Choose Format, Slide Color Scheme.

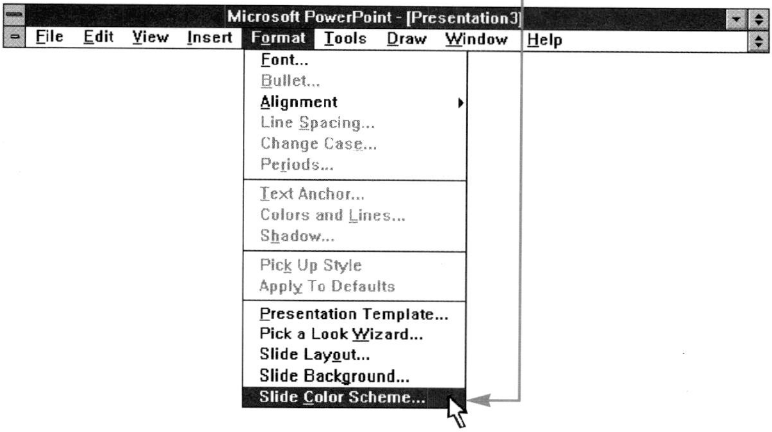

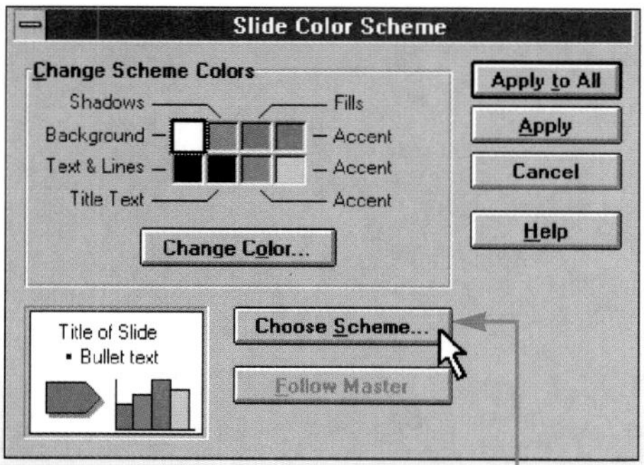

2 Click Choose Scheme.

more ▶

3 Select the background color.

Accent color options are determined by the background and text colors selected.

4 Select the text and line color.

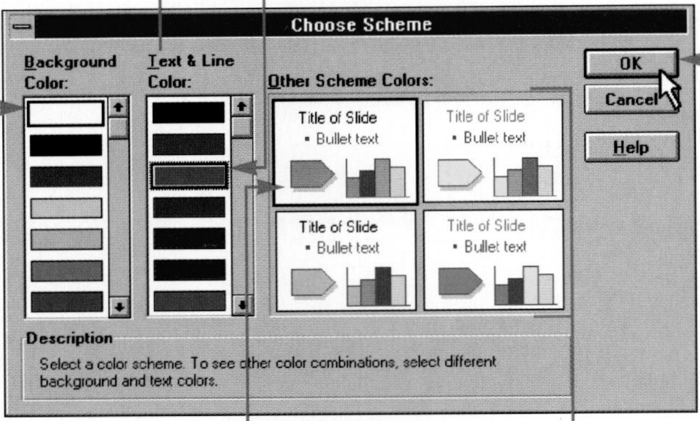

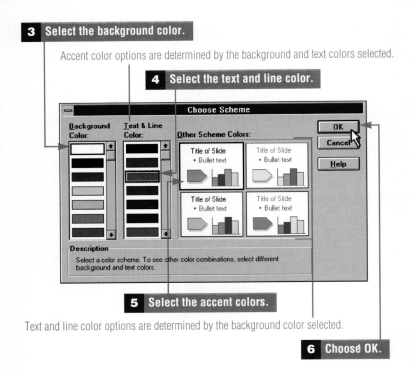

5 Select the accent colors.

Text and line color options are determined by the background color selected.

6 Choose OK.

7 Choose Apply to All.

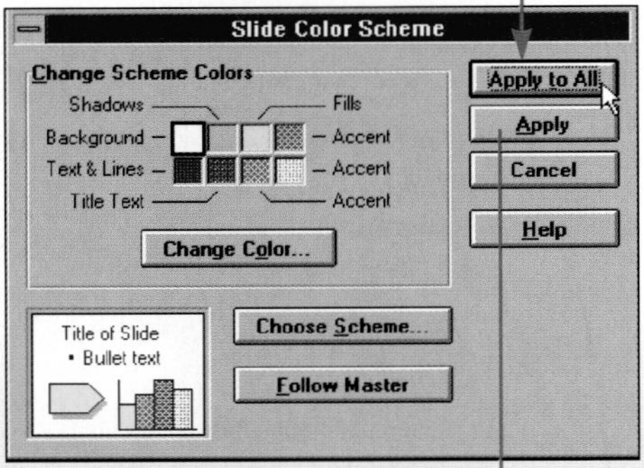

Choose Apply to select the color scheme for the current slide only.

Modifying a Color Scheme

You can modify the individual colors in a selected color scheme at any time. You have the option to apply the changes to the current slide or to the entire presentation.

1 Choose Format, Slide Color Scheme.

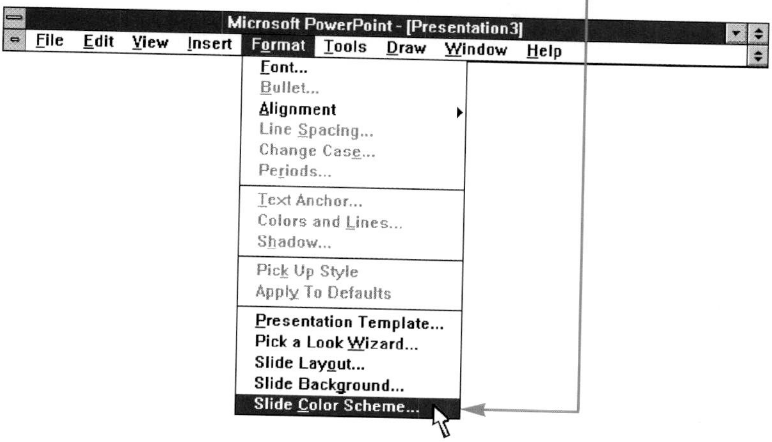

2 Select the color box for the element you want to edit.

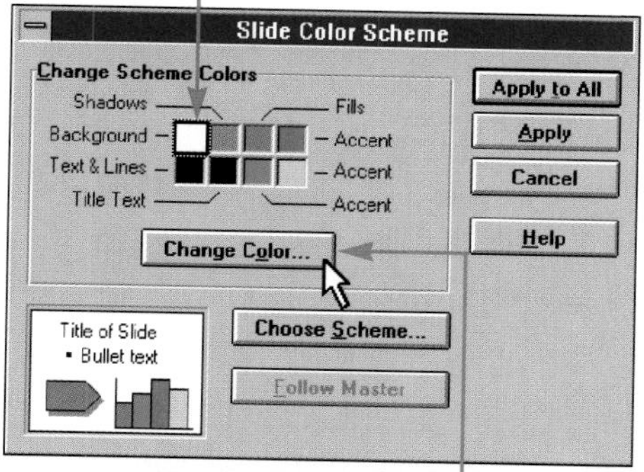

3 Choose Change Color.

more ▶

4 Select the desired color.

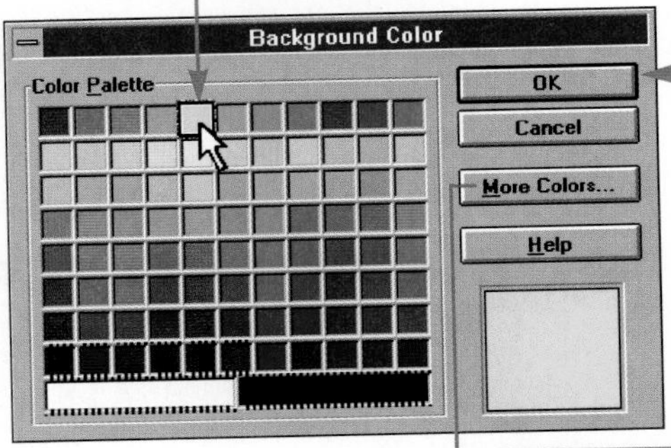

5 Choose OK.

Choose More Colors for additional color options.

6 Choose Apply to All.

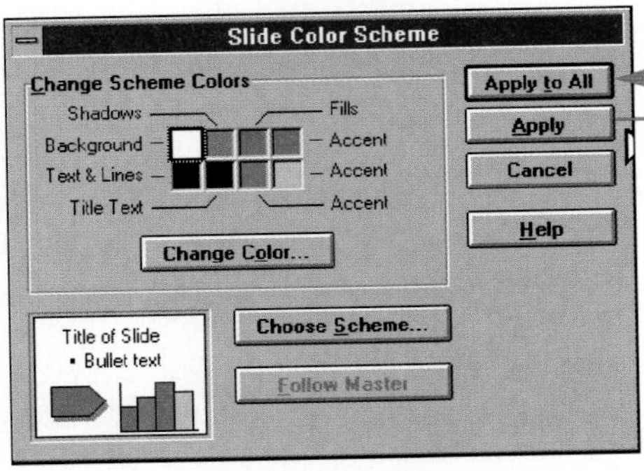

Choose Apply to change the color on the current slide only.

Using the Pick a Look Wizard

The Pick a Look Wizard assists you in designing the look of your presentation. You select the template and determine various fine-tuning options.

1 Click the Pick a Look Wizard button.

41%
Times New Roman
24

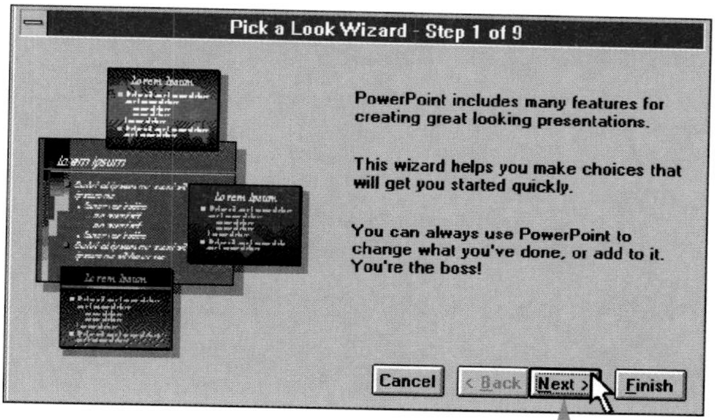
Pick a Look Wizard - Step 1 of 9
PowerPoint includes many features for creating great looking presentations.
This wizard helps you make choices that will get you started quickly.
You can always use PowerPoint to change what you've done, or add to it. You're the boss!
Cancel
< Back
Next >
Finish

2 Choose Next.

3 Select the type of output you need.

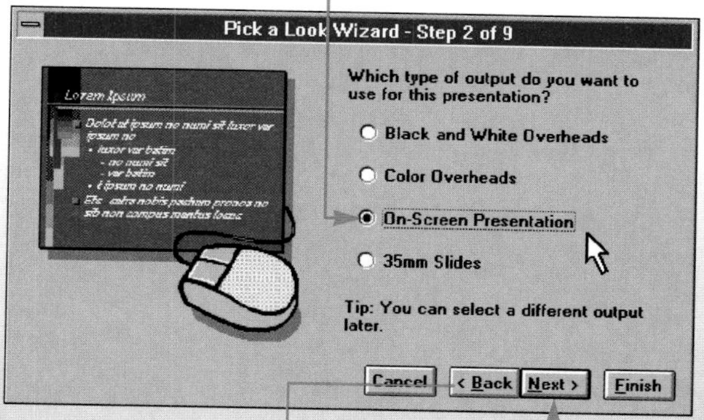
Pick a Look Wizard - Step 2 of 9
Which type of output do you want to use for this presentation?
Black and White Overheads
Color Overheads
On-Screen Presentation
35mm Slides
Tip: You can select a different output later.
Cancel
< Back
Next >
Finish

4 Choose Next.

Click the Back button on any screen to return to the preceding Pick a Look screen.

more ▶

5 Select the template for the presentation.

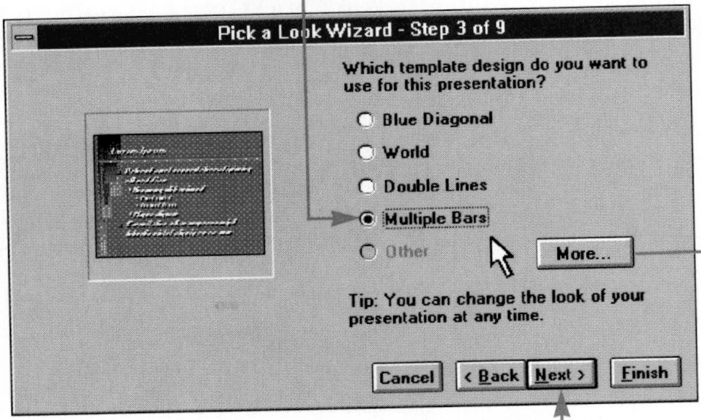

6 Choose Next.

Choose More to display additional presentation template options.

7 Select the options for printing your presentation.

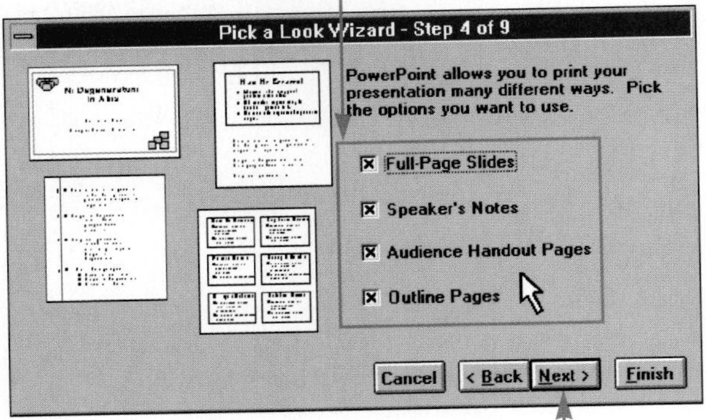

You can select multiple printing options.

8 Choose Next.

9 Select text items to include on your presentation display.

10 Enter the name text, if applicable.

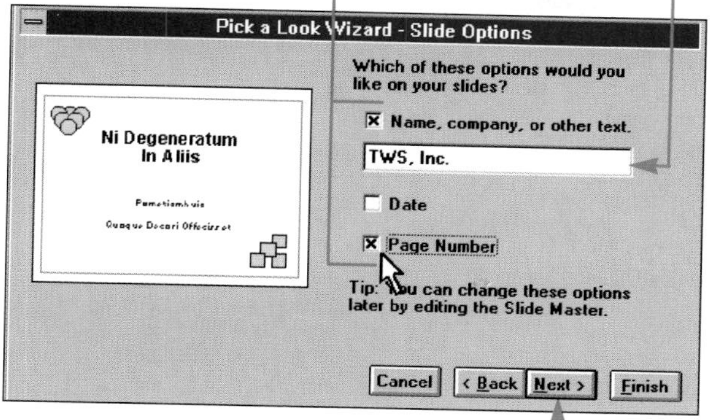
Pick a Look Wizard - Slide Options
Ni Degeneratum
In Aliis
Which of these options would you like on your slides?
Name, company, or other text.
TWS, Inc.
Date
Page Number
Tip: You can change these options later by editing the Slide Master.
Cancel
< Back
Next >
Finish

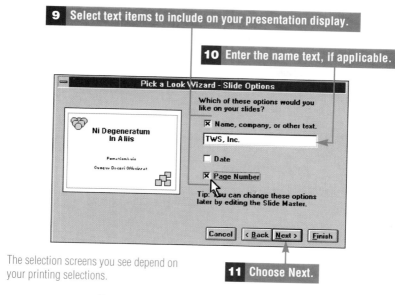

The selection screens you see depend on your printing selections.

11 Choose Next.

Repeat steps 9–13 on each Slide Options screen until you reach the final Pick a Look screen.

Pick a Look Wizard - Step 9 of 9
Congratulations! You have just picked the look for your presentation.
Press Finish and PowerPoint will make all the changes you've specified.
If you want to run this Wizard again, you can find it under the Format menu.
Cancel
< Back
Next >
Finish

12 Choose Finish.

Printing an Outline

You can print a copy of your presentation outline at any time. The printed outline includes only the outline text displayed in Outline view and follows the format that appears on-screen.

1 Click the Outline View button.

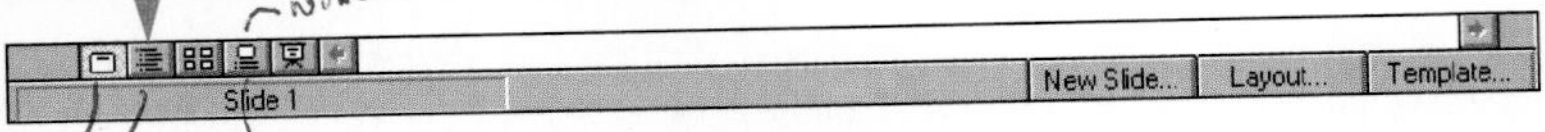

See "Outlining: Creating and Editing" for information related to outlines.

2 Choose File, Print.

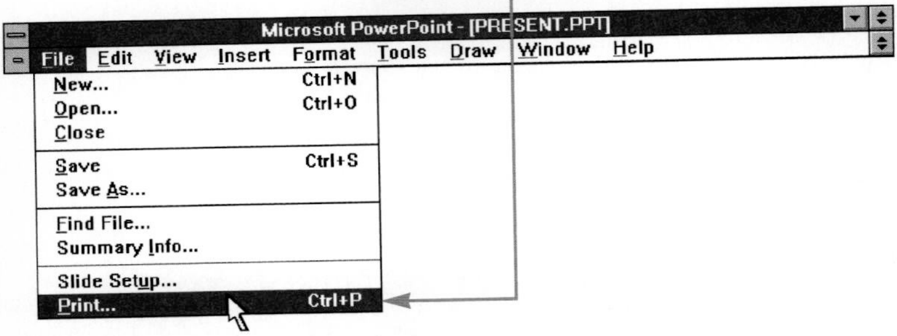
Microsoft PowerPoint - [PRESENT.PPT]
File Edit View Insert Format Tools Draw Window Help
New... Ctrl+N
Open... Ctrl+O
Close
Save Ctrl+S
Save As...
Find File...
Summary Info...
Slide Setup...
Print... Ctrl+P

3 Select Outline View.

4 Indicate the number of copies.

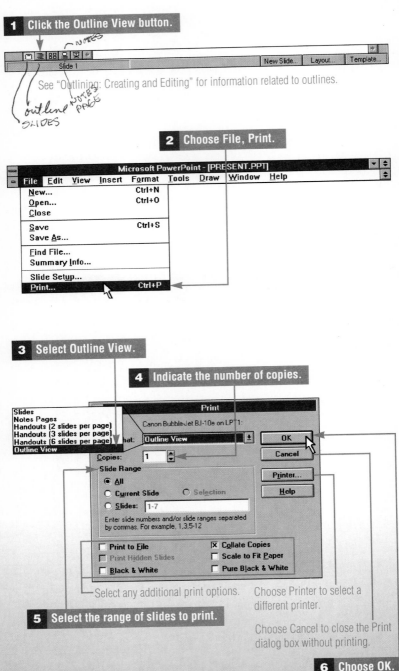

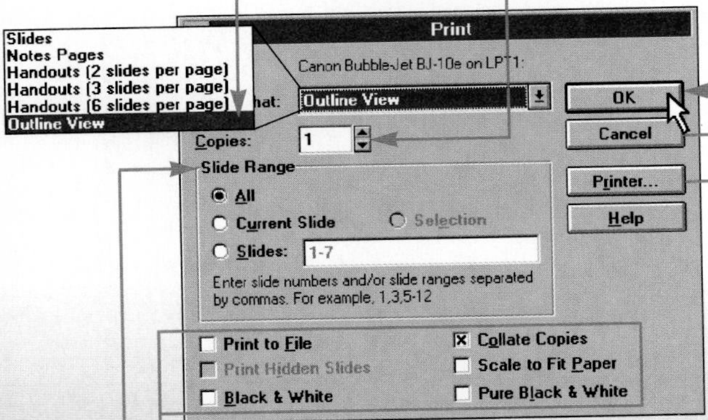
Print
Slides
Notes Pages
Handouts (2 slides per page)
Handouts (3 slides per page)
Handouts (6 slides per page)
Outline View
Canon BubbleJet BJ-10e on LPT1:
Outline View
OK
Cancel
Copies: 1
Printer...
Help
Slide Range
All
Current Slide
Selection
Slides: 1-7
Enter slide numbers and/or slide ranges separated by commas. For example, 1,3,5-12
Print to File
Print Hidden Slides
Black & White
Collate Copies
Scale to Fit Paper
Pure Black & White

Select any additional print options.

Choose Printer to select a different printer.

5 Select the range of slides to print.

Choose Cancel to close the Print dialog box without printing.

6 Choose OK.

Printing Audience Handouts

Audience handouts print two, three, or six presentation slides per page. Select the type of handout depending on the size you want the slides to print at and the amount of note-taking space you want on the page.

1 Choose File, Print.

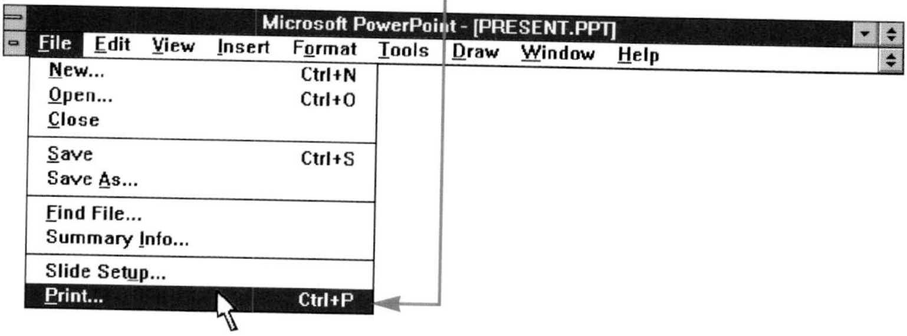

2 Select one of the Handouts options.

3 Indicate the number of copies.

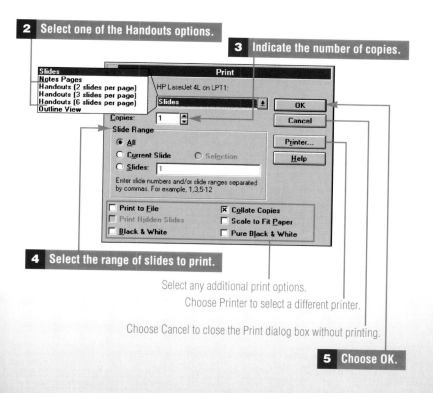

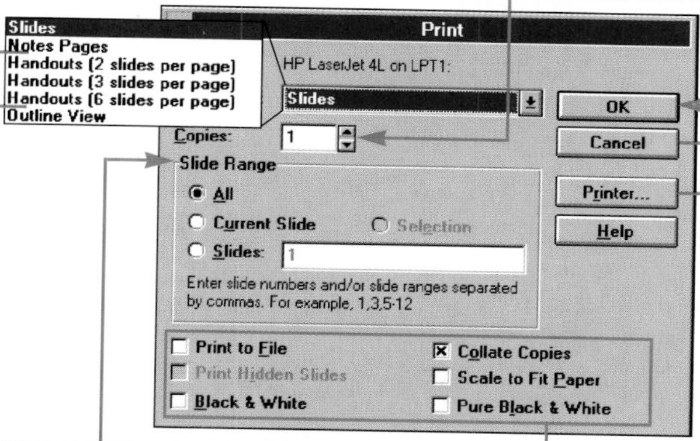

4 Select the range of slides to print.

Select any additional print options.

Choose Printer to select a different printer.

Choose Cancel to close the Print dialog box without printing.

5 Choose OK.

Printing Pages with Notes

You can print copies of your slides that include any information entered on the Notes Page format for the slides. When printed, the Notes Page includes the slide at the top of the page and the notes at the bottom of the page.

1 Choose File, Print.

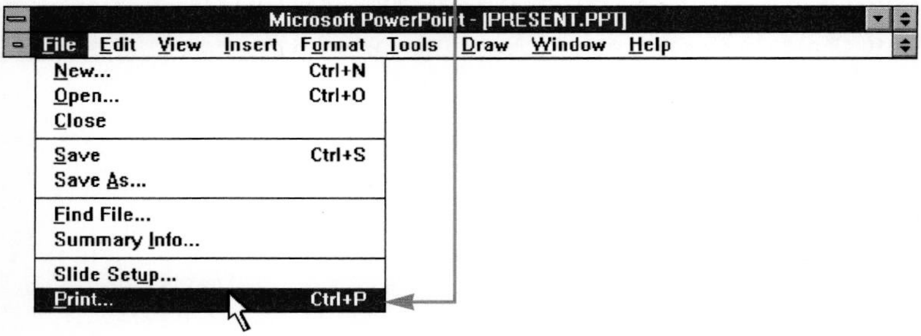

2 Select Notes Pages.

3 Indicate the number of copies.

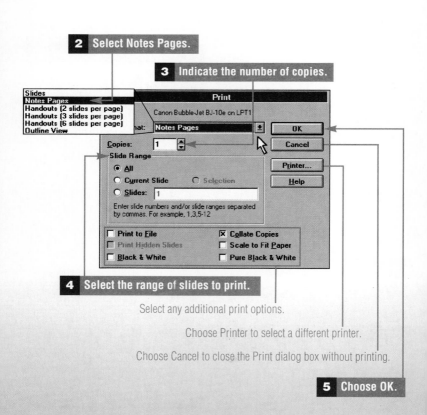

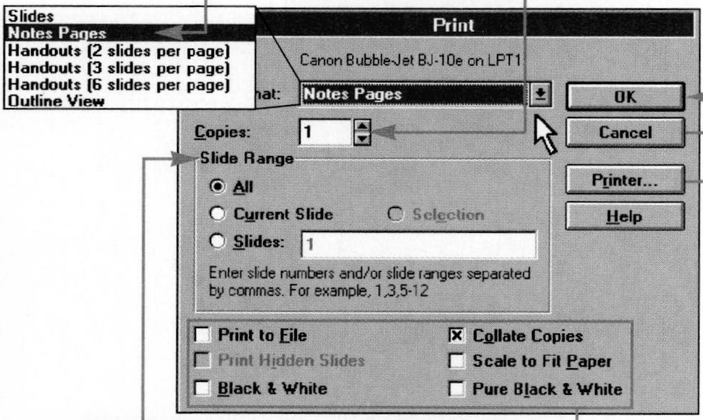

4 Select the range of slides to print.

Select any additional print options.

Choose Printer to select a different printer.

Choose Cancel to close the Print dialog box without printing.

5 Choose OK.

Printing Overheads

The Slides option prints one presentation slide per page. You can use this option to create overheads for displaying your presentation.

1 Choose File, Print.

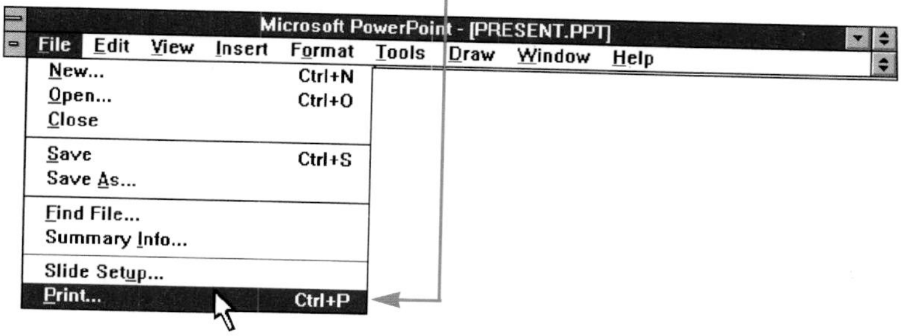

2 Select the Slides options.

3 Indicate the number of copies.

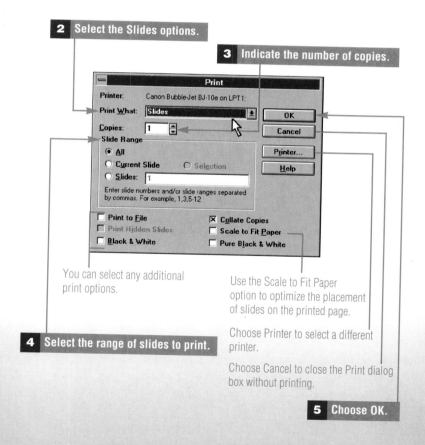

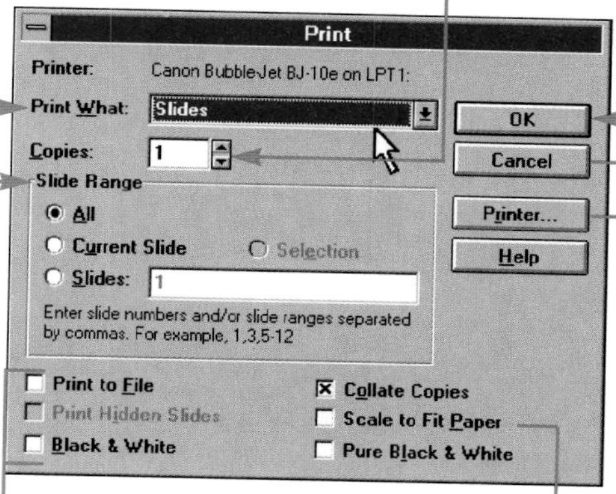

You can select any additional print options.

Use the Scale to Fit Paper option to optimize the placement of slides on the printed page.

Choose Printer to select a different printer.

Choose Cancel to close the Print dialog box without printing.

4 Select the range of slides to print.

5 Choose OK.

Copying Data to the Clipboard

The Windows Clipboard is a temporary storage area used to copy and move object data from one location to another. To use the Clipboard, you must first copy data to it.

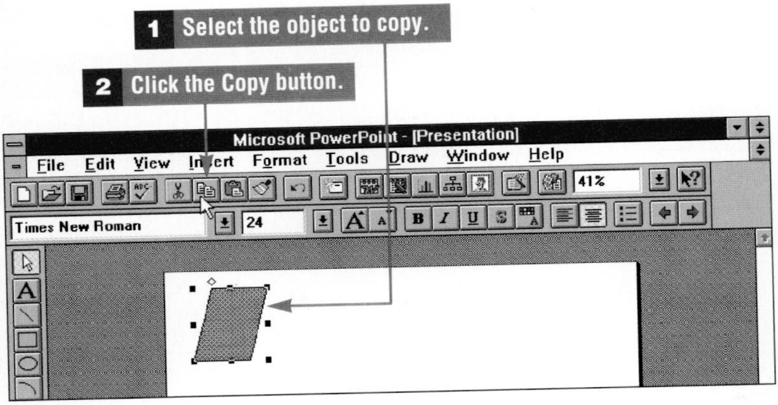

Pasting Data from the Clipboard

To insert data from the Clipboard at a specific location, you use the Paste option. You can paste copied data to another slide in the same presentation, or to a slide in a different presentation.

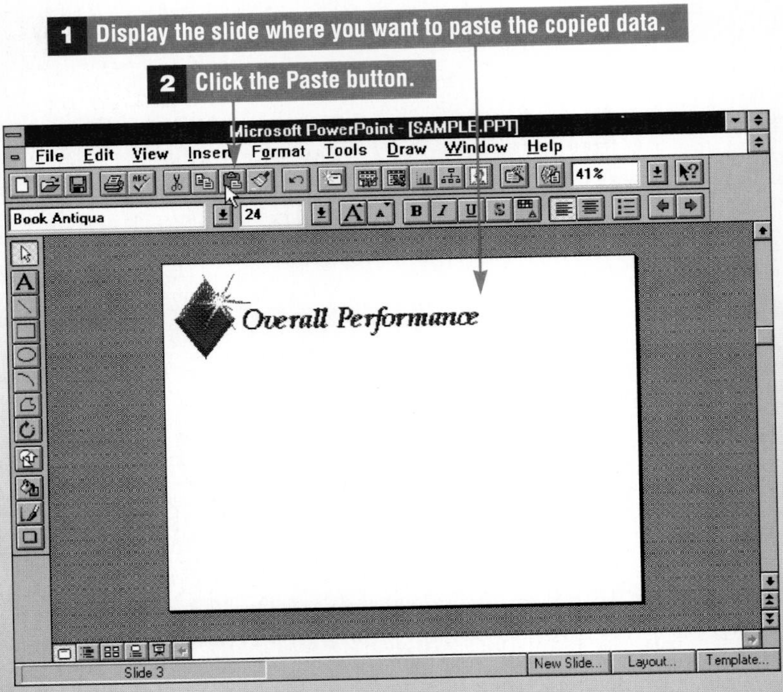

Copying Slides from Another Presentation

Using the Windows Clipboard, you can share slides between presentations. You select the slide and copy it to the Clipboard; then you paste the slide data in the other presentation.

1 Open the presentations you want to copy from and to.

2 Choose Window, Arrange All.

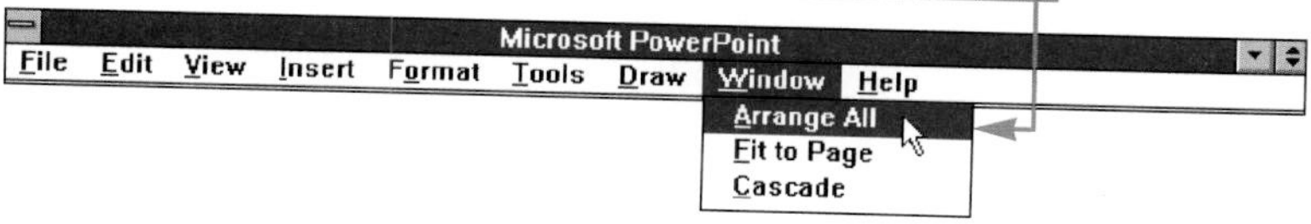

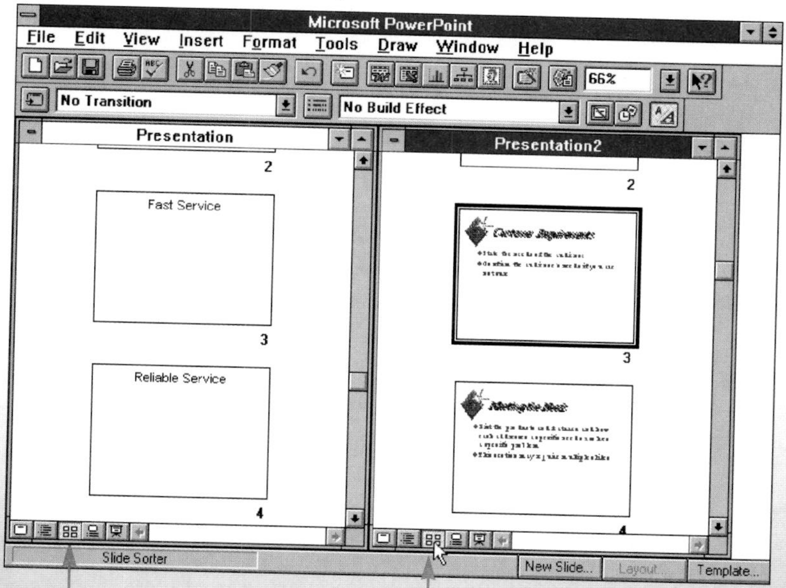

3 Change to Slide Sorter view in both windows.

more ▶

4 Select the slide to copy.

5 Click the Copy button.

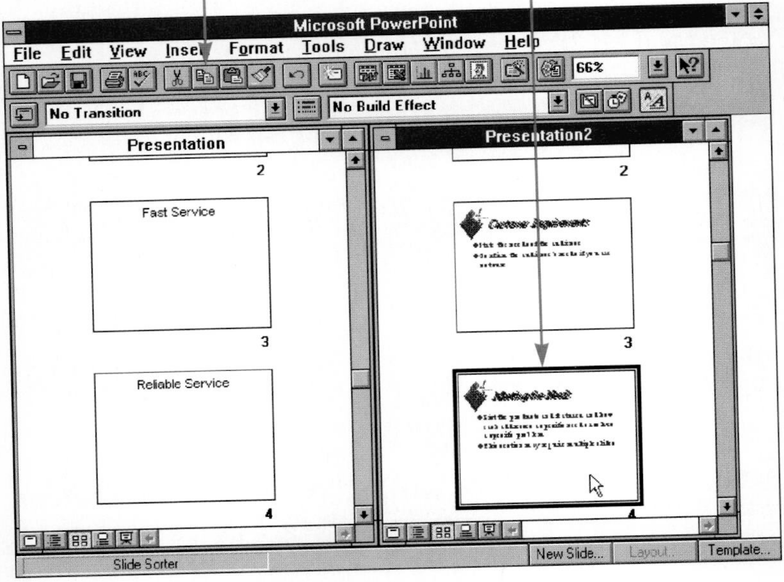

You also can select and copy multiple slides.

6 Select the slide that you want to precede the copied slide.

7 Click the Paste button.

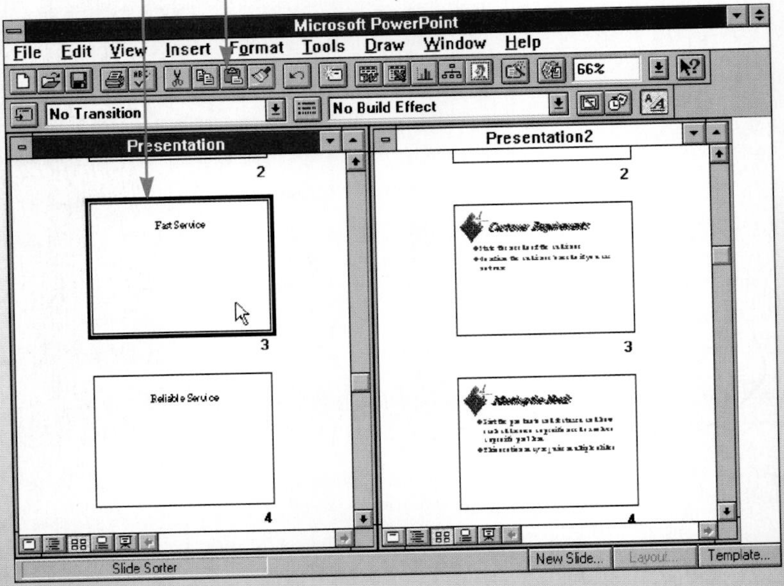

Importing a Microsoft Word Table

You can create a Microsoft Word table and import it to any slide in your presentation. The table retains its appearance and data as entered and formatted in Microsoft Word.

1 Click the Insert Microsoft Word Table button.

From a slide layout with a table placeholder, you can double-click the table placeholder.

2 Drag across the grid to select the number of table columns and rows.

This table will be two columns by two rows.

3 Open an existing table using the Word menu or toolbar.

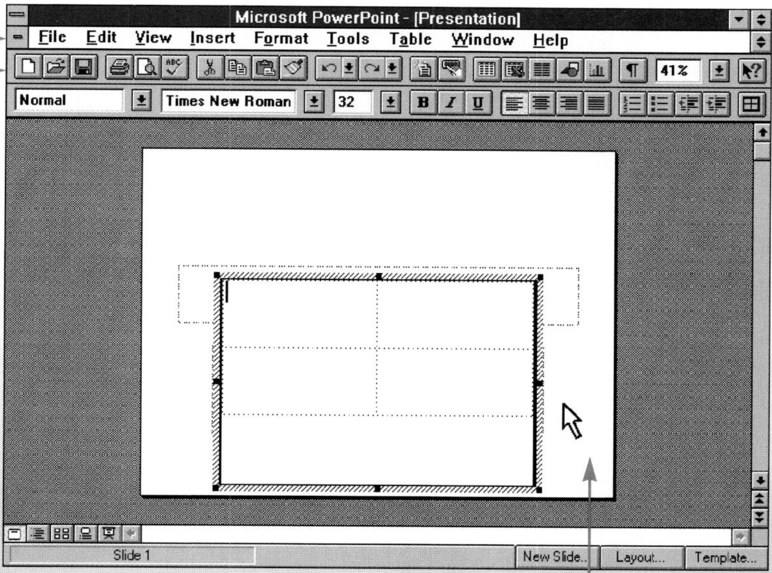

4 Click anywhere outside the table to return to PowerPoint.

Importing Outline Text

You can create the outline for your presentation in another application and then import the text into PowerPoint. Level 1 headings become slide titles and the remaining outline levels become bulleted items up to five levels deep.

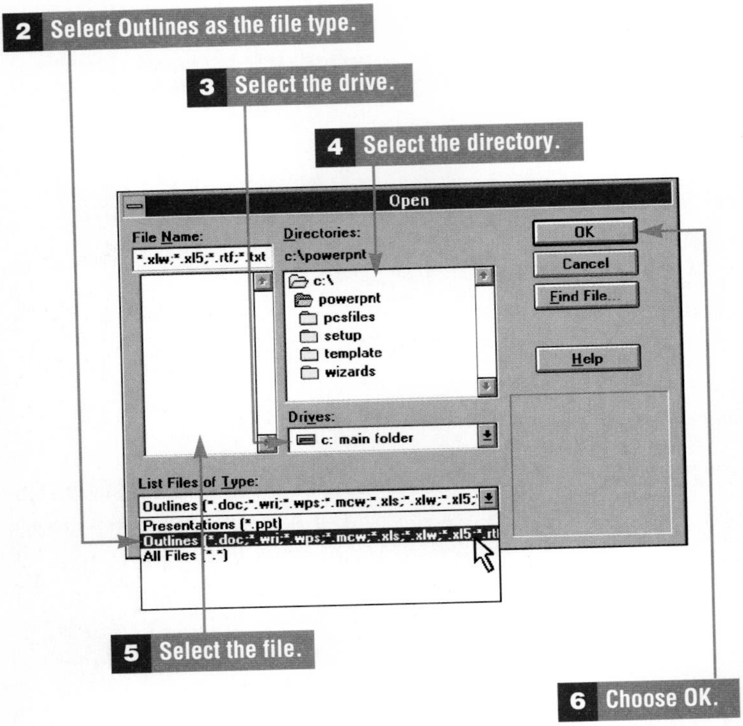

Saving a Presentation as a Word Outline

The Report It feature lets you work with your PowerPoint presentation outline as a Microsoft Word document. Using this feature automatically launches Word.

1 Click the Report It button.

2 Use the Word menus and toolbars to edit and save the outline.

3 Click the PowerPoint button to return to PowerPoint with your outline.

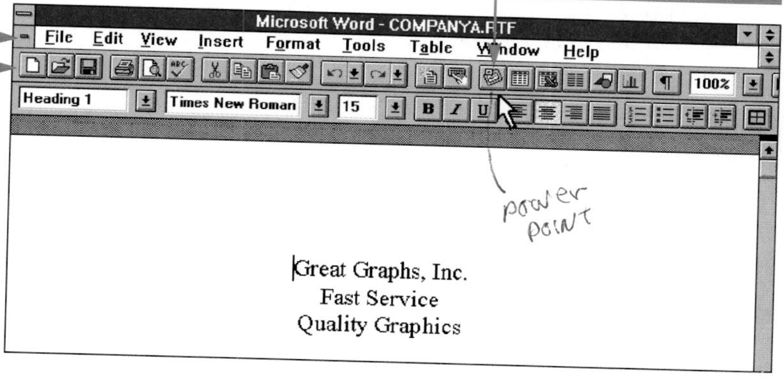

Linking Data from Another Application to PowerPoint

To ensure that your presentation data is always up to date, you can link data from another application to a slide in your presentation. When you edit the data in the other application, the data is updated in PowerPoint as well.

To link selected data from a file

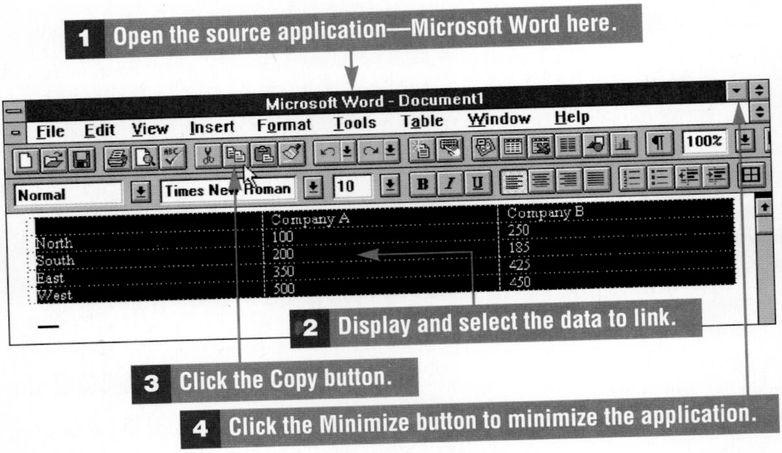
1 Open the source application—Microsoft Word here.
Microsoft Word - Document1
2 Display and select the data to link.
3 Click the Copy button.
4 Click the Minimize button to minimize the application.

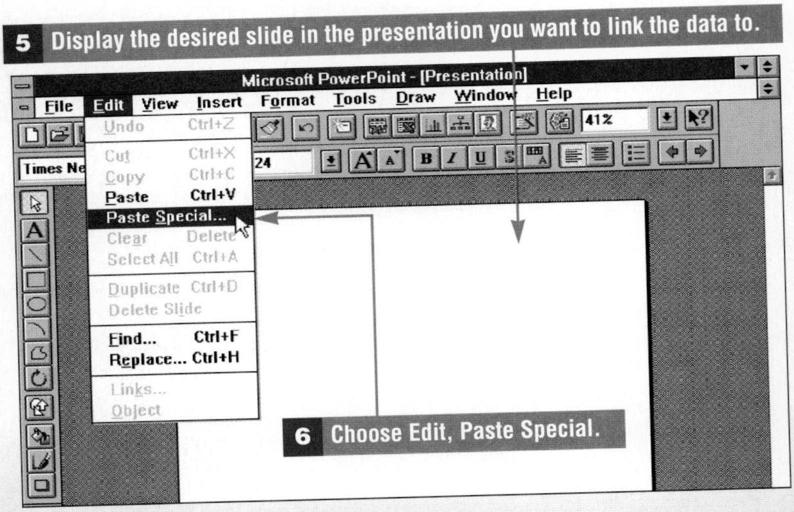
5 Display the desired slide in the presentation you want to link the data to.
Microsoft PowerPoint - [Presentation]
Paste Special...
6 Choose Edit, Paste Special.

To link an entire file

1 Choose Insert, Object.

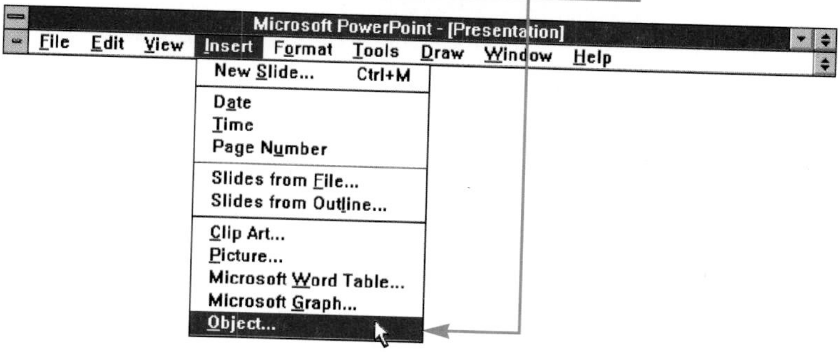

2 Choose Create from File.

3 Choose Browse.

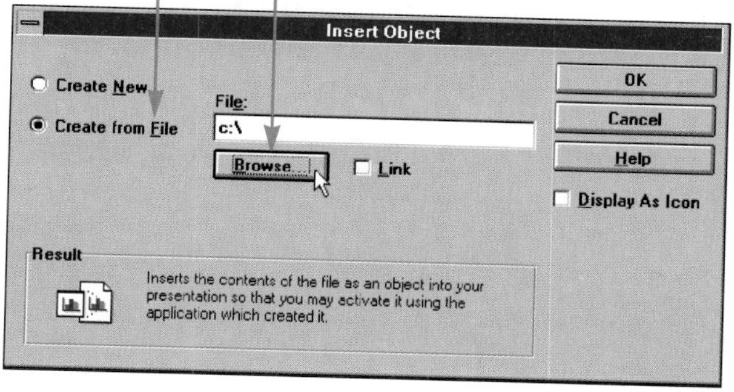

4 Select the drive.

5 Select the directory.

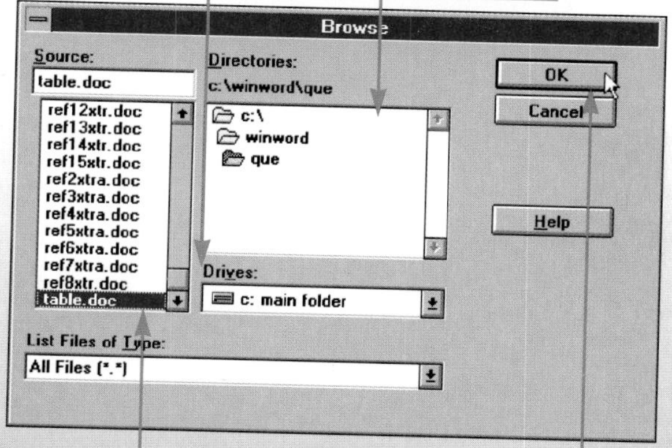

6 Select the file to link.

7 Choose OK.

more ▶

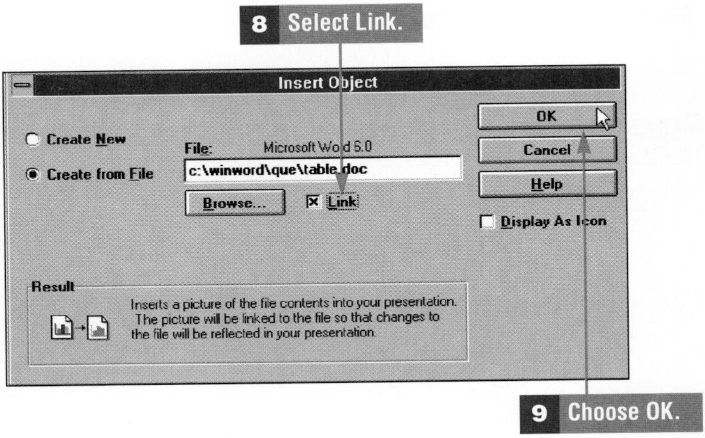

Updating a Link Manually

When you link data from another application to PowerPoint, the link is defined as an automatic update link. With an automatic link, the data is updated automatically each time you enter PowerPoint. You have the option to change the link to manual update. With manual update, you must use the Update Now option for the data to be refreshed.

Microsoft PowerPoint - [Presentation]
File Edit View Insert Format Tools Draw Window Help
Undo Ctrl+Z
Cut Ctrl+X
Copy Ctrl+C
Paste Ctrl+V
Paste Special...
Clear Delete
Select All Ctrl+A
Duplicate Ctrl+D
Delete Slide
Find... Ctrl+F
Replace... Ctrl+H
Links...
Object

1 Choose Edit, Links.

2 Select the link to update.

3 Choose Update Now.

Links

Links:	Type	Update
c:\winword\que\table.doc	Document	Automatic
c:\...\que\table.doc!DDE_LINK1	Document	Manual

Close
Update Now
Open Source
Change Source...
Break Link

Source: c:\winword\que\table.doc!DDE_LINK1
Type: Microsoft Word 6.0 Document
Update: Automatic Manual

Help

4 Choose Close.

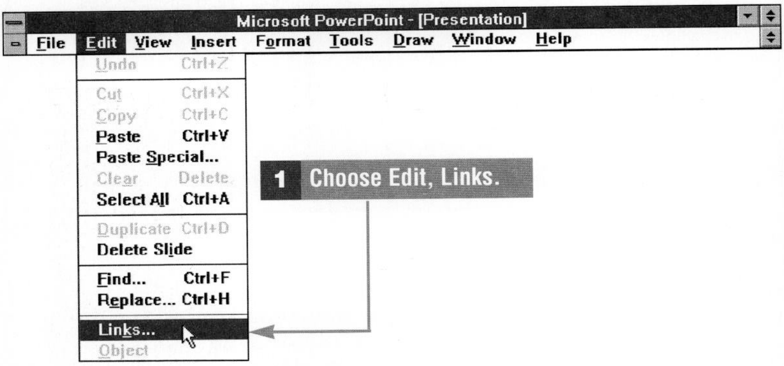

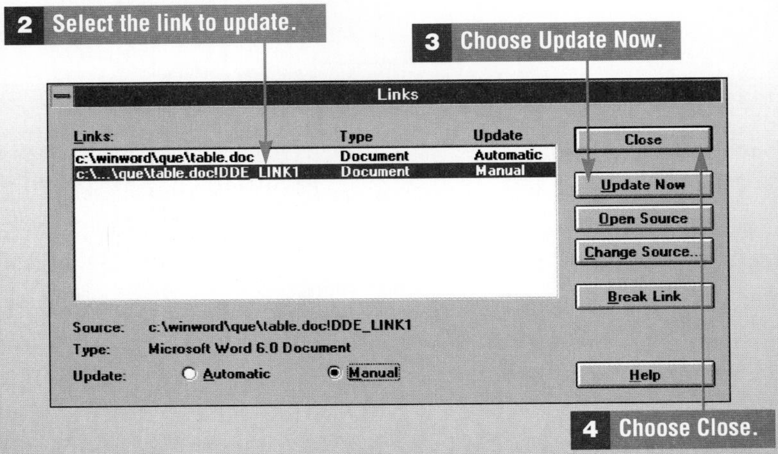

Breaking a Link

After you establish a link between PowerPoint and another application, you can break the link. When you break a link, however, PowerPoint converts the linked data to an uneditable object that cannot be relinked.

1 Choose Edit, Links.

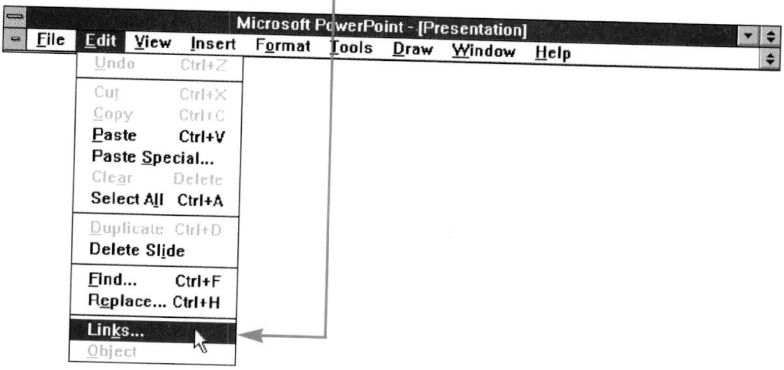

2 Select the link to break.

3 Choose Break Link.

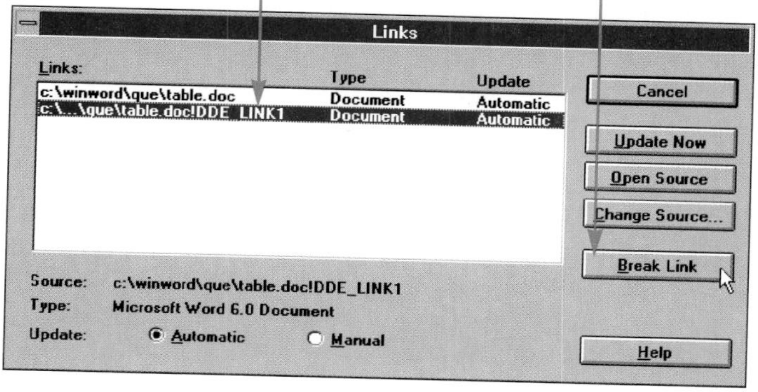

4 Choose OK.

Embedding an Object

Using PowerPoint's embedding capability, you can insert an object created in another application into your presentation. Doing so allows you to access the original application from within PowerPoint to edit the embedded object.

1 Display the slide on which to embed the object.

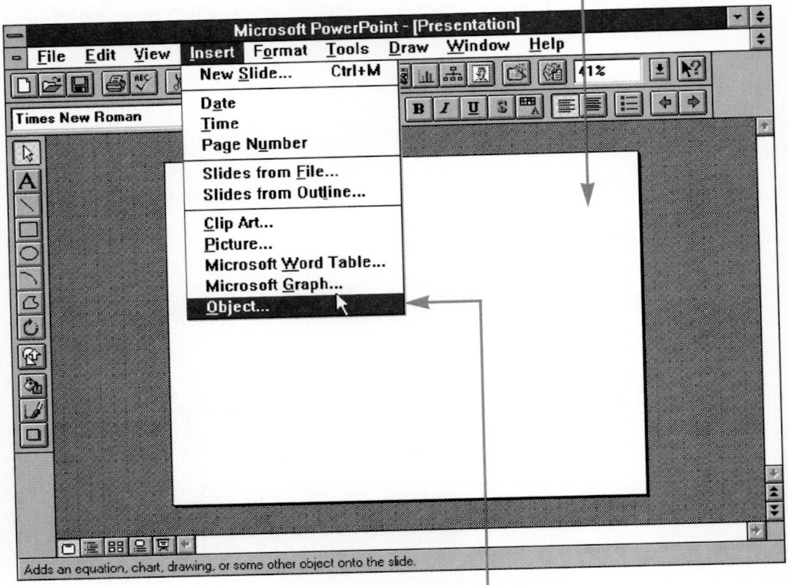

2 Choose Insert, Object.

3 Select Create from File.

4 Choose Browse.

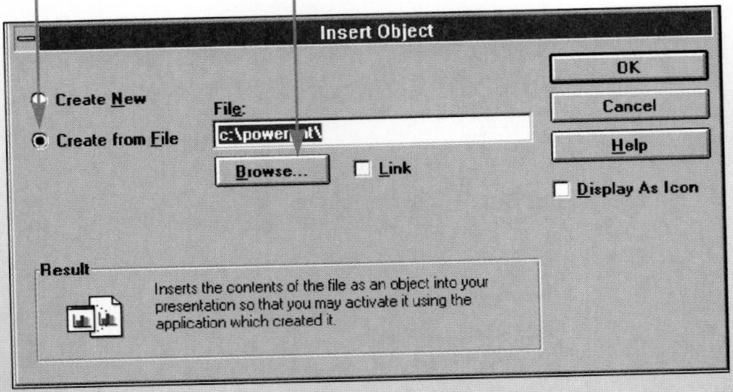

5 Select the drive.

6 Select the directory.

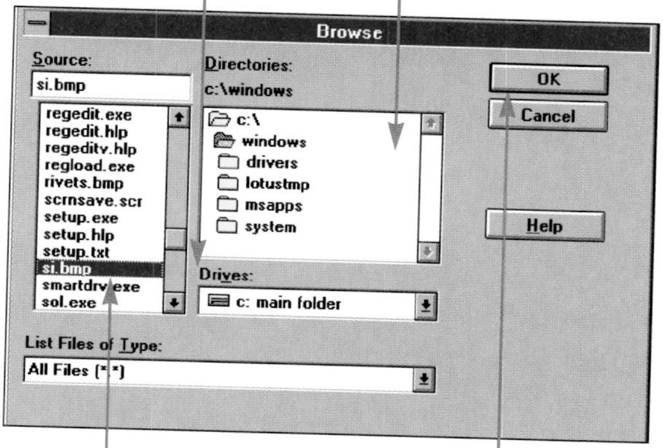

7 Select the file to embed.

8 Choose OK.

9 Choose OK.

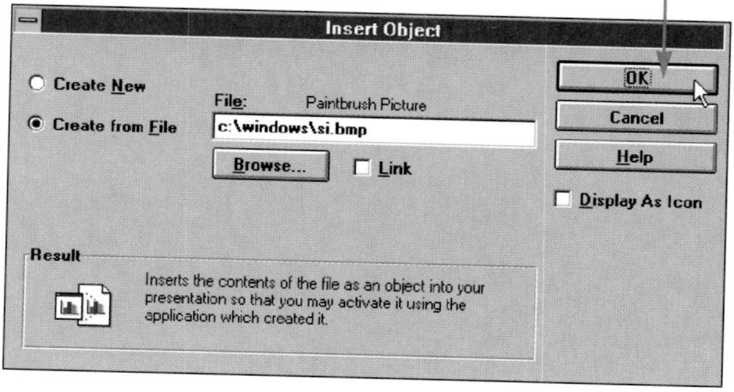

PowerPoint embeds the object on the current slide.

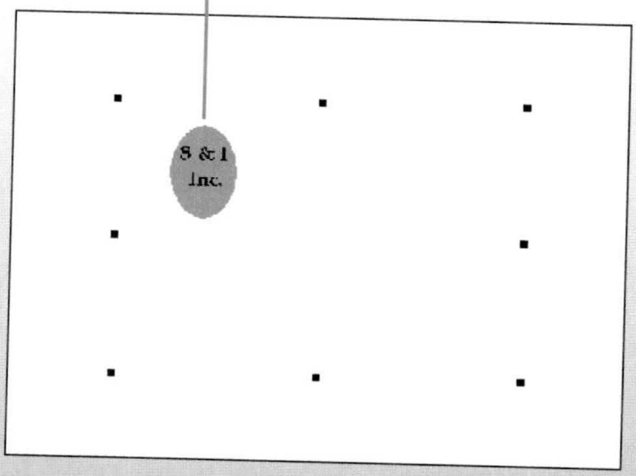

Editing an Embedded Object

Once you embed an object in a PowerPoint presentation, you can access the application used to create the object from within PowerPoint. This allows you to edit the object without exiting PowerPoint.

1 Double-click the embedded object.

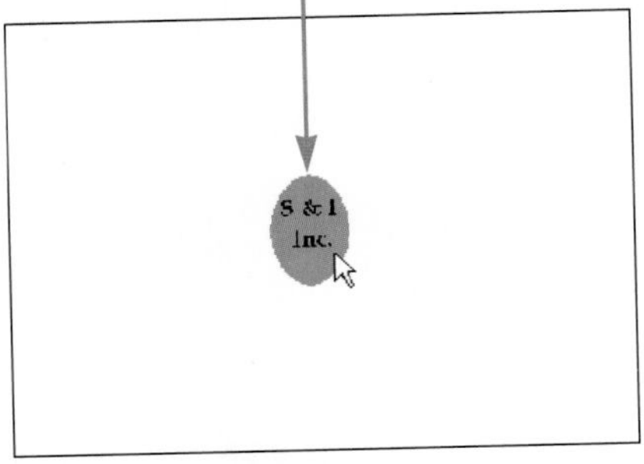

2 Edit the object in its original application.

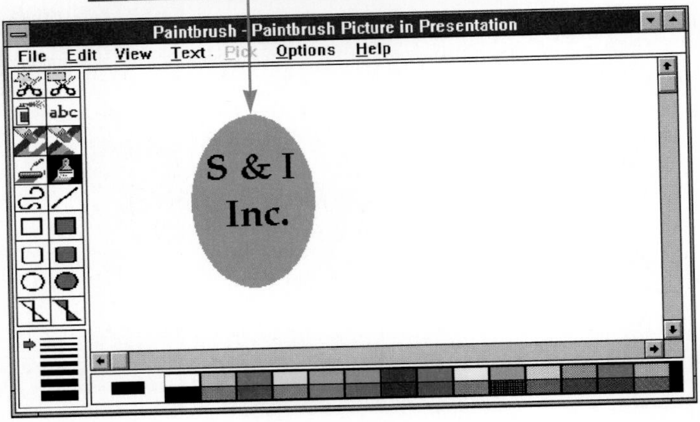

3 Choose File, Exit & Return to Presentation.

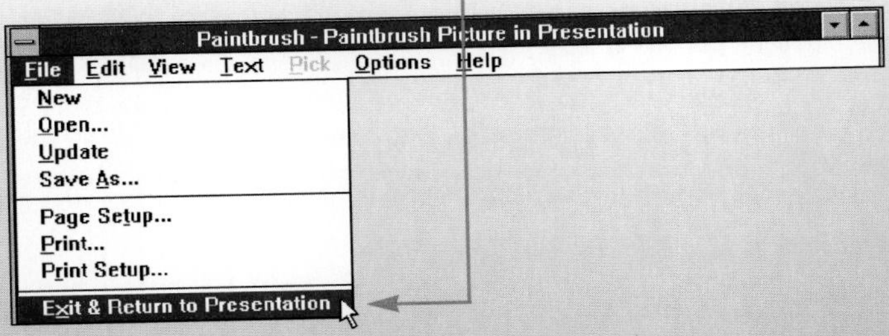

E-Mailing Your Presentation File

You can send a copy of your presentation to one or more other PowerPoint users with Microsoft Mail. To send your presentation only, use the Send feature. Using the Routing feature is like using a routing slip; the presentation is sent to each user in order and then returned to you with the others' comments.

To send a presentation

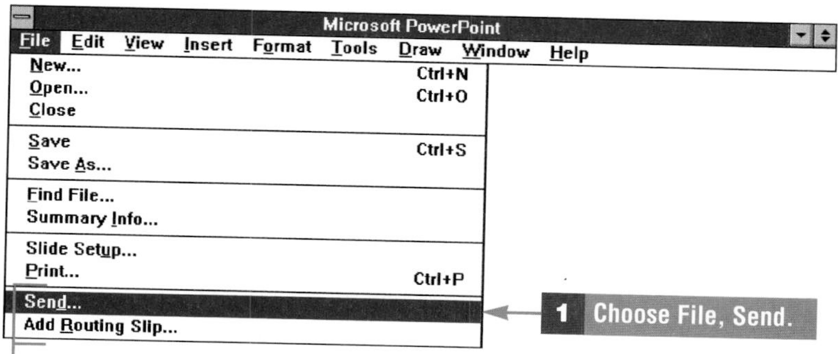

1 Choose File, Send.

These options are added to the File menu if Mail is installed.

If you don't have Mail running, this dialog box opens.

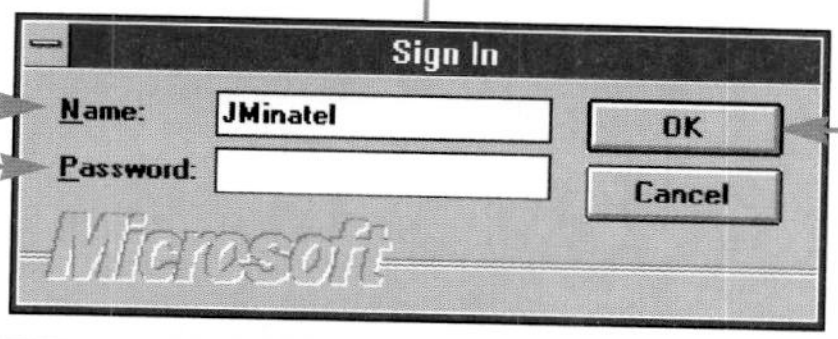

2 Enter your user name and password.

3 Choose OK.

If Mail is running, skip to step 4.

The PowerPoint file name is entered automatically as the subject.

4 Click Address.

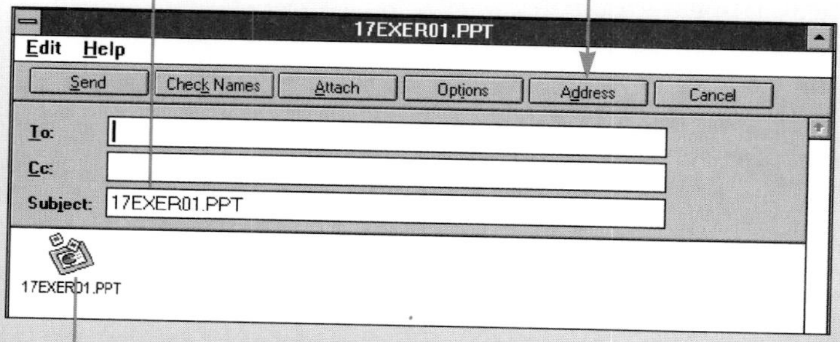

An icon representing the file appears in the contents area.

more ▶

5 Select the names to add to the recipient lists.

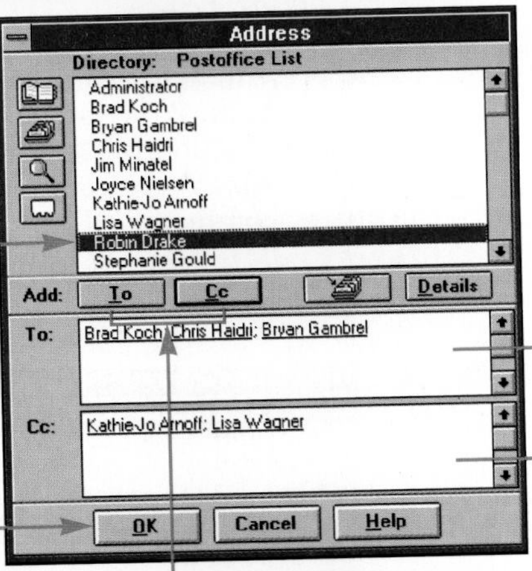

6 Click To or Cc to add the name.

Recipients are added to these lists.

7 Repeat steps 5 and 6 for all recipients.

8 Choose OK.

9 Choose Send.

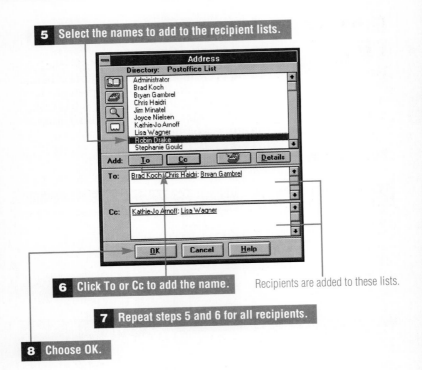

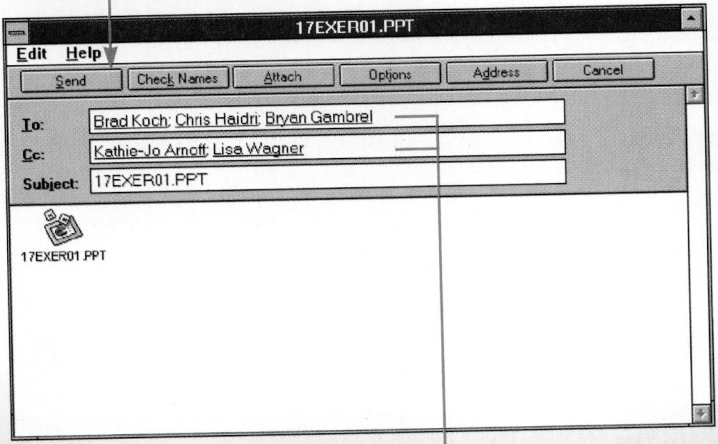

Recipients' names are shown here.

To route a presentation

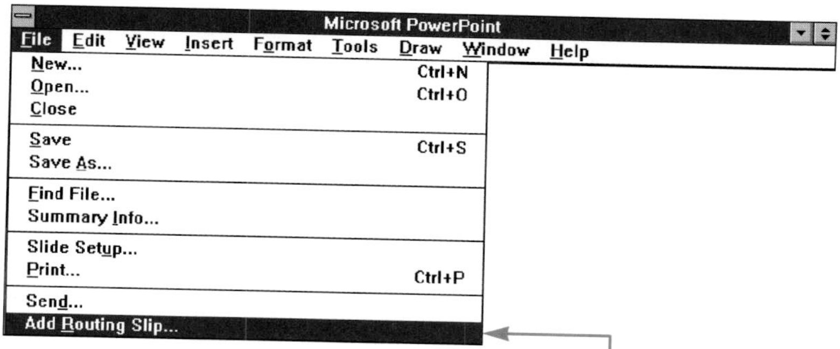

1 Choose File, Add Routing Slip.

2 Choose Address.

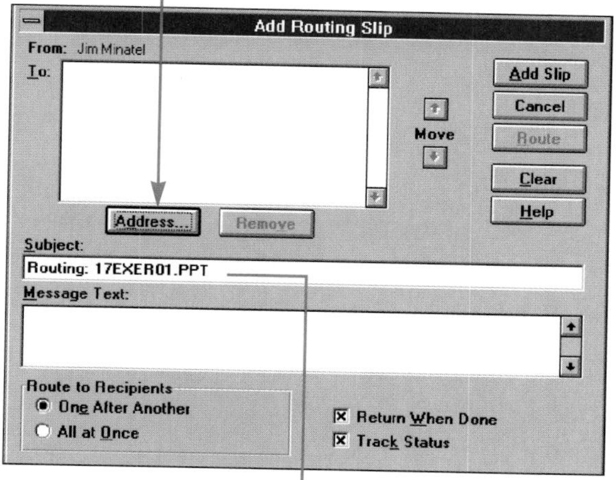

The PowerPoint file name is entered automatically as the subject.

more ▶

3 Select the name to add to the routing slip.

4 Choose Add.

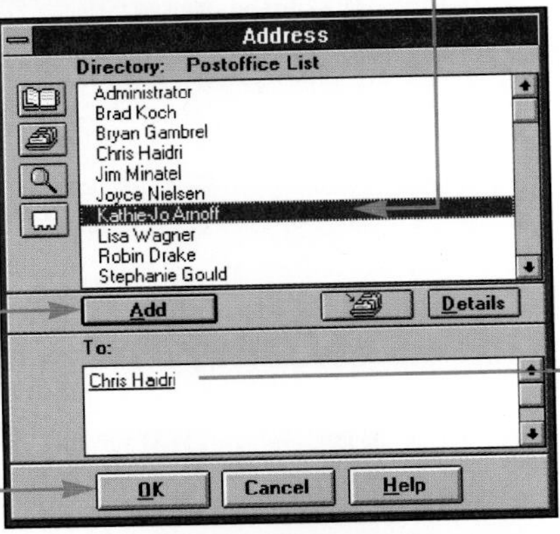

5 Repeat steps 3 and 4 for all recipients.

6 Choose OK.

Recipients' names are added here in the order you choose.

7 Select a routing order option.

8 Choose Route to begin routing.

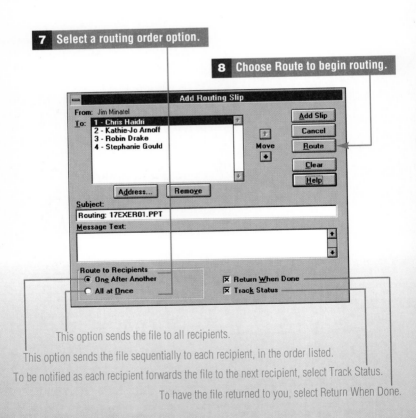

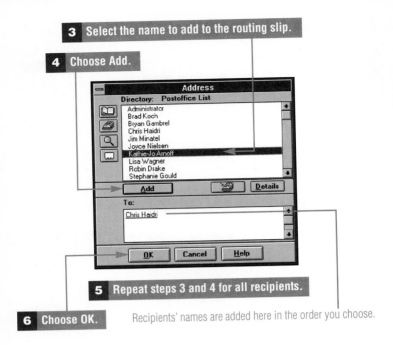

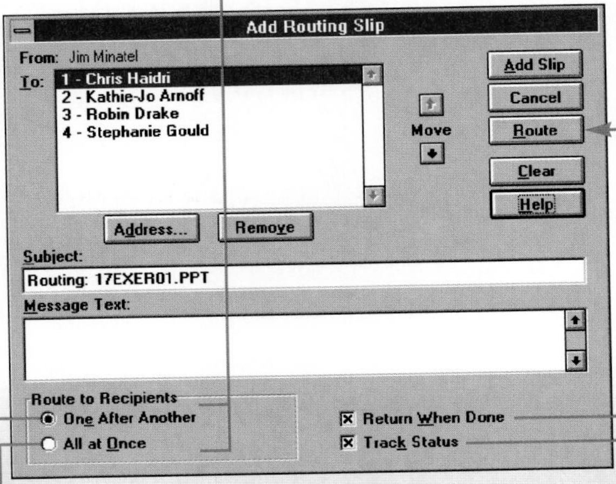

This option sends the file to all recipients.

This option sends the file sequentially to each recipient, in the order listed.

To be notified as each recipient forwards the file to the next recipient, select Track Status.

To have the file returned to you, select Return When Done.

Adding a New Slide to a Presentation

You can add additional slides to your presentation at any time. When using the New Slide option, the new slide is placed immediately following the currently selected slide.

1 Choose Insert, New Slide.

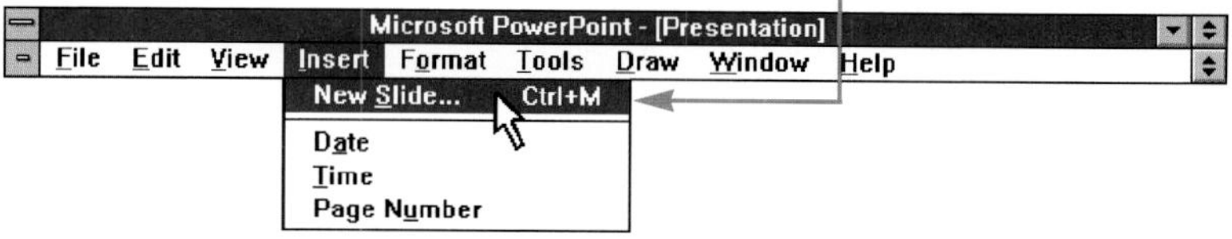

You also can click the New Slide button on the status bar.

2 Select the layout for the slide.

3 Choose OK.

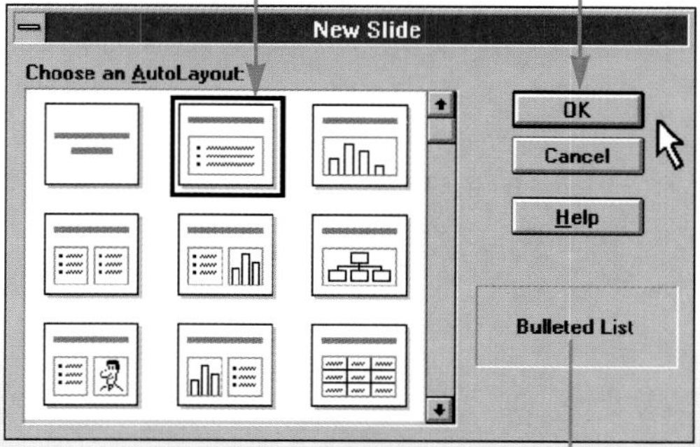

Description of the slide layout

Deleting a Presentation Slide

You can delete a slide from your presentation at any time.

To delete a slide in Slide view or Notes Pages view

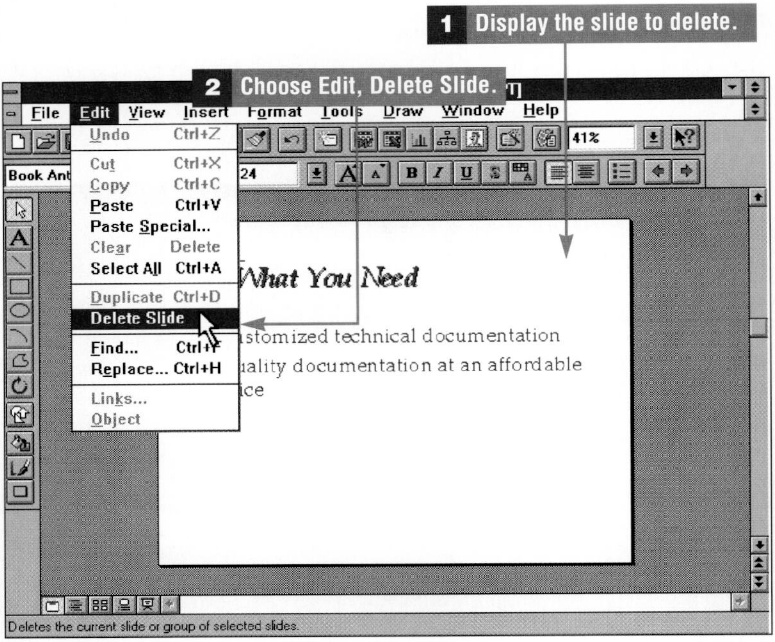

To delete a slide in Slide Sorter view

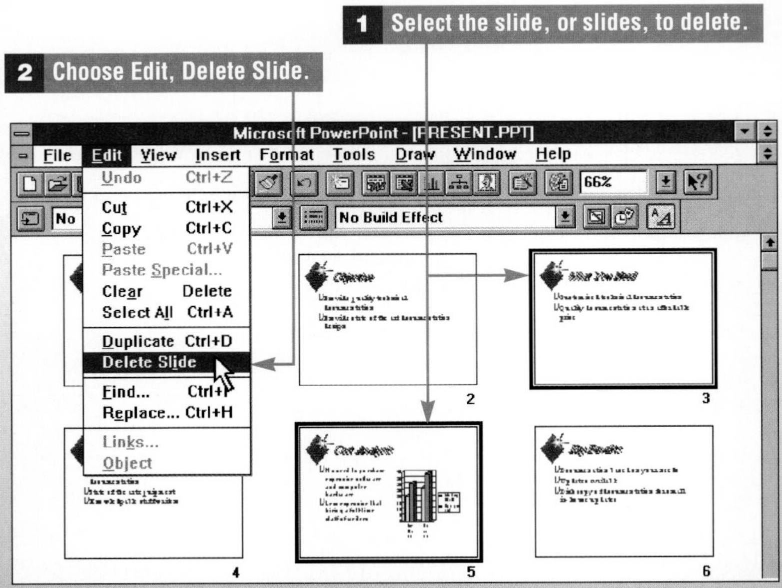

You also can press the Delete key to delete the selected slides in Slide Sorter view.

Changing Slide Order

You can easily rearrange the slides in your presentation in either Outline or Slide Sorter view.

To change slide order in Outline view

1 Select the slide to move.

2 Position the pointer on the slide icon.

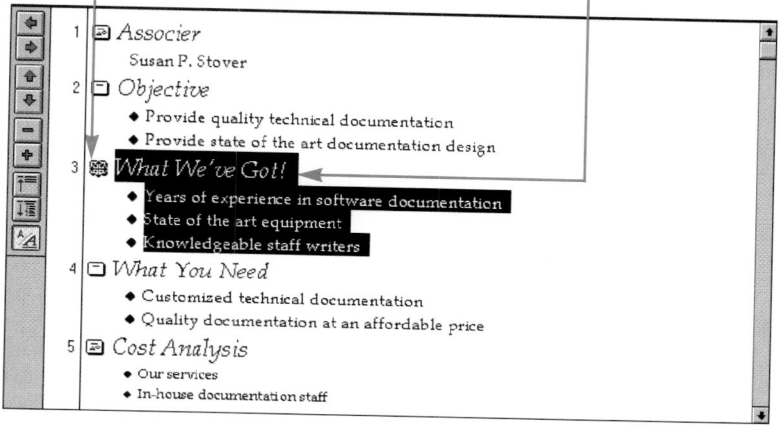
1 Associer
Susan P. Stover
2 Objective
◆ Provide quality technical documentation
◆ Provide state of the art documentation design
3 What We've Got!
◆ Years of experience in software documentation
◆ State of the art equipment
◆ Knowledgeable staff writers
4 What You Need
◆ Customized technical documentation
◆ Quality documentation at an affordable price
5 Cost Analysis
◆ Our services
◆ In-house documentation staff

3 Drag the slide to the new location.

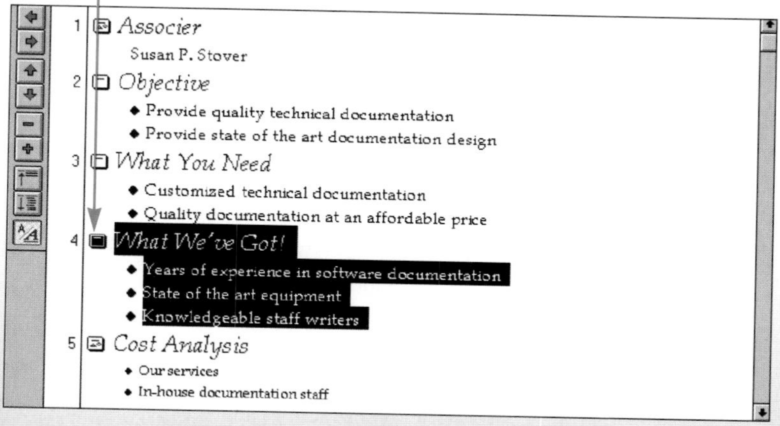
1 Associer
Susan P. Stover
2 Objective
◆ Provide quality technical documentation
◆ Provide state of the art documentation design
3 What You Need
◆ Customized technical documentation
◆ Quality documentation at an affordable price
4 What We've Got!
◆ Years of experience in software documentation
◆ State of the art equipment
◆ Knowledgeable staff writers
5 Cost Analysis
◆ Our services
◆ In-house documentation staff

As you drag, the pointer becomes a two-headed arrow and the horizontal line indicates the current position.

To change slide order in Slide Sorter view

1 Select the slide to move.

2 Drag the slide to the new location.

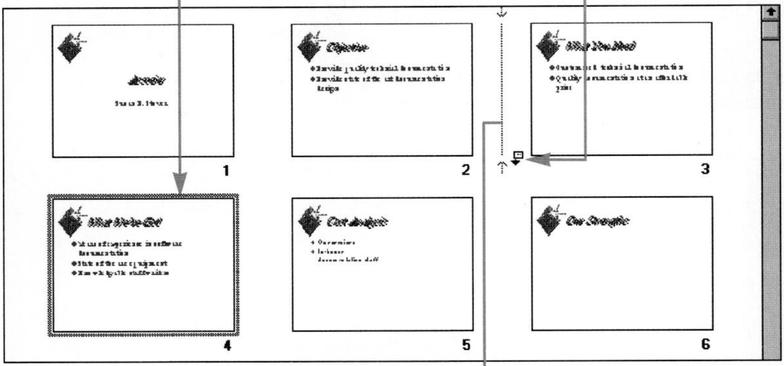

The vertical line indicates the slide's new position.

Selecting a New Layout for a Slide

You can change the layout of a slide without losing the text and graphics already included on the slide. You change the layout in Slide view.

1 Choose Format, Slide Layout.

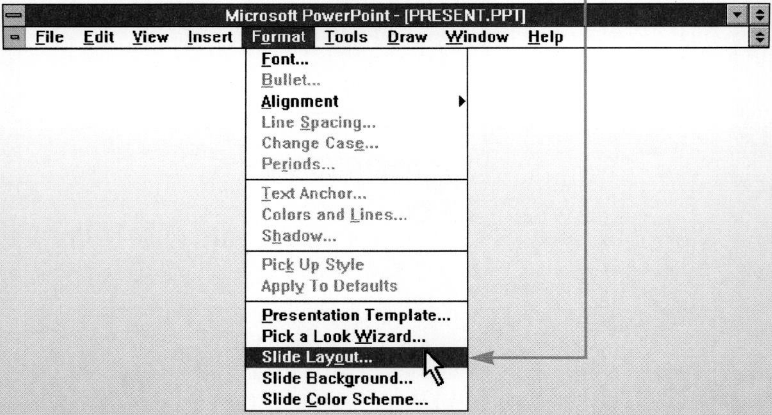

You also can click the Layout button on the status bar.

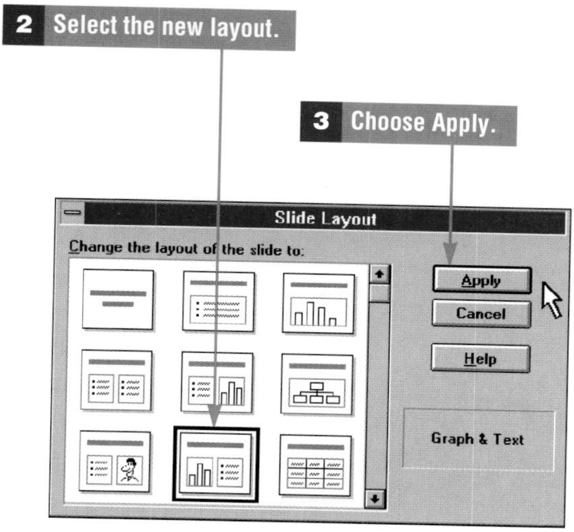

Changing Slide Backgrounds

You can select the color and adjust the shading of the slide background. You also can determine whether to include Slide Master background objects on the slide.

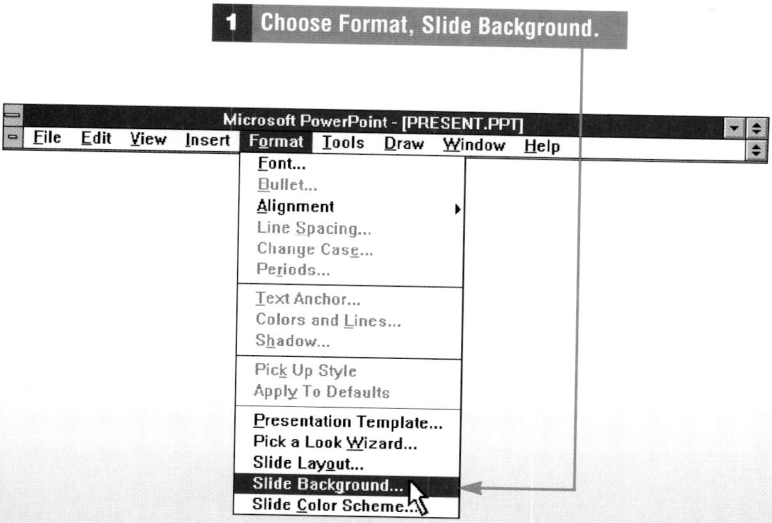

more ▶

2 Indicate whether to include Slide Master objects.

3 Select the shading style.

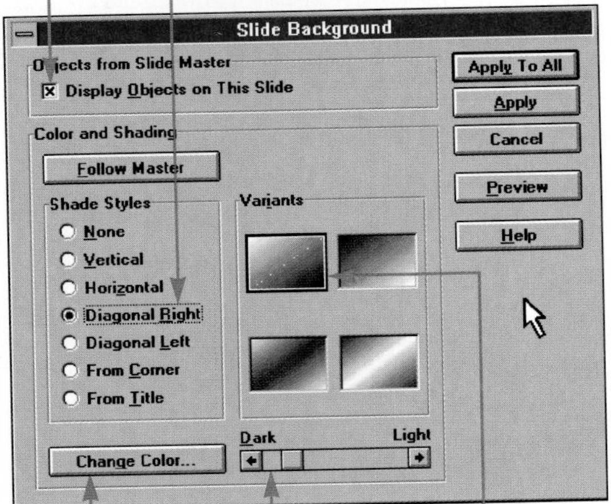

4 Select the shading variation.

5 Adjust the color intensity.

6 Choose Change Color to select a new background color.

If you choose Change Color, this dialog box opens.

If you don't want to change colors, skip to step 9.

7 Select the new color.

8 Choose OK.

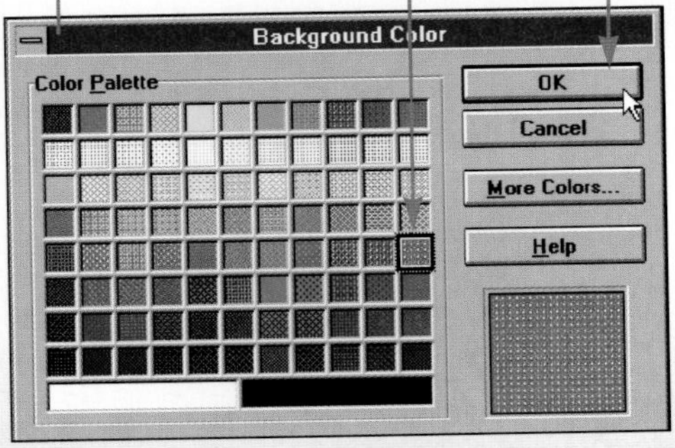

9 Choose Apply to All.

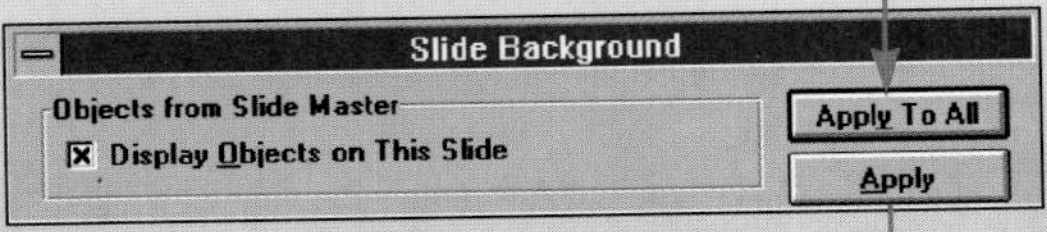

Choose Apply to change only the current slide.

Changing Slide Format and Orientation

You should select the slide format and orientation before printing or displaying your slide show. This ensures that your slides appear in proper proportion for the selected format.

1 Choose File, Slide Setup.

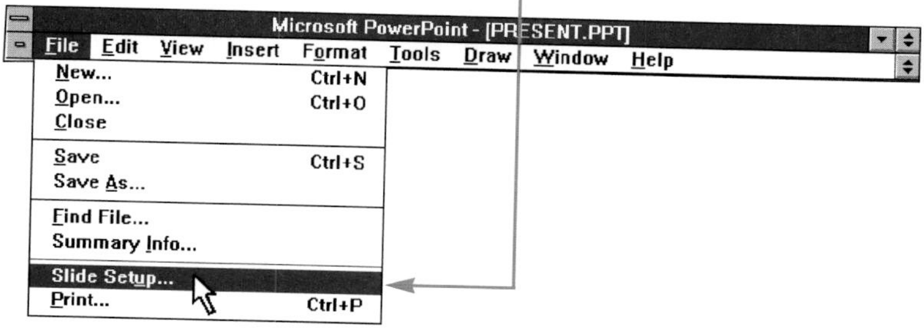

2 Select the sizing option for the slides.

3 Select the orientation for slides.

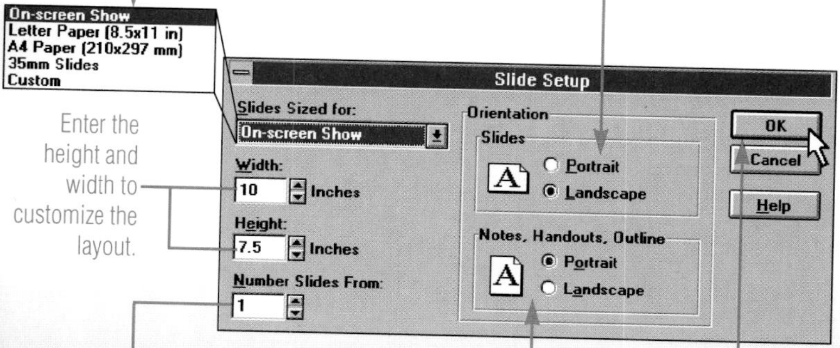

Enter the height and width to customize the layout.

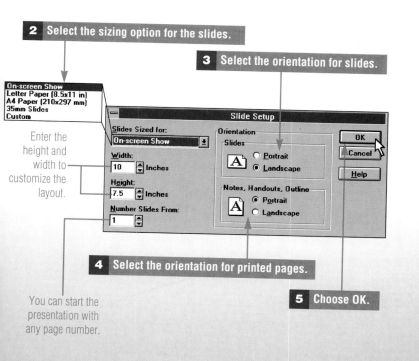

You can start the presentation with any page number.

4 Select the orientation for printed pages.

5 Choose OK.

Adding Header and Footer Text

Use headers and footers to add printed text to the top and bottom of each printed presentation page. For example, you can include your company name or a theme in a header or footer.

To add a header or footer

1 Choose View, Master.

2 Select a master—use Slide Master here.

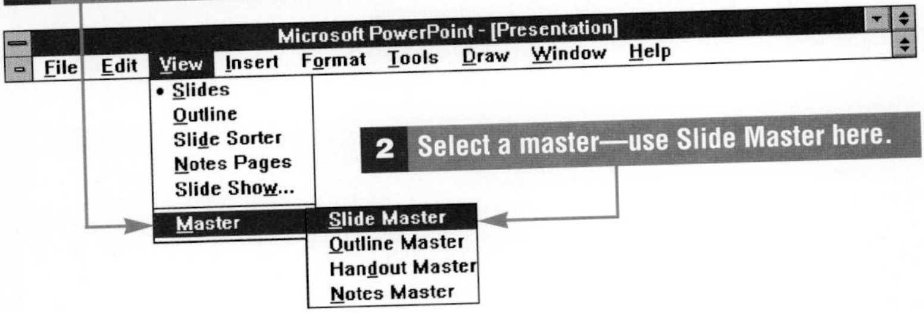

3 Click the Text tool.

4 Click where you want to begin header or footer text.

5 Type normally to add text.

6 Click outside the text area when finished.

Be careful not to click inside master text areas.

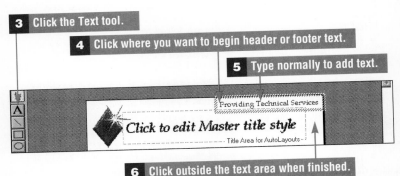

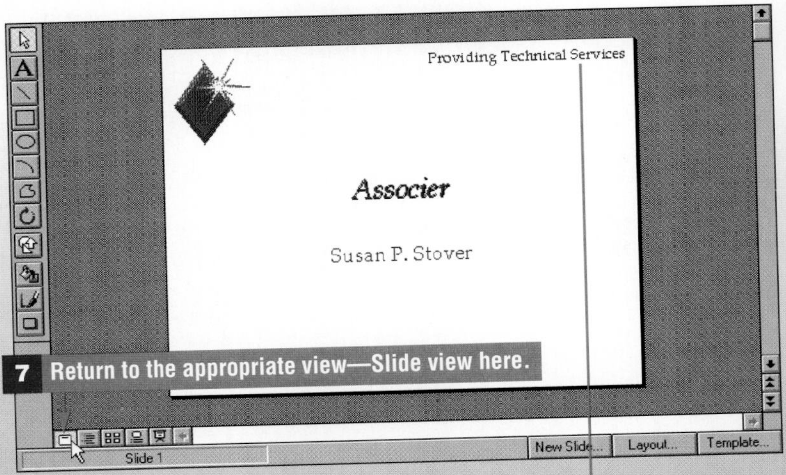

7 Return to the appropriate view—Slide view here.

The header or footer text appears on your presentation page.

To add a multiple-line header or footer

1 Choose View, Master.

2 Select a master—use Slide Master here.

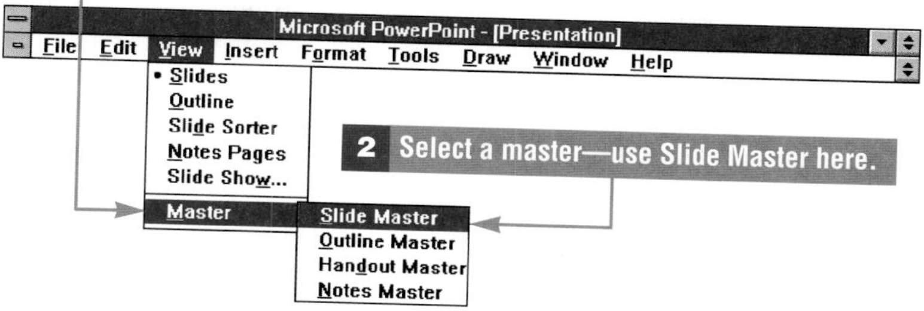

3 Click the Text tool.

4 Click and drag to define the text area.

Click to edit Master title style
Title Area for AutoLayouts

5 Release the mouse button.

6 Type normally to add text.

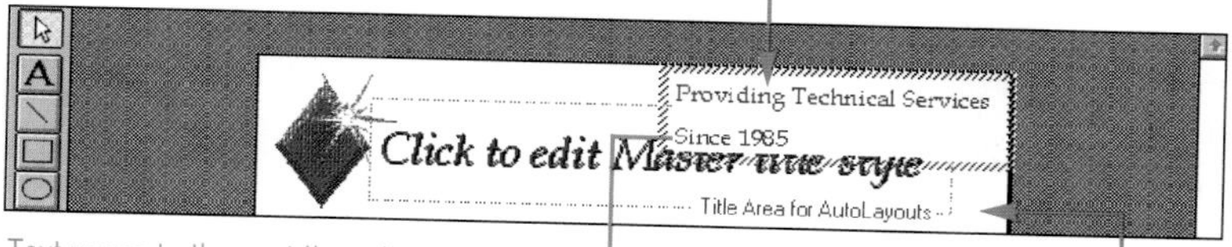
Providing Technical Services
Since 1985
Click to edit Master title style
Title Area for AutoLayouts

Text wraps to the next line when you reach the right end of the text area.

You also can press Enter to add a new line of text.

7 Click outside the text area when finished.

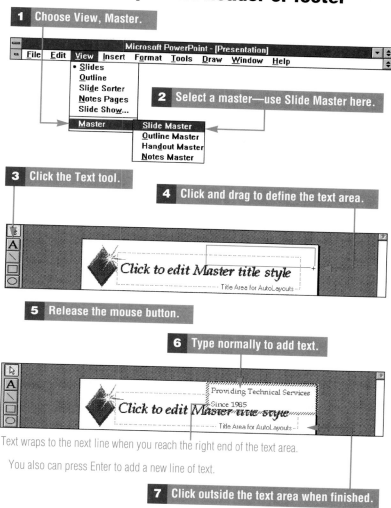

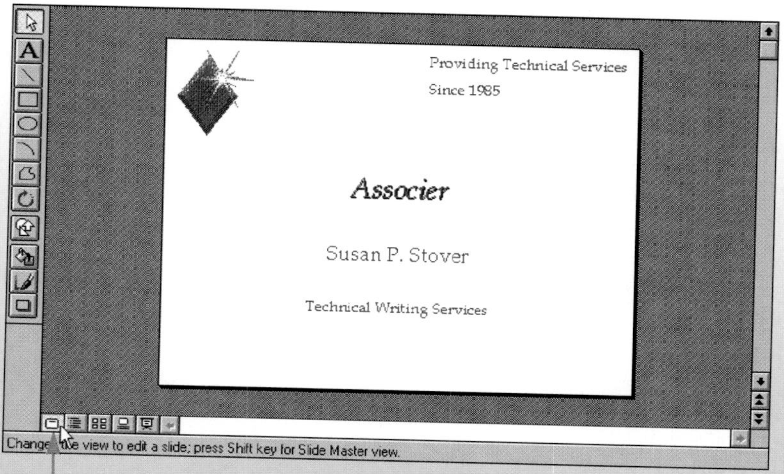
Providing Technical Services
Since 1985
Associer
Susan P. Stover
Technical Writing Services
Change the view to edit a slide; press Shift key for Slide Master view.

8 Return to the appropriate view—Slide View here.

Adding a Date, Time, or Page Number

Entering date, time, and page number codes allows you to print the current date, time, or page number without having to edit the information each time you print.

To enter the date, time, or page number in a text area

1 Click the Text tool.

2 Click where you want to start the text area.

3 Choose Insert.

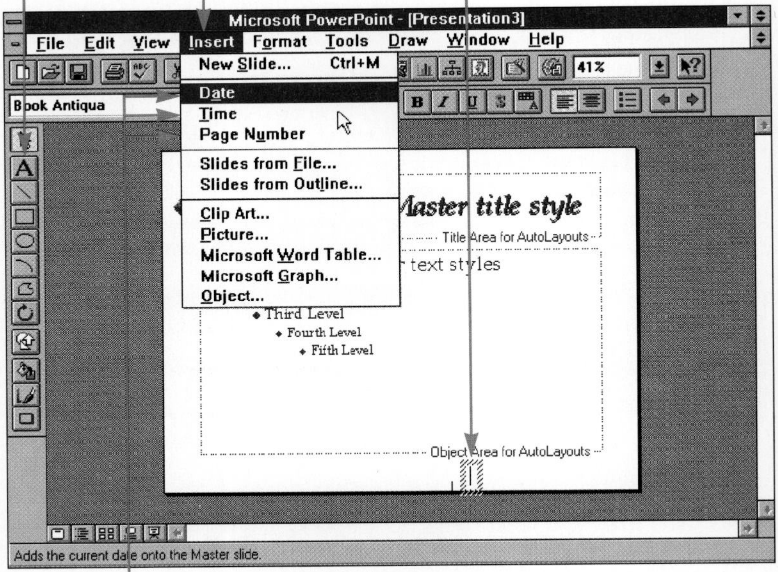

4 Choose Date, Time, or Page Number.

You also can add a date, time, or page number to an existing text area.

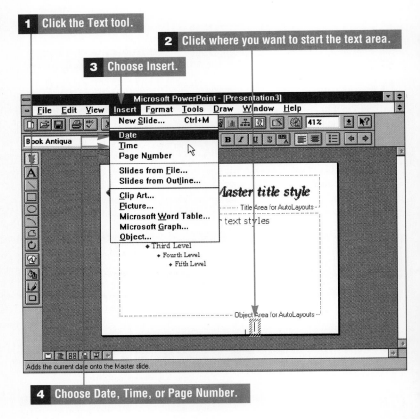

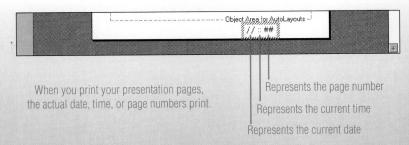

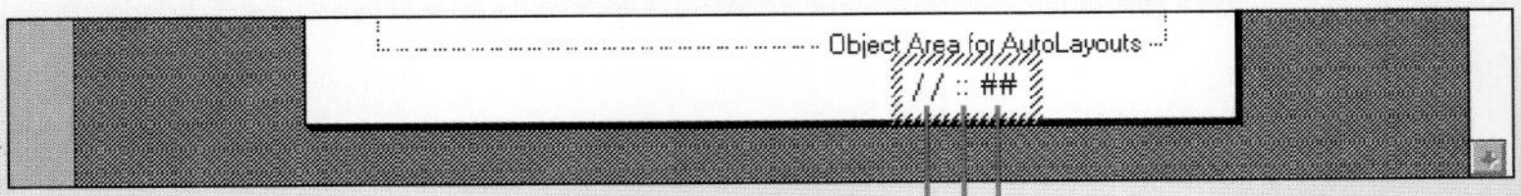

When you print your presentation pages, the actual date, time, or page numbers print.

Represents the page number

Represents the current time

Represents the current date

To place the date, time, or page number on a master

1 Choose Insert.

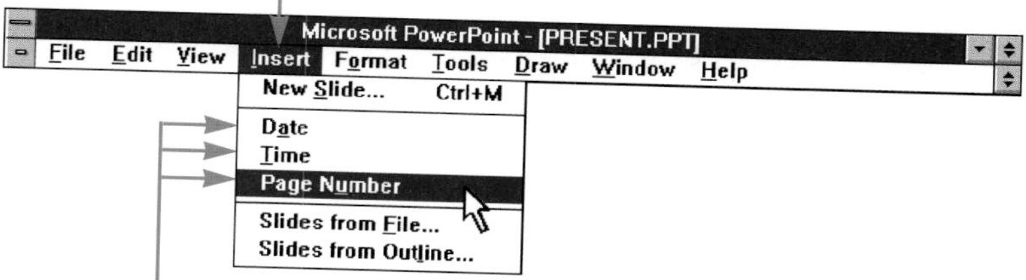

2 Choose Date, Time, or Page Number.

3 Click the shaded border and drag to the desired location.

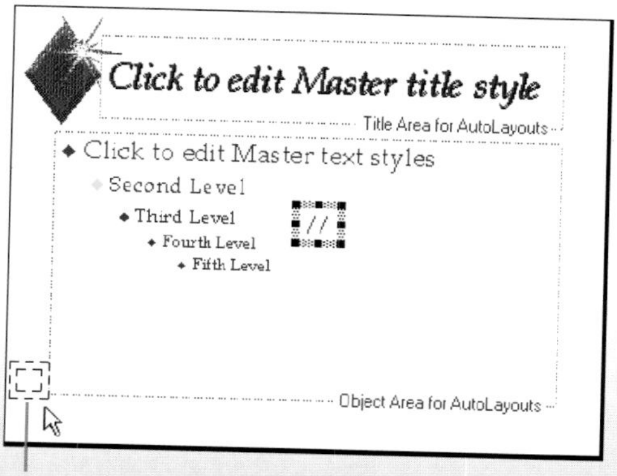

The outline shows the current location as you drag.

4 Release the mouse button.

Adding Speaker Notes to a Slide

Use the Notes Page View option to include notes for a slide. These notes appear in the bottom half of the page when you print with Notes Pages selected in the Print dialog box's Print What box.

1 Choose View, Notes Pages.

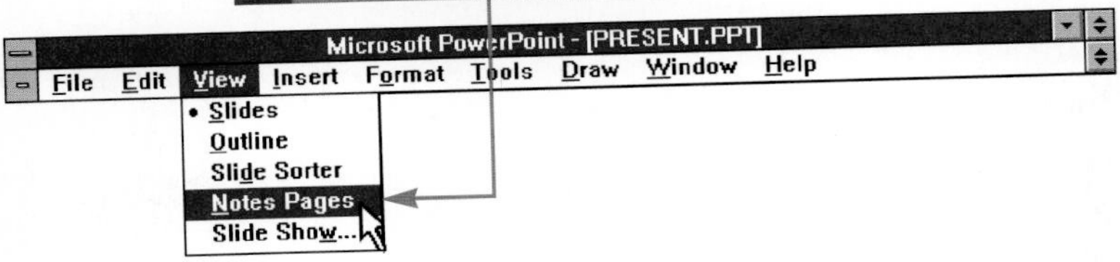

2 Click in the notes text area.

3 Click the Zoom Control arrow.

4 Choose a higher Zoom percentage.

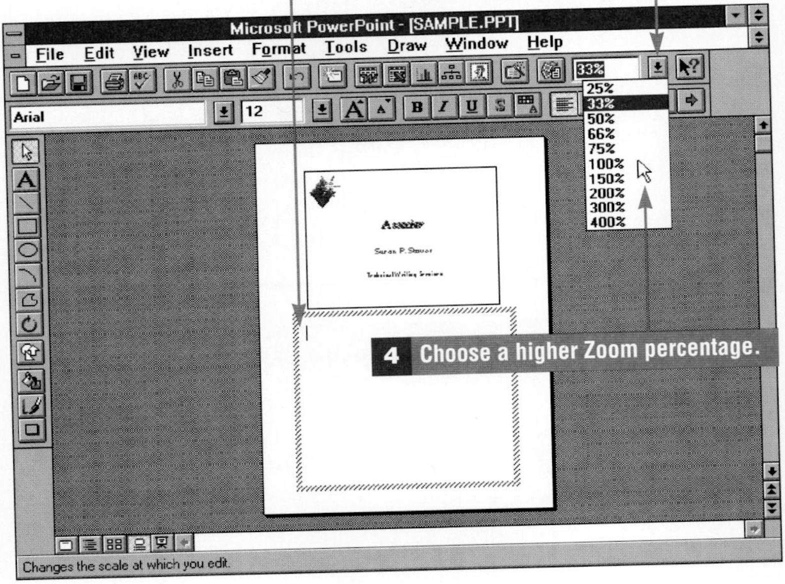

Increasing the Zoom percentage makes the text easier to read.

5 Type normally to enter notes.

6 Return the Zoom percentage to 33%.

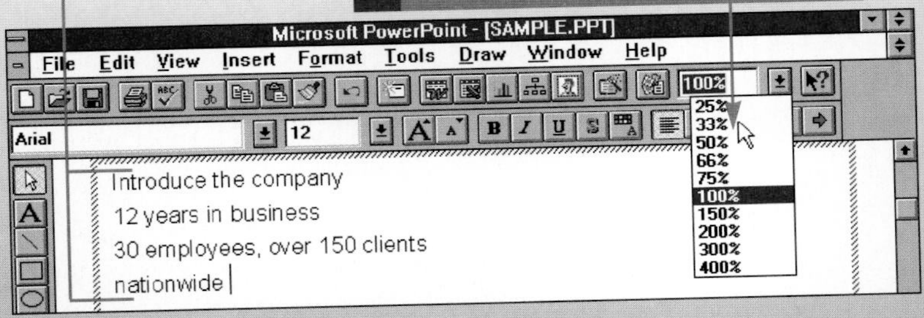

Viewing and Editing the Slide Master

Edit the Slide Master to change the look of the entire presentation. You can format title text and master text, change the color of the slide background, and add background items.

To view the Slide Master

1 Choose View, Master, Slide Master.

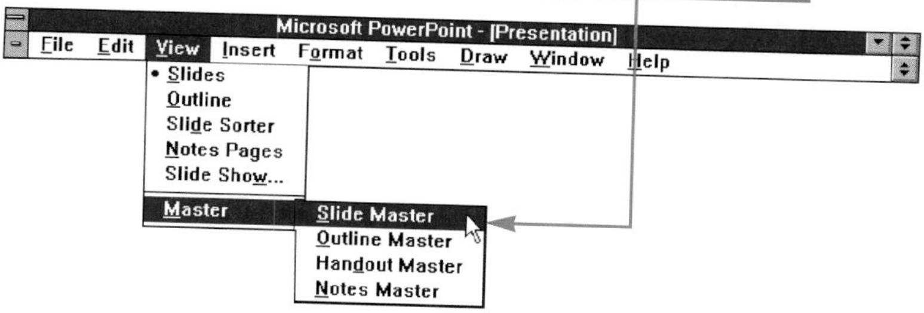

To edit the Slide Master

1 Select the title text to change slide title attributes.

2 Select the title text area to change its attributes.

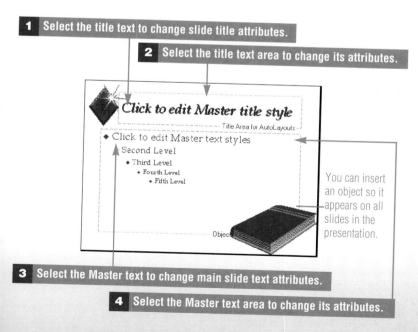

You can insert an object so it appears on all slides in the presentation.

3 Select the Master text to change main slide text attributes.

4 Select the Master text area to change its attributes.

See "Graphics: Adding and Editing" for information on inserting graphics.

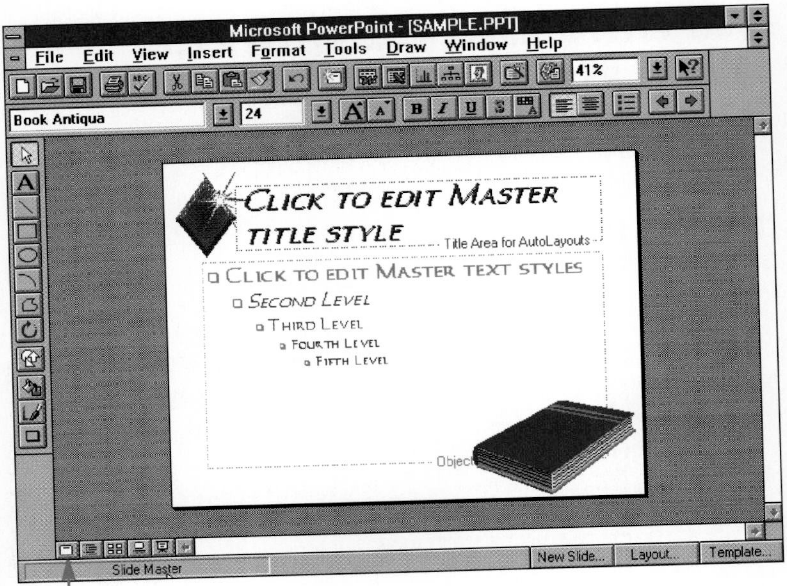
Microsoft PowerPoint - [SAMPLE.PPT]
File Edit View Insert Format Tools Draw Window Help
41%
Book Antiqua
24
CLICK TO EDIT MASTER TITLE STYLE
Title Area for AutoLayouts
CLICK TO EDIT MASTER TEXT STYLES
SECOND LEVEL
THIRD LEVEL
FOURTH LEVEL
FIFTH LEVEL
New Slide...
Layout...
Template...
Slide Master

5 Click the Slide View button.

Creating Building Slides

A build slide is a slide that displays a bulleted list, with bulleted items added sequentially to the slide, one at a time, until the list is complete. Rather than create a series of slides yourself, you can create one slide with the complete list and let PowerPoint generate the build slide. You can create a build slide in any view.

1 Display the slide to build.

2 Choose Tools, Build.

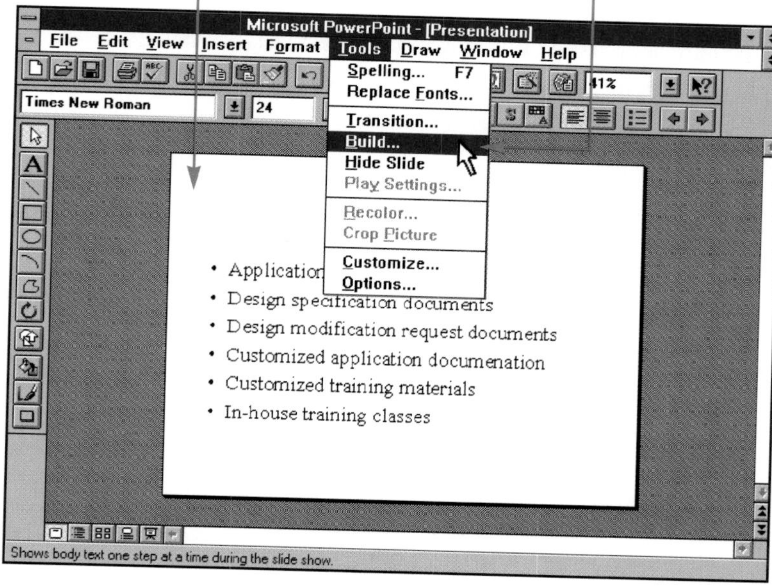

3 Select the Build options.

Use Dim Previous Points to dim previous list items.

Use Build Body Text to create a simple build slide.

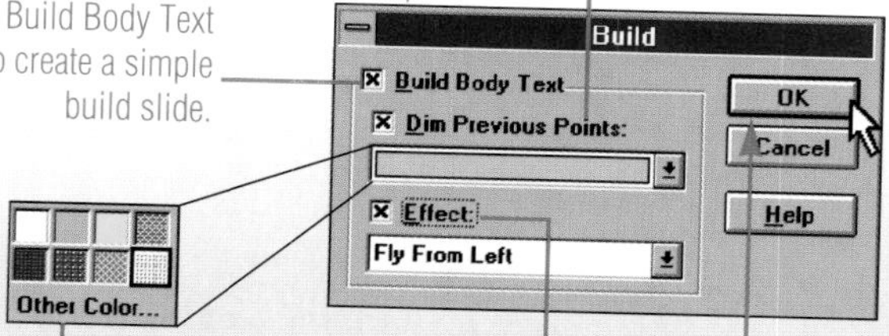

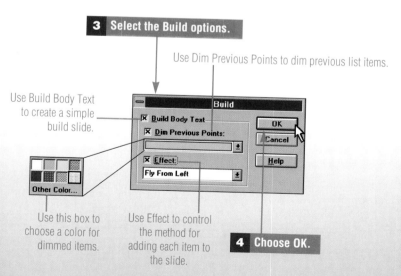

Use this box to choose a color for dimmed items.

Use Effect to control the method for adding each item to the slide.

4 Choose OK.

Changing Transition Methods

You control the manner in which slides appear on-screen during a slide show. You can advance all the slides with the same effect, or you can vary the effects of transition.

1 Switch to Slide Sorter view.

2 Select the slide whose transition you want to change.

3 Click the Transition button.

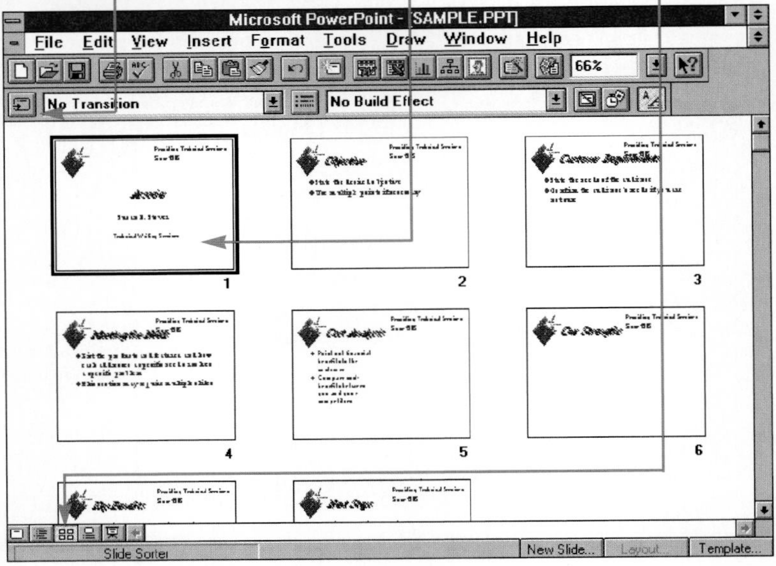

4 Select the transition effect.

5 Select the transition speed.

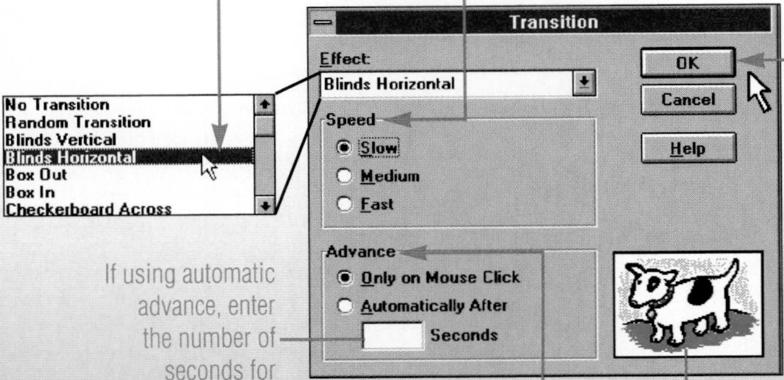

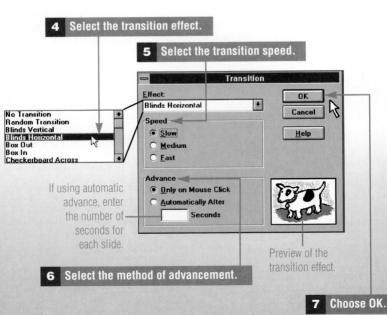

If using automatic advance, enter the number of seconds for each slide.

Preview of the transition effect.

6 Select the method of advancement.

7 Choose OK.

Running the Slide Show Manually

You can set the slide show so you control the advancement from one slide to the next, using either the mouse or the keyboard.

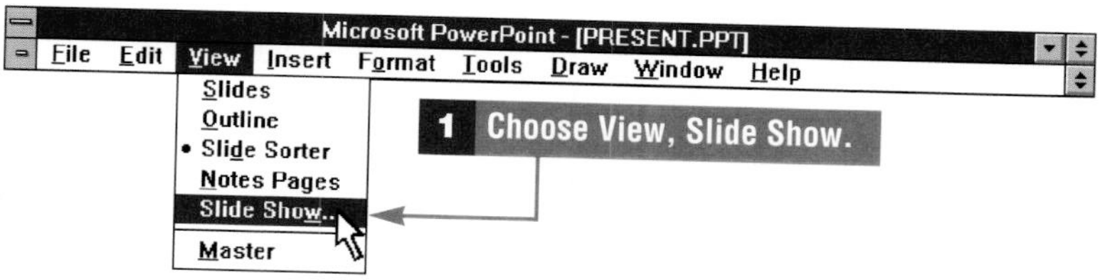

1 Choose View, Slide Show.

2 Indicate the slides to include in the slide show.

Enter a range of slides to display in the slide show.

Select All to display the entire slide presentation.

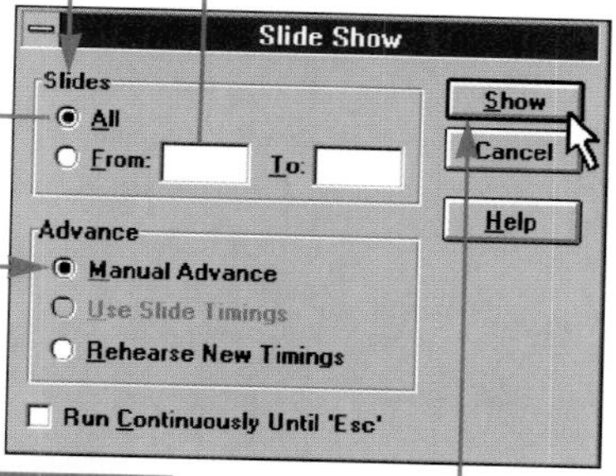

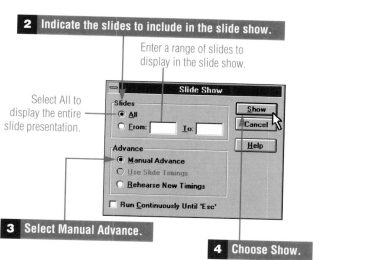

3 Select Manual Advance.

4 Choose Show.

5 Click the mouse to advance the slides.

You also can press Page Down to advance the slides. Press Esc at any time to end the slide show.

Running the Slide Show Continuously

Ordinarily a slide show ends after all the slides have displayed. You can choose, however, to have the slide show run in a continuous loop, cycling through the slides until you end the show manually by pressing Esc.

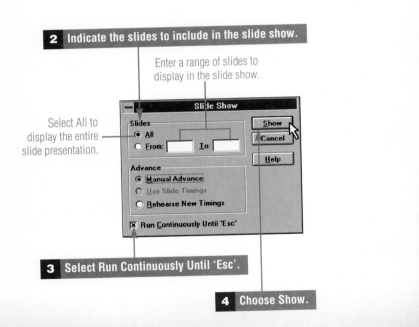

1 Choose View, Slide Show.

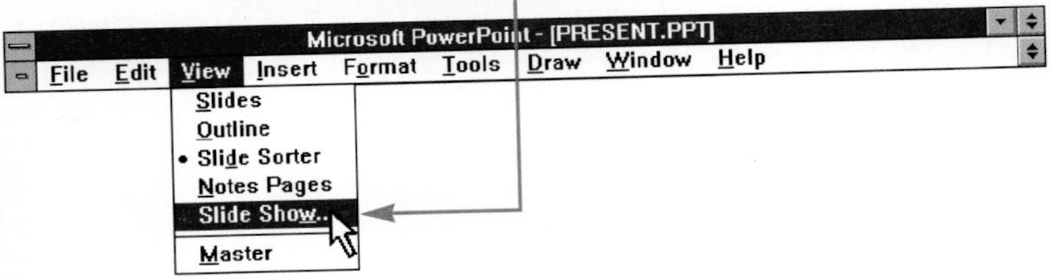

2 Indicate the slides to include in the slide show.

Enter a range of slides to display in the slide show.

Select All to display the entire slide presentation.

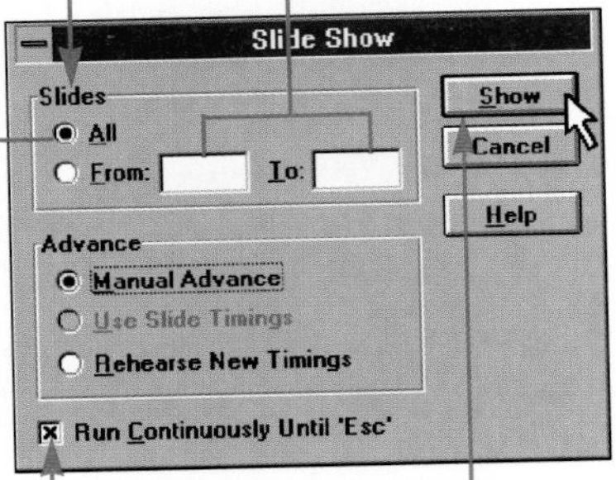

3 Select Run Continuously Until 'Esc'.

4 Choose Show.

Using the Drawing Tool during a Slide Show

While running your slide show, you can use the Freehand Annotation drawing tool to bring attention to specific items on your slides. The drawing remains on-screen until you advance to the next slide. It does not effect the original slides at all.

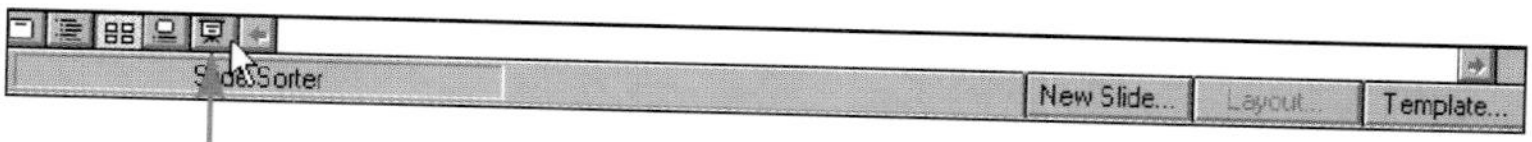

1 Click the Slide Show button.

2 Click the Freehand Annotation icon.

The pointer changes to pencil.

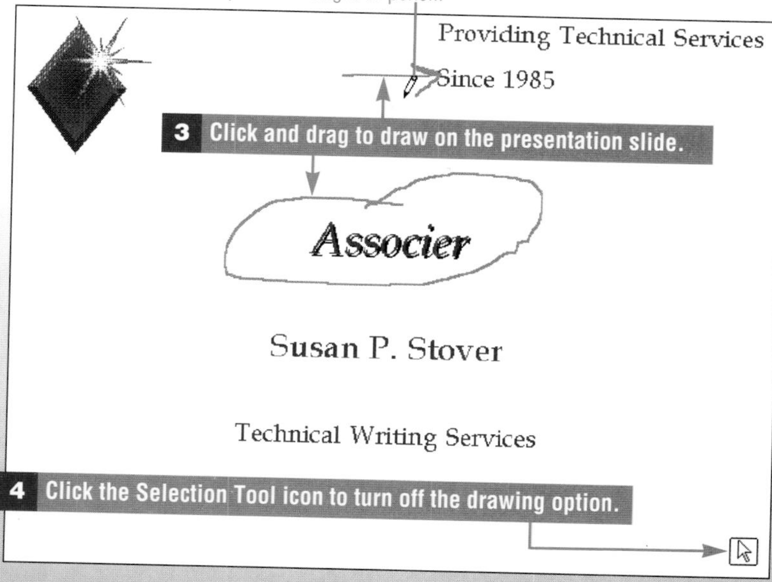

3 Click and drag to draw on the presentation slide.

4 Click the Selection Tool icon to turn off the drawing option.

Creating Hidden Slides

Create a hidden slide so you have the option of whether to include that slide in the slide show.

1 Select the slide to hide.

2 Click the Hide Slide button.

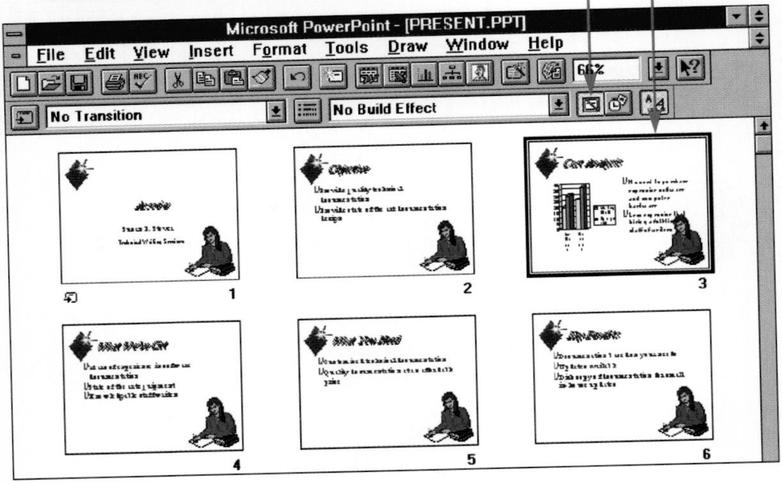

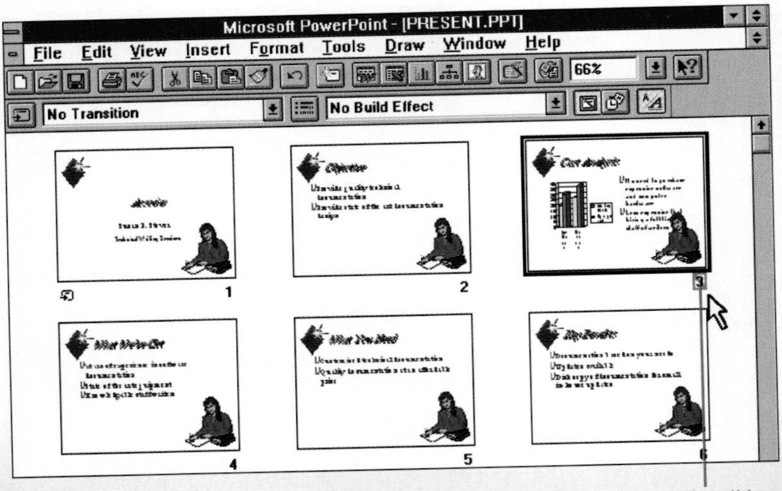

The number of the hidden slide appears in a box with a line through it in Slide Sorter view.

Displaying Hidden Slides

When you run a slide show, you have the option to display hidden slides.

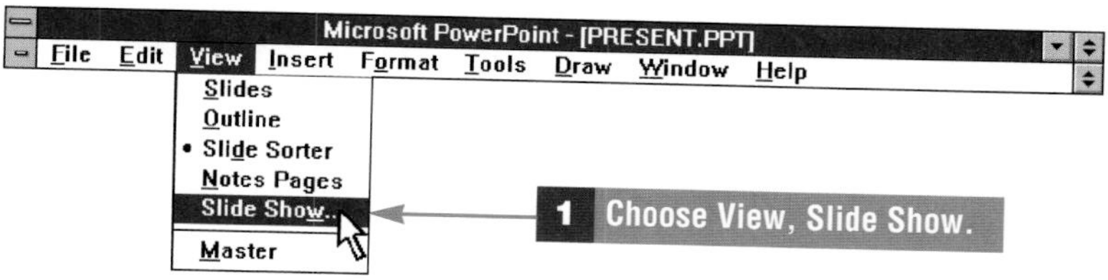

1 Choose View, Slide Show.

2 Select the display options.

3 Choose Show.

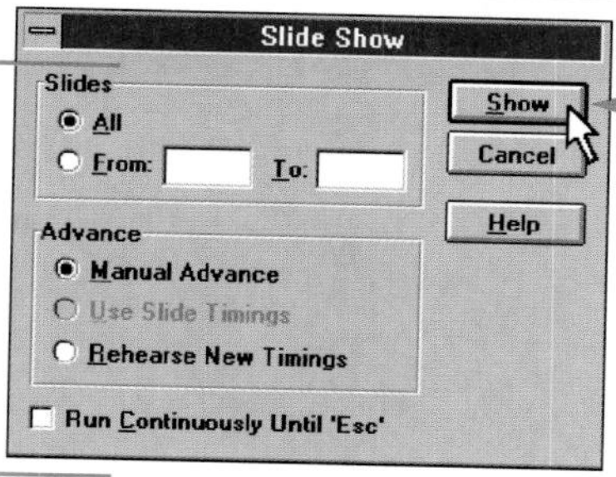

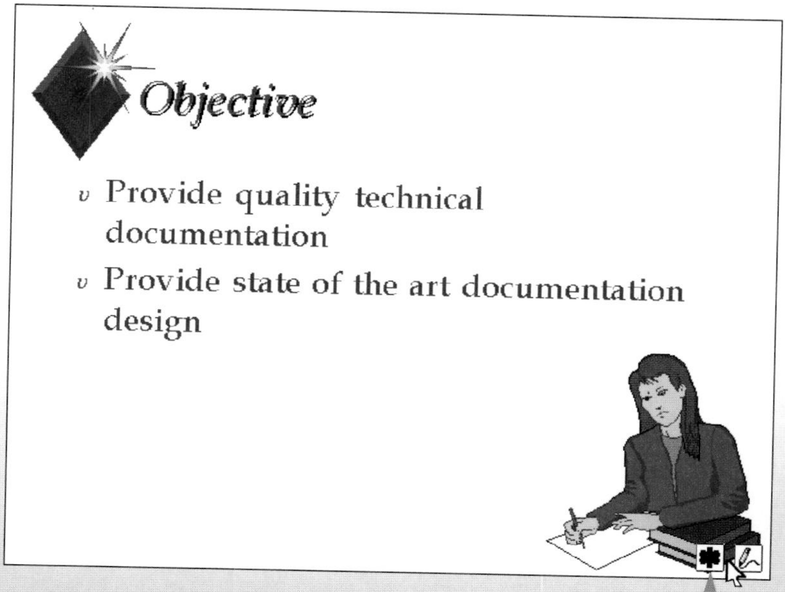

4 Click the Hidden Slide icon on the slide preceding the hidden slide.

Rehearsing a Slide Show for Timing

You can rehearse the presentation and time each slide. PowerPoint uses the rehearsal times when advancing your slides during a show.

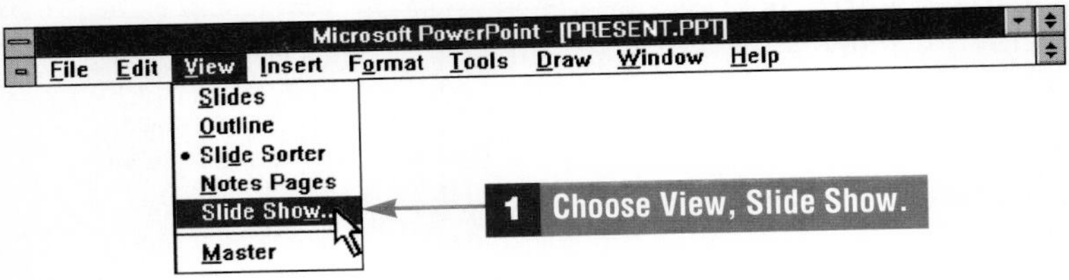

1 Choose View, Slide Show.

2 Select Rehearse New Timings.

3 Choose Show.

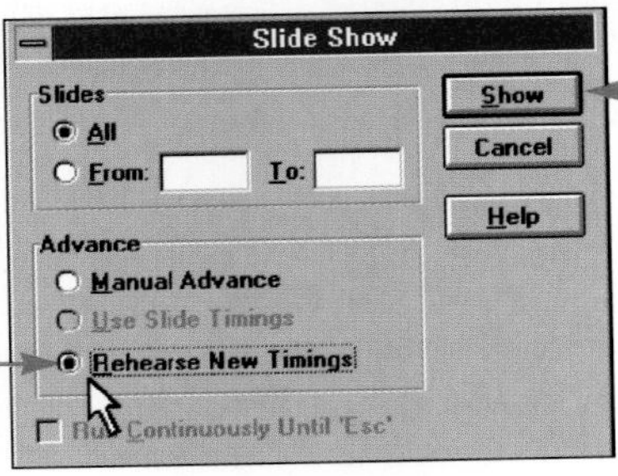

4 Click anywhere on the slide to advance when you are ready.

The clock shows the elapsed time for the slide.

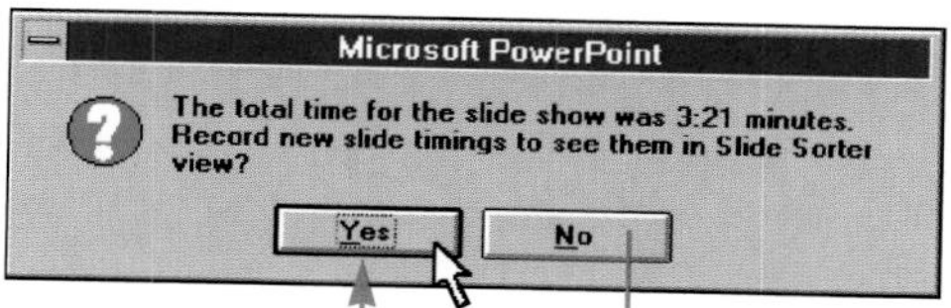

5 Choose Yes.

If the time is unsatisfactory, choose No to close the window without saving the rehearsal times.

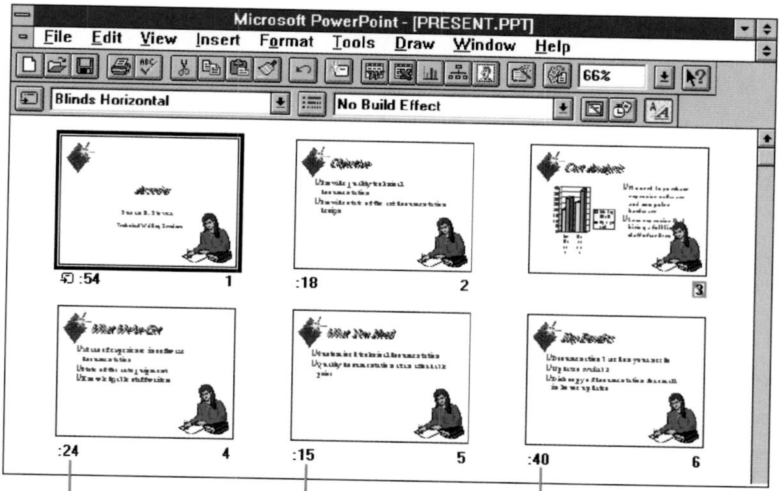

The time for each slide appears below the slide in Slide Sorter view.

Adding a Table to a Slide

You can add a table to any slide, regardless of whether the slide layout includes a table placeholder. You actually create and edit the tables in Microsoft Word 6 for Windows, so you must have that application in order to use the Table feature.

To add a table using a table placeholder

1 Double-click the table placeholder.

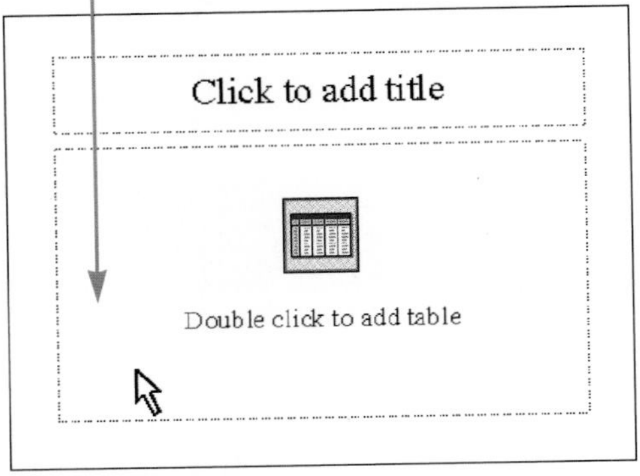

See "Adding a New Slide to a Presentation" to learn how to add a slide with a particular layout.

2 Enter the number of columns and rows for the table.

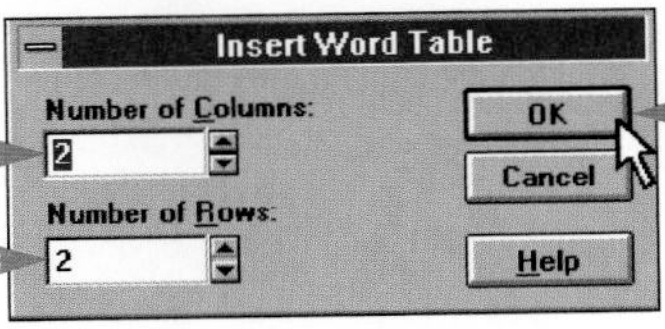

3 Choose OK.

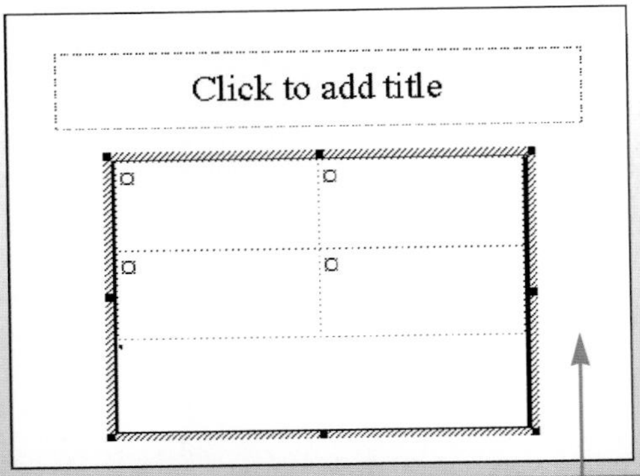

4 Click anywhere outside the table to return to PowerPoint.

To add a table to any slide

1 Click the Insert Microsoft Word Table button.

2 Drag across the grid to select the number of table columns and rows.

This table will be two columns by two rows.

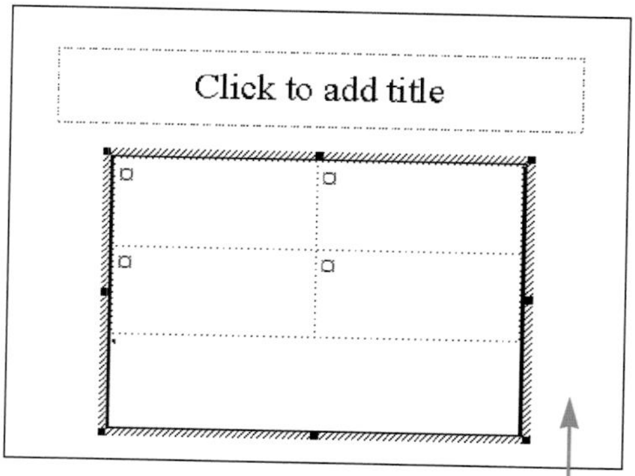

3 Click anywhere outside the table to return to PowerPoint.

Entering Table Data

Once you create a Microsoft Word table, you enter data in any or all of the table cells. Entering data is done from Microsoft Word 6.

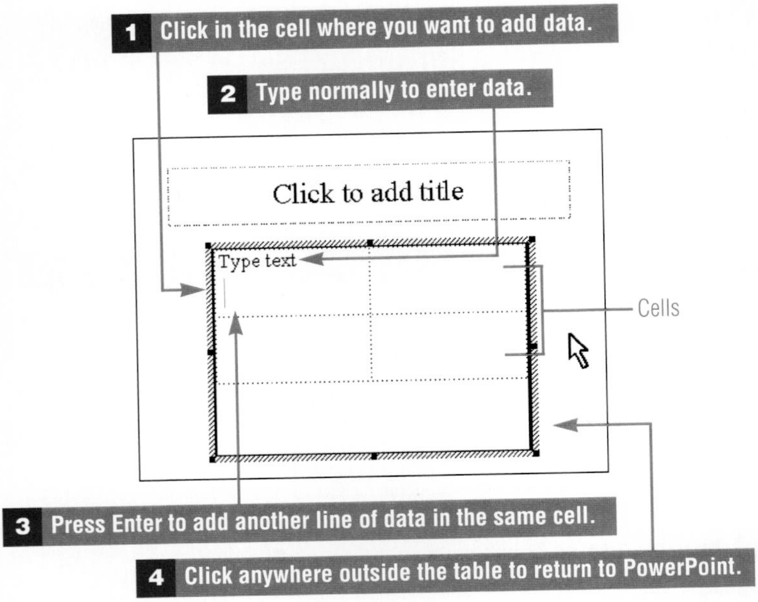

1 Click in the cell where you want to add data.
2 Type normally to enter data.
Click to add title
Type text
Cells
3 Press Enter to add another line of data in the same cell.
4 Click anywhere outside the table to return to PowerPoint.

You can click in any cell to select it.

Press Tab to advance to the next cell in the table.

Editing Table Data

Just like any other text on a PowerPoint slide, you can edit the data in a Microsoft Word table at any time.

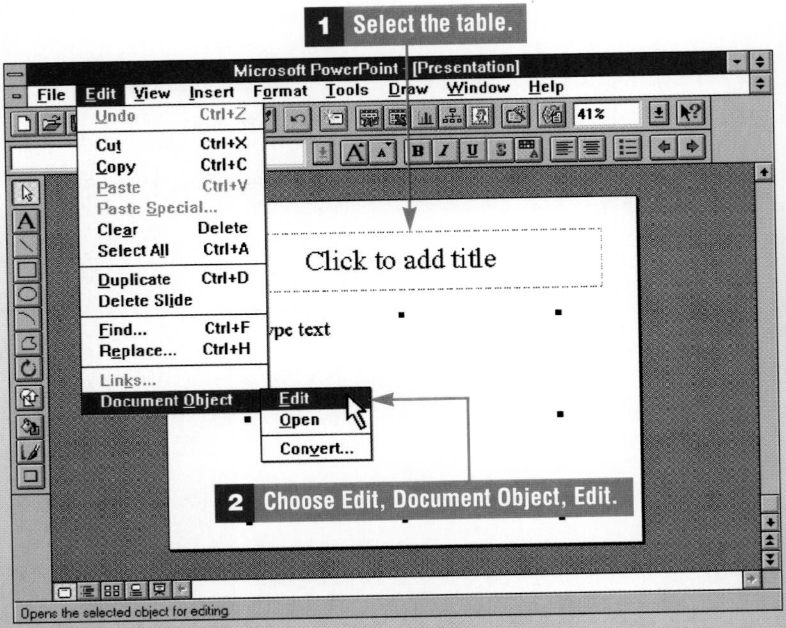

3 Click in the cell containing data to edit.

4 Edit the text in the selected cell.

Edit the text as you would in any Word 6 table.

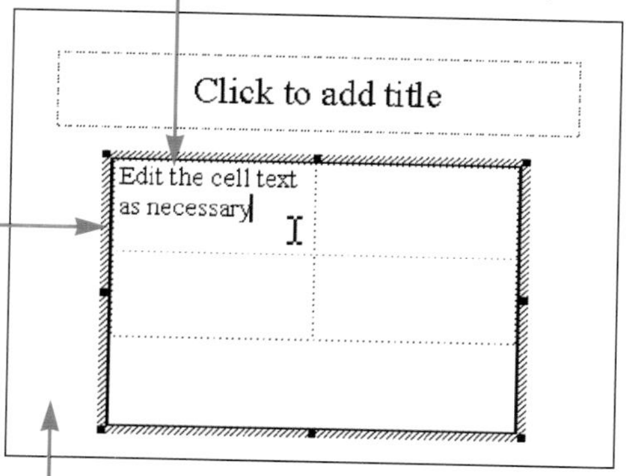

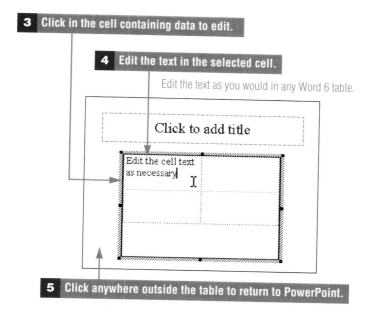

5 Click anywhere outside the table to return to PowerPoint.

Changing the Table Appearance

Using the Microsoft Word 6 menus and buttons, you can change the appearance of a table in your presentation.

To insert a row

1 Click in a cell in the row that you want just below the new row.

2 Choose Table, Insert Rows.

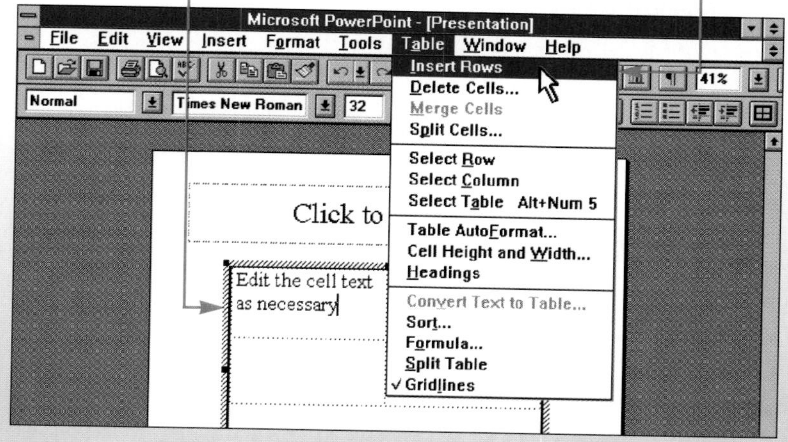

more ▶

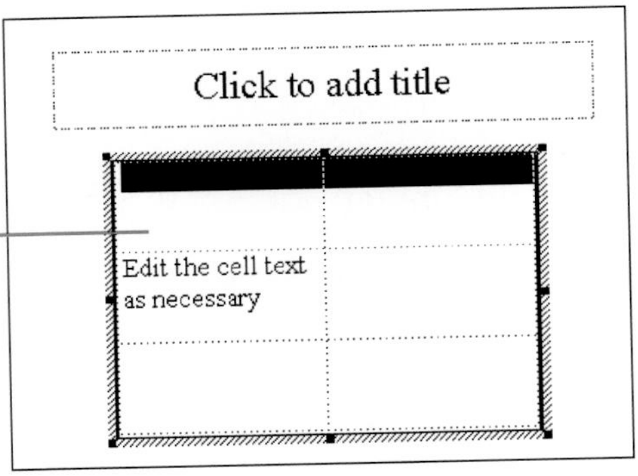

The new row is inserted.

To insert a column

1 Click in a cell in the column to the right of the new column.

2 Choose Table, Select Column.

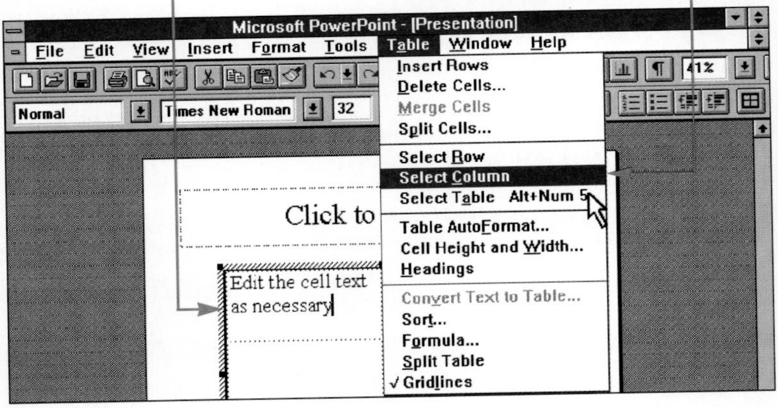

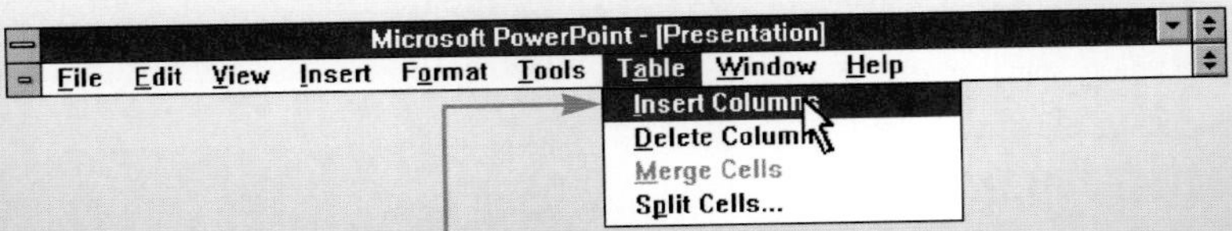

3 Choose Table, Insert Columns.

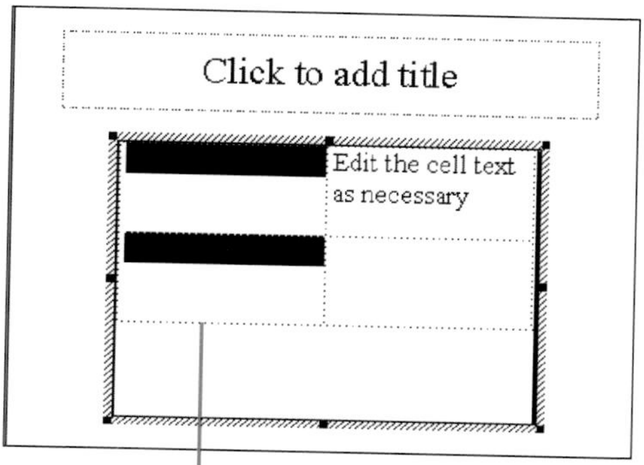

The new column is inserted.

To delete a row

1 Click in a cell in the row you want to delete.

2 Choose Table, Select Row.

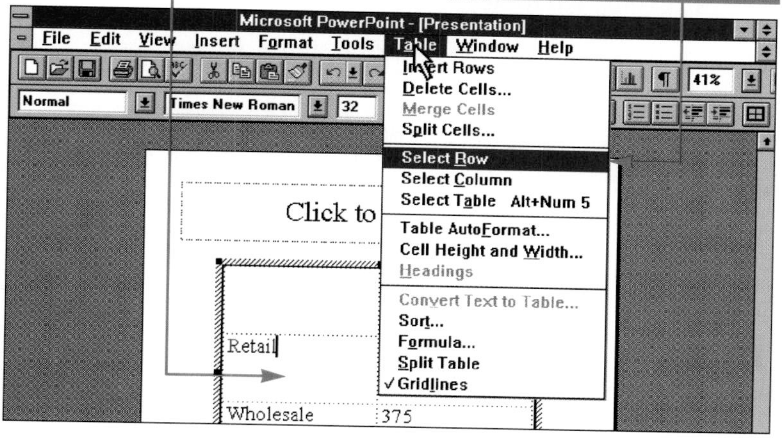

3 Choose Table, Delete Rows.

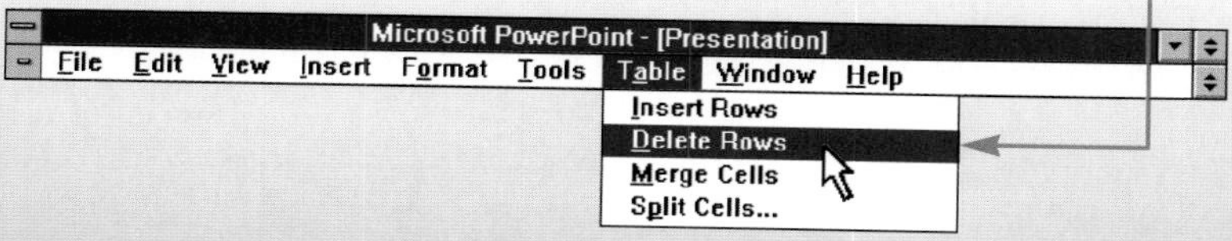

To delete a column

1 Click in a cell in the column you want to delete.

2 Choose Table, Select Column.

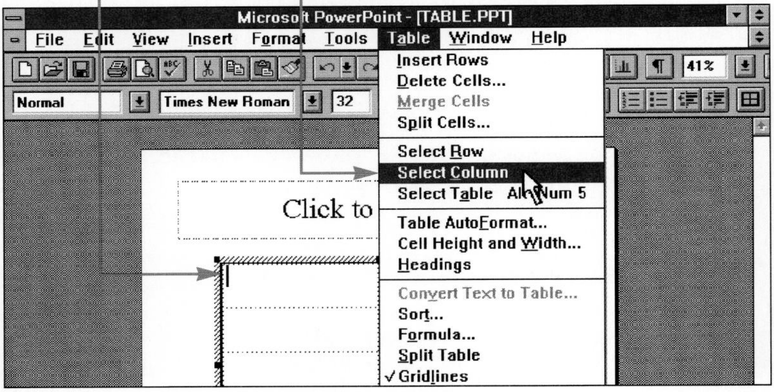

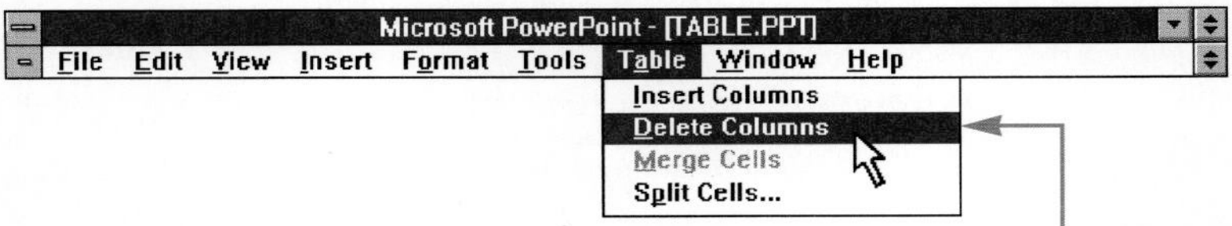

3 Choose Table, Delete Columns.

To format cells

1 Select the row or column to format.

2 Choose Table, Cell Height and Width.

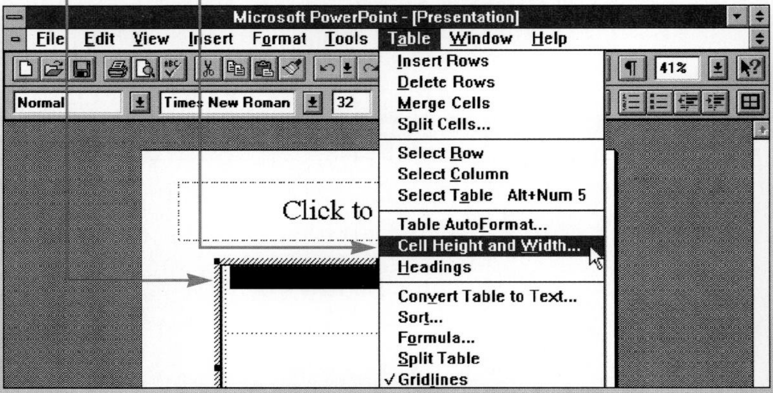

3 Click Row.

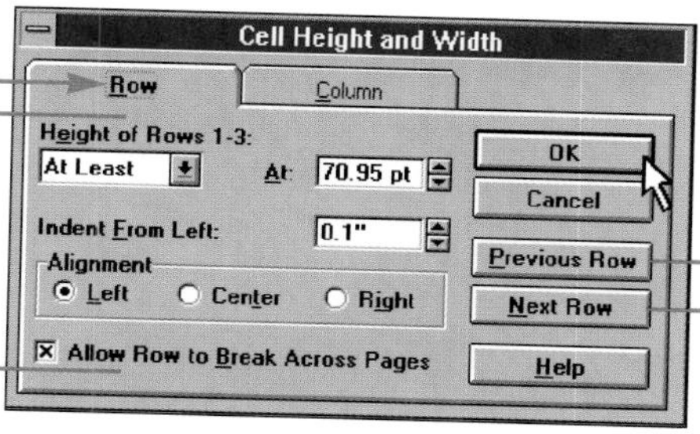

4 Select the formatting options for the selected row.

You can use Previous Row or Next Row to select a different row to format.

5 Click Column.

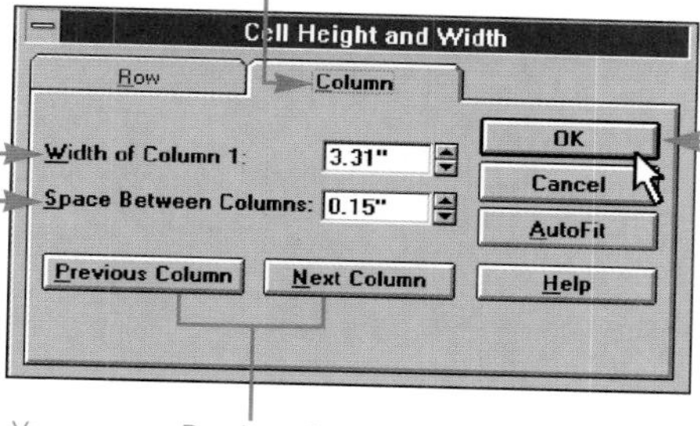

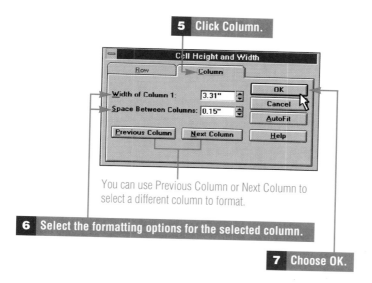

You can use Previous Column or Next Column to select a different column to format.

6 Select the formatting options for the selected column.

7 Choose OK.

To format table text

1 Select the table text to format.

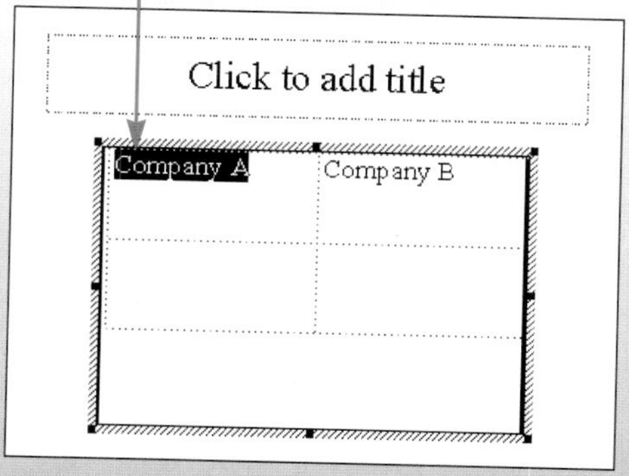

more ▶

2 Choose Format, Font.

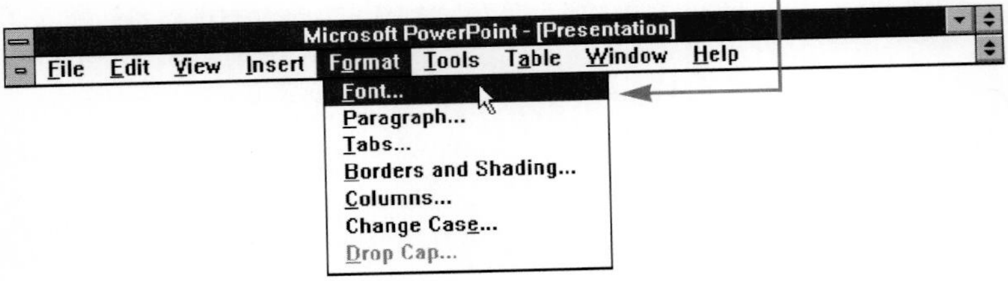

3 Select the desired formatting options.

4 Choose OK.

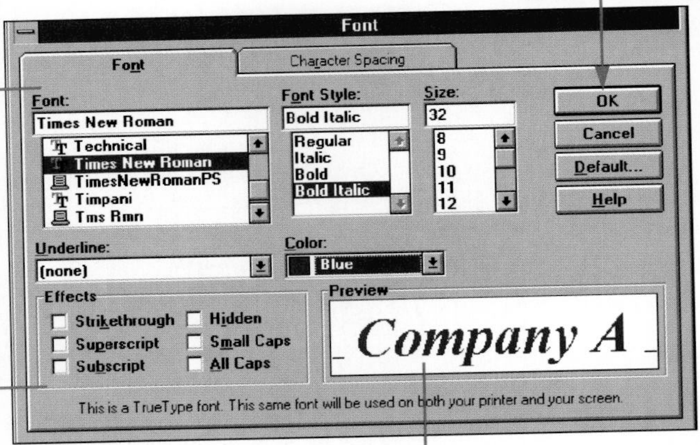

Preview of how text will appear with the current settings

5 Click anywhere on the table to deselect the text.

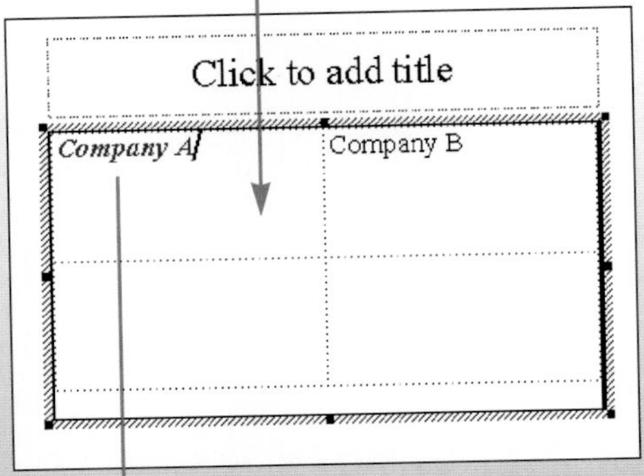

The formatting changes are applied to the text.

To apply AutoFormats

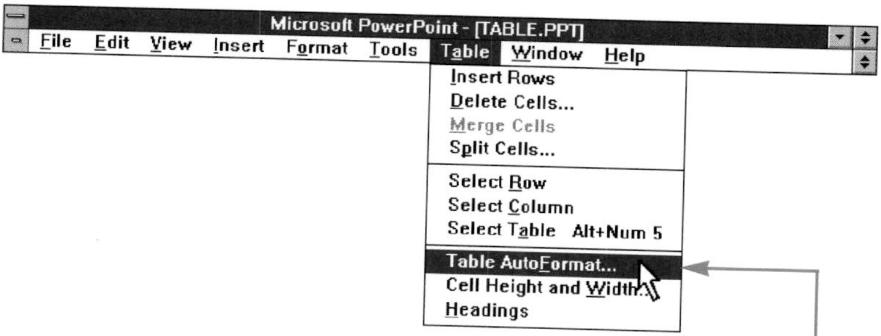

1 Choose Table, Table AutoFormat.

2 Select the desired format.

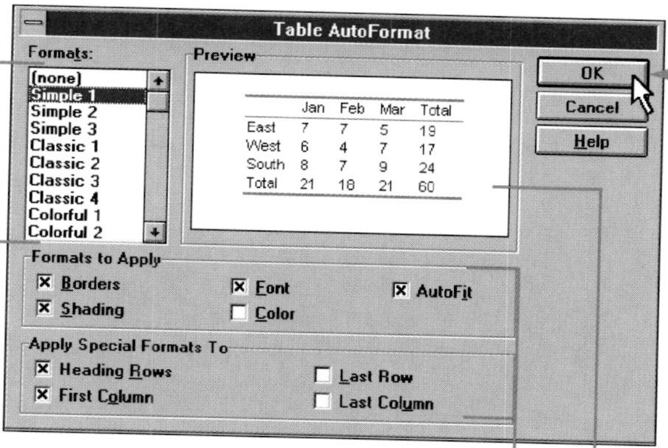

3 Select the format settings.

You can preview the table format.

4 Choose OK.

A finished table

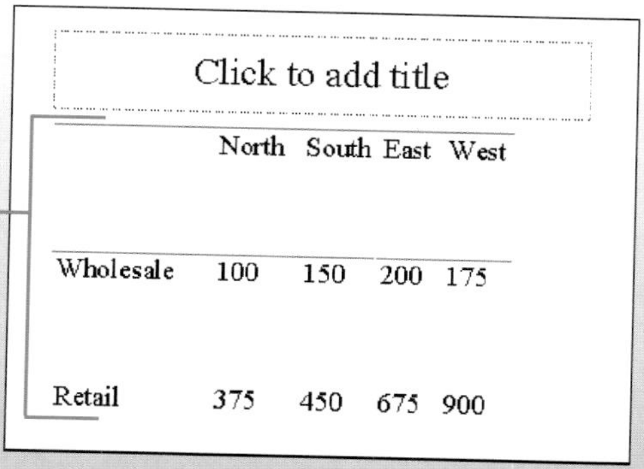

Adding Text on a Slide

In addition to entering text in text placeholders on slide layouts, you can enter text on any slide or master. This text can be either a one-line caption or word-wrapping text.

To enter a text caption

1 Click the Text tool.

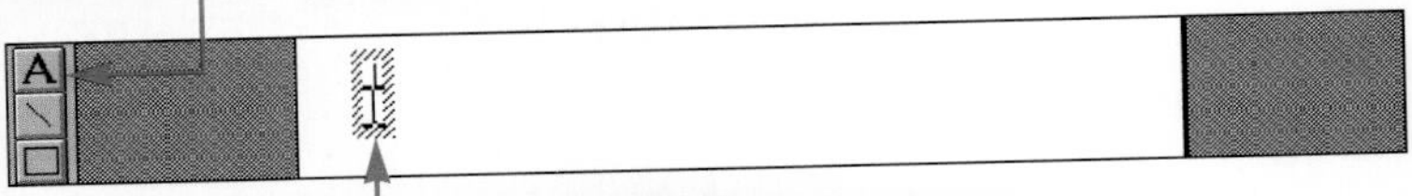

2 Click where you want to begin the text.

3 Type normally.

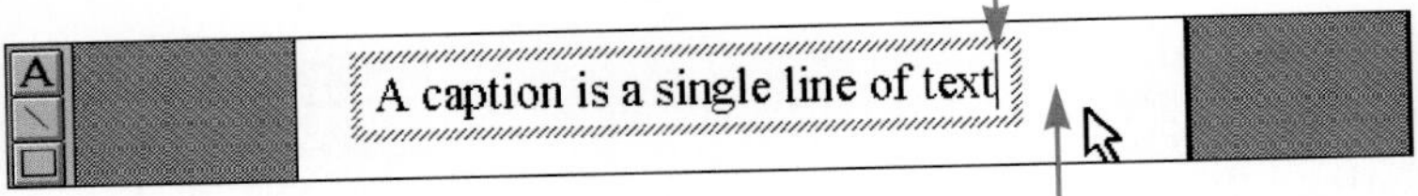
A caption is a single line of text

4 Click outside the text area when finished.

To add word wrapping text

1 Click the Text tool.

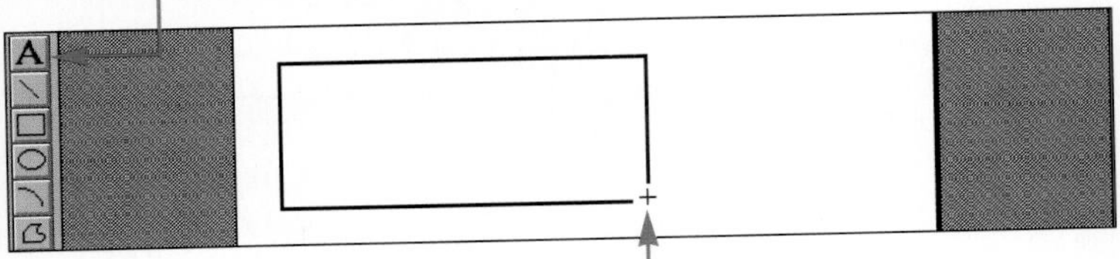

2 Click and drag to create the text area.

3 Release the mouse button.

4 Type normally.

Text automatically wraps to the next line at the end of the text area.

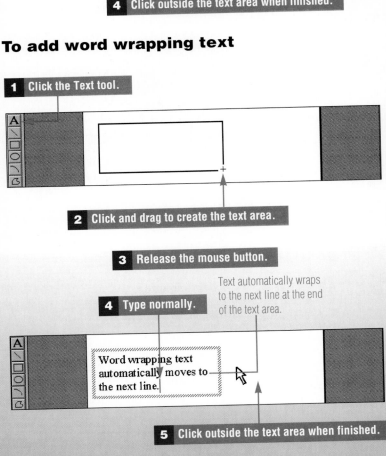

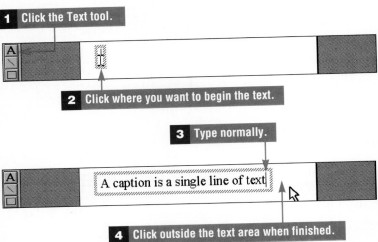

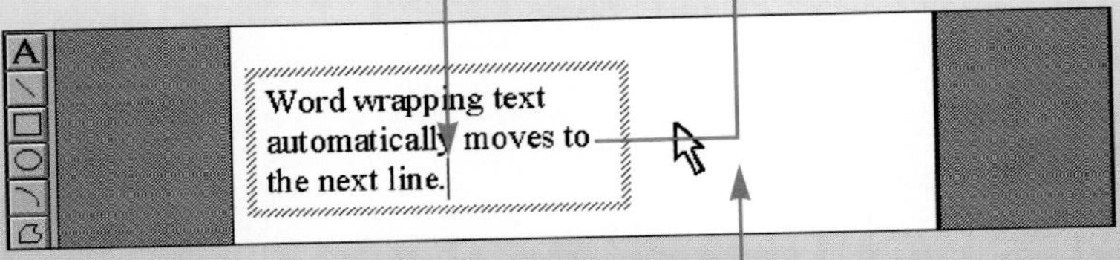
Word wrapping text
automatically moves to
the next line.

5 Click outside the text area when finished.

Selecting Text

In order to edit or format text, you must first select the text.

1 Click at the beginning of the text to select.

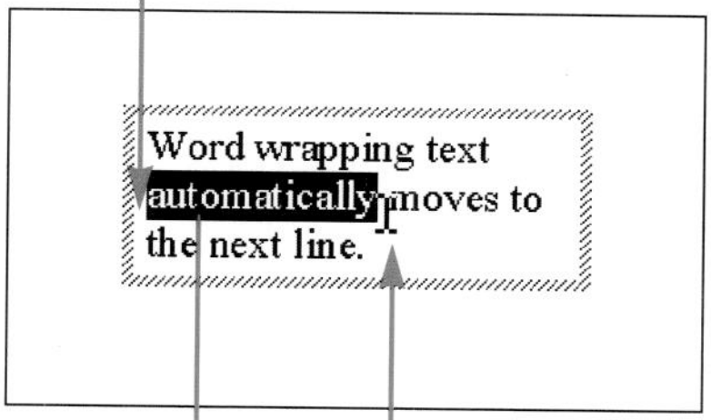
Word wrapping text
automatically moves to
the next line.

2 Drag to highlight the text.

The selected text is highlighted.

3 Release the mouse button.

Editing Text

Rather than retype an entire text selection, you can add, edit, and delete words and characters as necessary.

To insert text

1 Position the mouse pointer at the location to insert text.

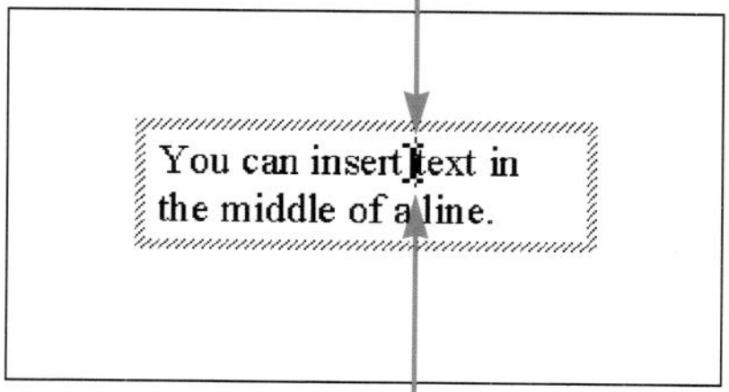
You can insert text in
the middle of a line.

2 Click to position the insertion point.

3 Type normally to insert text at the insertion point.

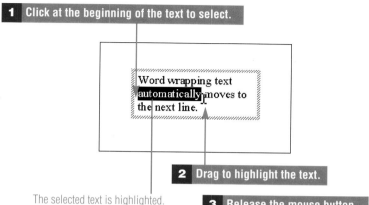

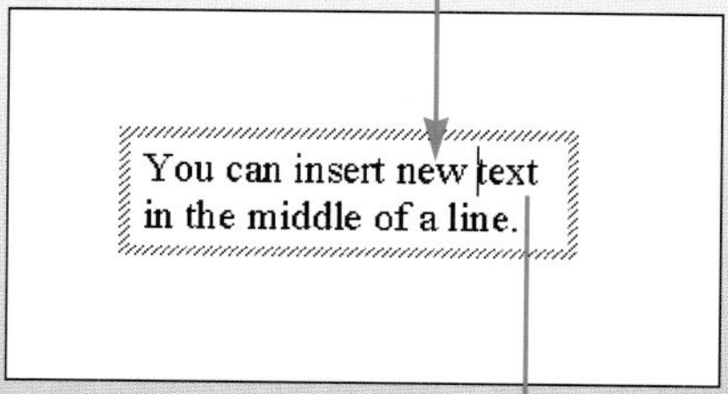
You can insert new text
in the middle of a line.

New text pushes existing text to the right.

To delete a character

1 Position the insertion point to the left of the character to delete.

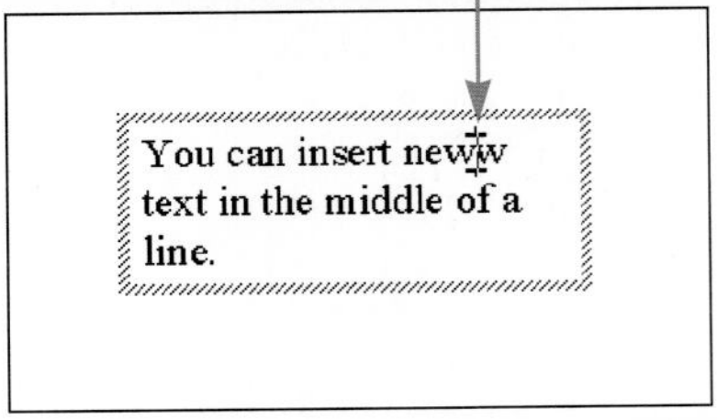
You can insert newjw
text in the middle of a
line.

2 Press Delete.

The character to the right of the insertion point is deleted.

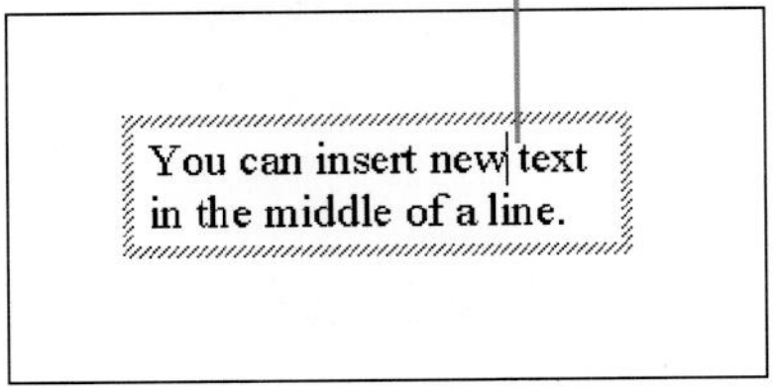
You can insert new text
in the middle of a line.

To delete a text selection

1 Select the text to delete.

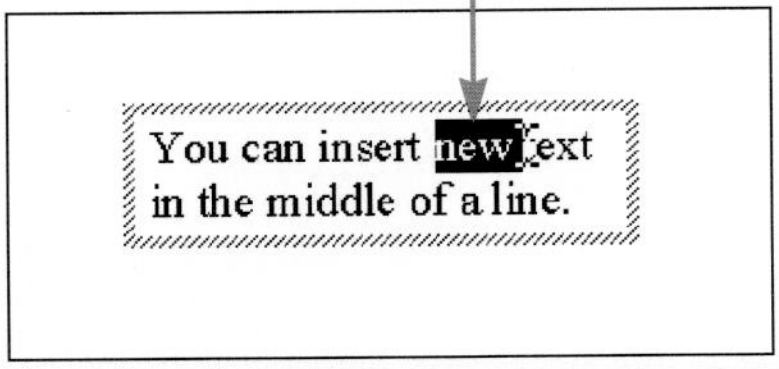
You can insert new text
in the middle of a line.

2 Press Delete.

The selected text is deleted.

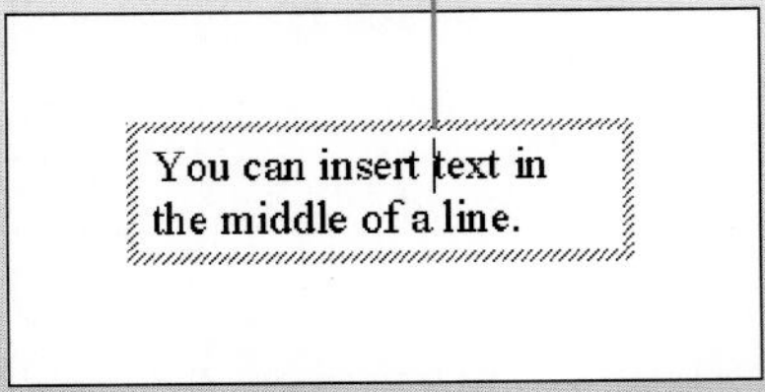
You can insert text in
the middle of a line.

To replace text

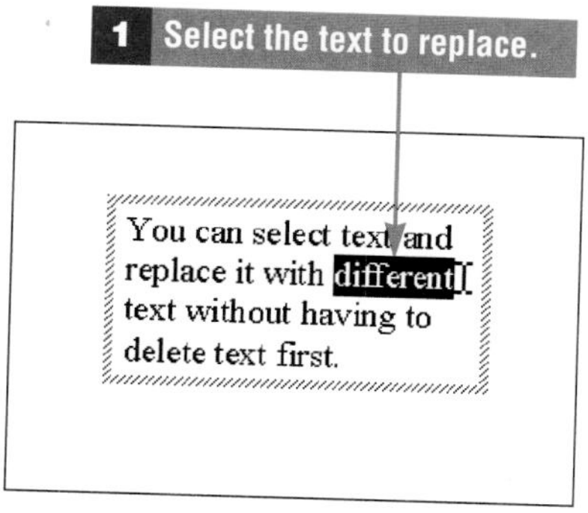
1 Select the text to replace.
You can select text and replace it with different text without having to delete text first.

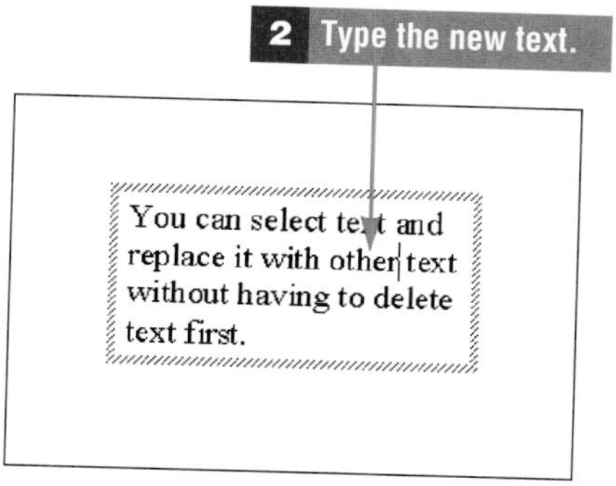
2 Type the new text.
You can select text and replace it with other text without having to delete text first.

The new text replaces the selected text.

Copying Text

Use the drag-and-drop method to copy text within a slide. Use the Windows Clipboard to copy text from one slide to another.

To copy text using drag and drop

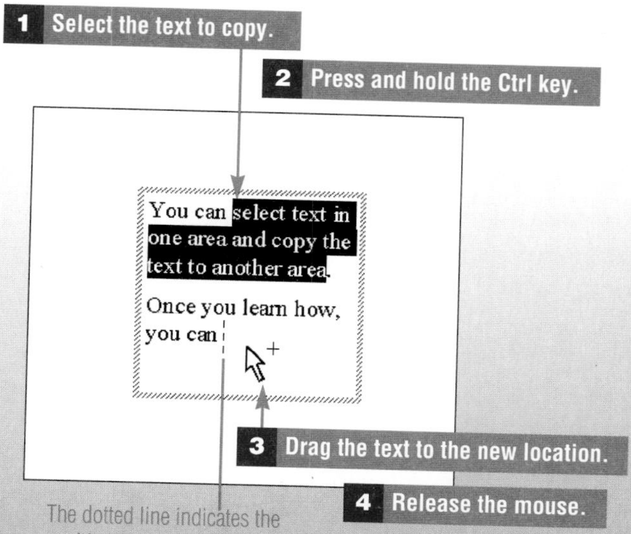
1 Select the text to copy.
2 Press and hold the Ctrl key.
You can select text in one area and copy the text to another area.
Once you learn how, you can
3 Drag the text to the new location.
4 Release the mouse.

The dotted line indicates the position for the copied text.

more ▶

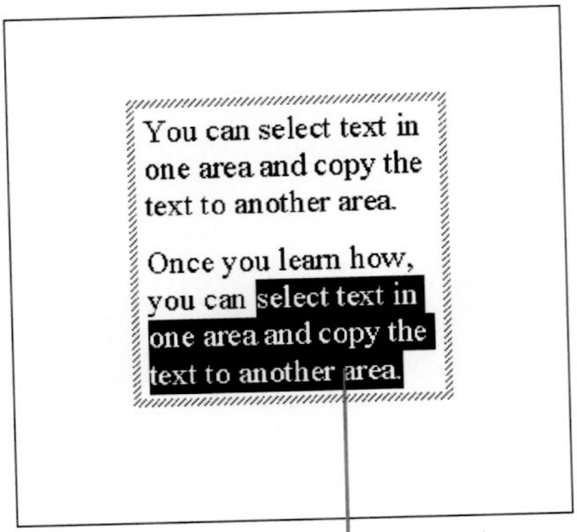
You can select text in one area and copy the text to another area.
Once you learn how, you can select text in one area and copy the text to another area.

The text is copied to the new location.

To copy text using the Clipboard

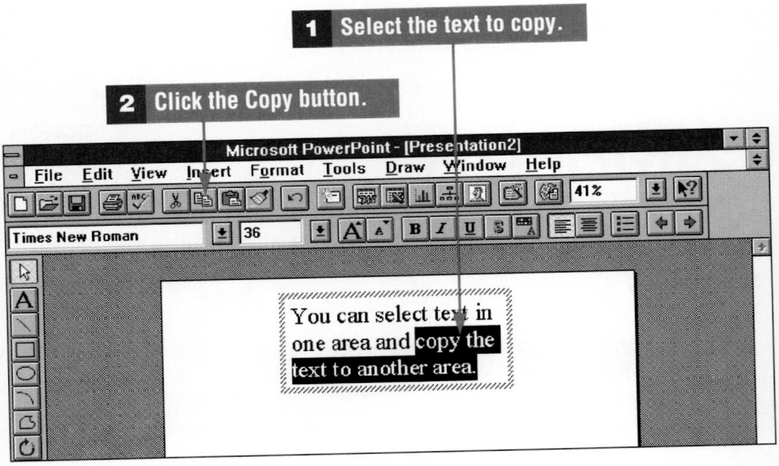
1 Select the text to copy.
2 Click the Copy button.
Microsoft PowerPoint - [Presentation2]
File Edit View Insert Format Tools Draw Window Help
Times New Roman
36
41%
You can select text in one area and copy the text to another area.

3 Position the insertion point where you want to place the copied data.

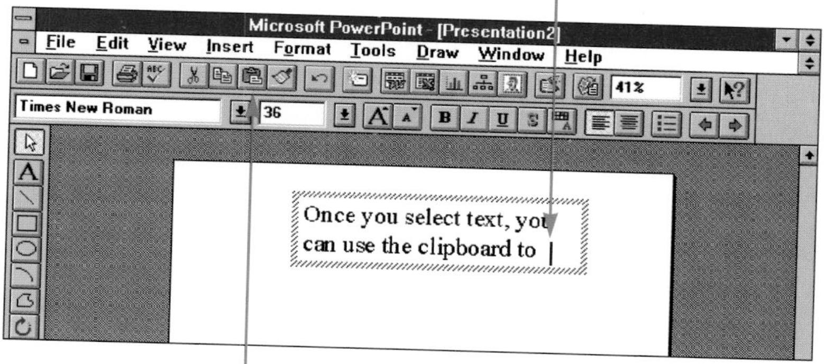

4 Click the Paste button.

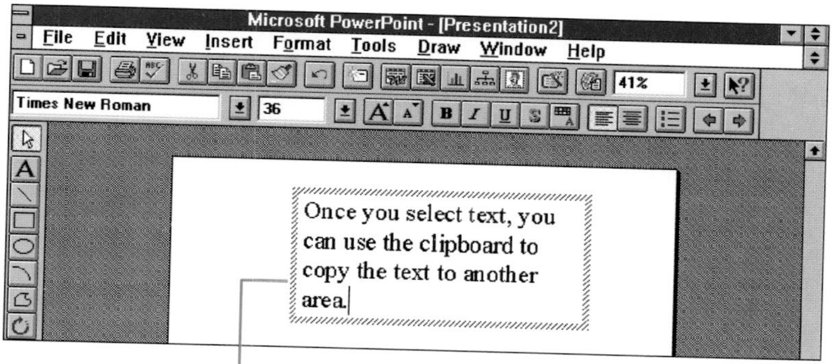

The copied text is pasted at the insertion point's location.

Moving Text

Rather than delete and retype text, you can move text from one location to another.

To move text using drag and drop

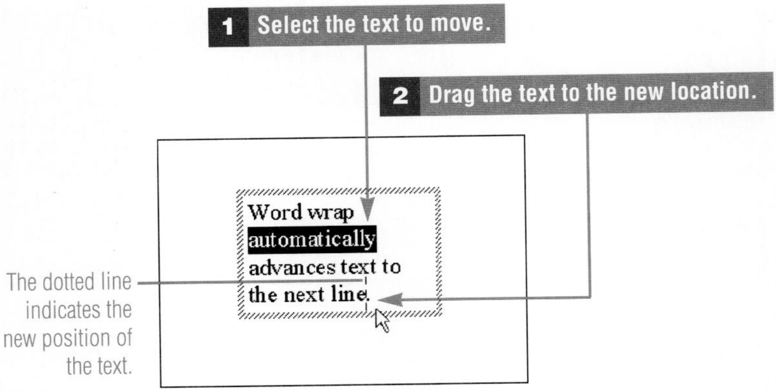
1 Select the text to move.
2 Drag the text to the new location.
Word wrap
automatically
advances text to
the next line.
The dotted line indicates the new position of the text.

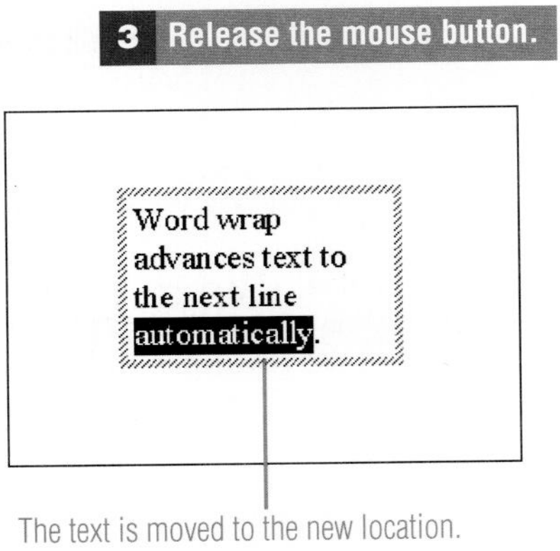

To move text using the Clipboard

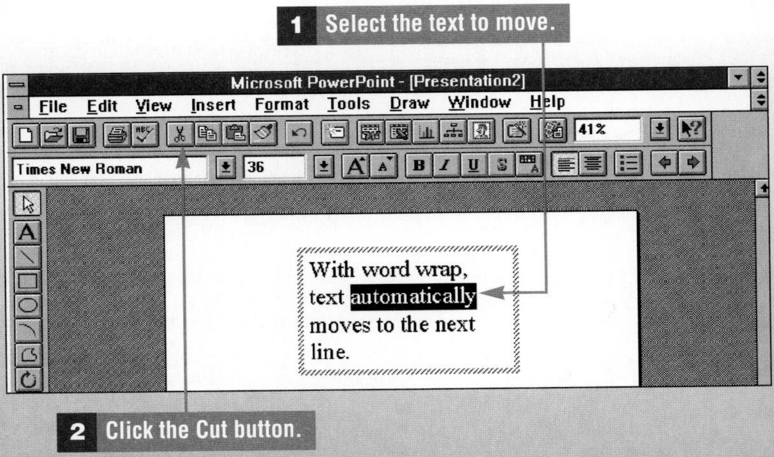

3 Position the insertion point at the new text location.

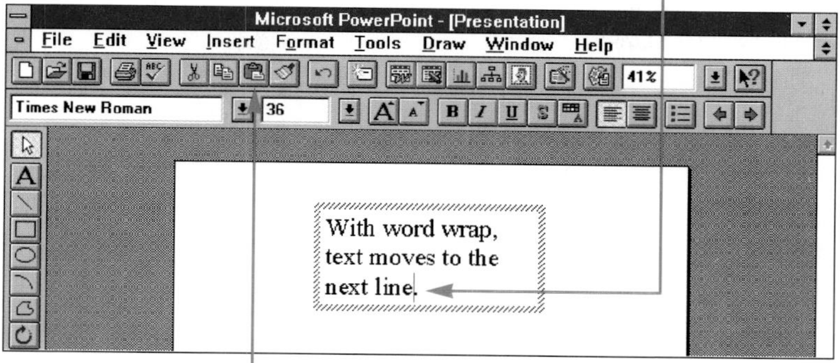

4 Click the Paste button.

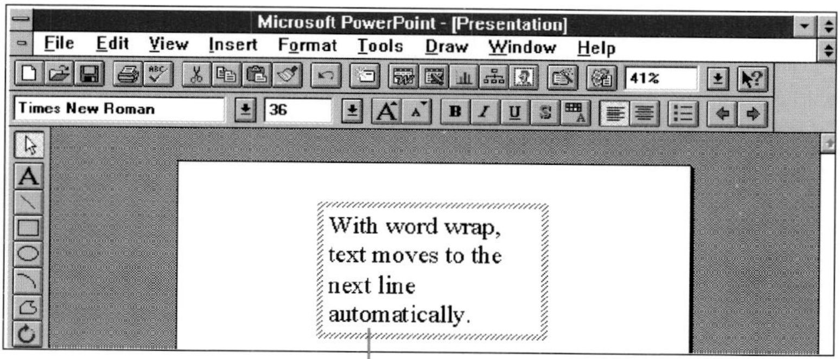

The text is pasted at the insertion point's location.

Checking Spelling

PowerPoint has a built-in spell checker that helps you catch mistakes in your presentation text.

1 Click the Spelling button.

more ▶

2 Look at the word that the program doesn't recognize.

3 Select an action for the word.

Select a suggested alternative word.

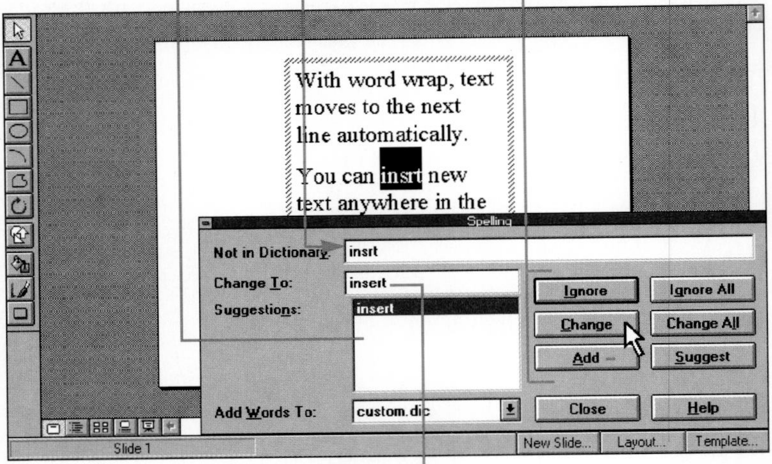

Edit the word manually in the Change To text box.

Spell-Check Action	Function
Ignore	Skips over this occurrence of the word without making any changes.
Ignore All	Skips over all occurrences of the word during the current spell check.
Change	Replaces the selected word with the text in the Change To box.
Change All	Replaces all occurrences of the word with the text in the Change To box.
Add	Includes the selected word in your dictionary for future reference.
Close	Stops the spell-check process.

4 Choose OK.

Selecting a Font and Text Attributes

You can change the font and attributes of selected text in a slide at any time.

1 Select the text to change.

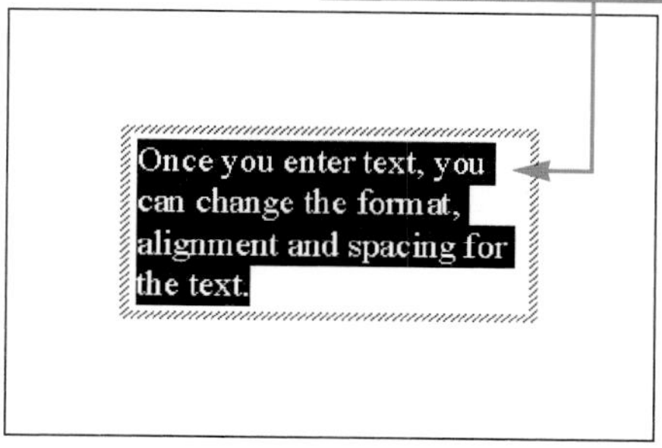

2 Choose Format, Font.

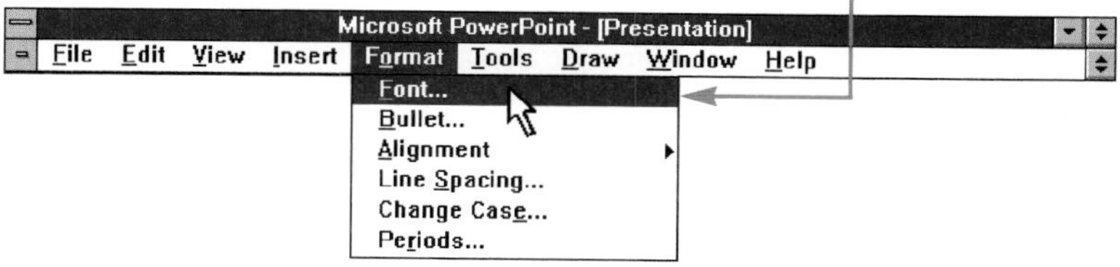

3 Select the font.

4 Select the font style.

5 Select the point size.

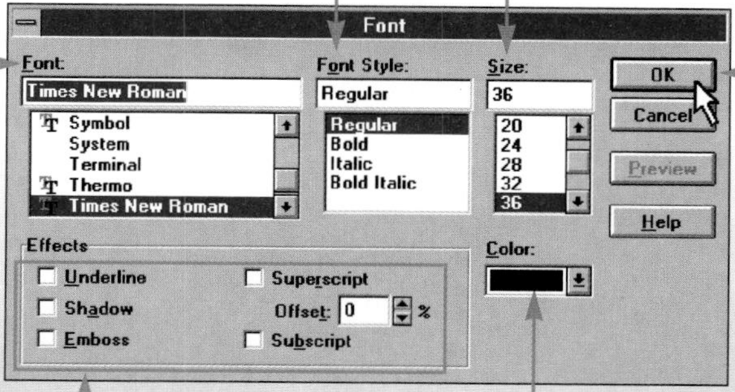

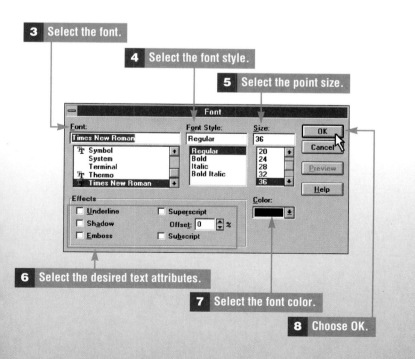

6 Select the desired text attributes.

7 Select the font color.

8 Choose OK.

Replacing a Font

Use the Replace Font option to change a font selection throughout the presentation without having to select and edit each text entry individually.

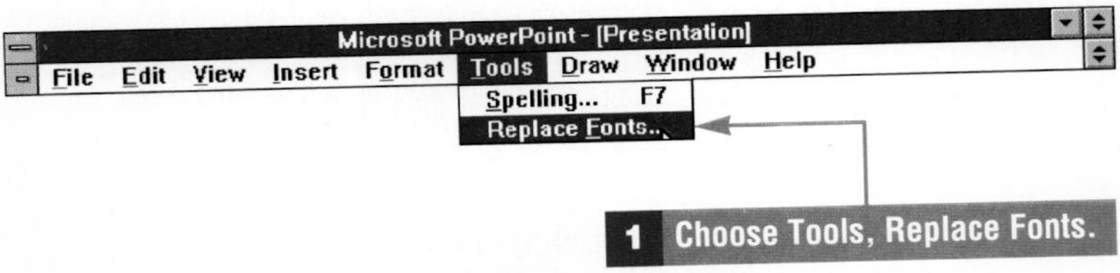

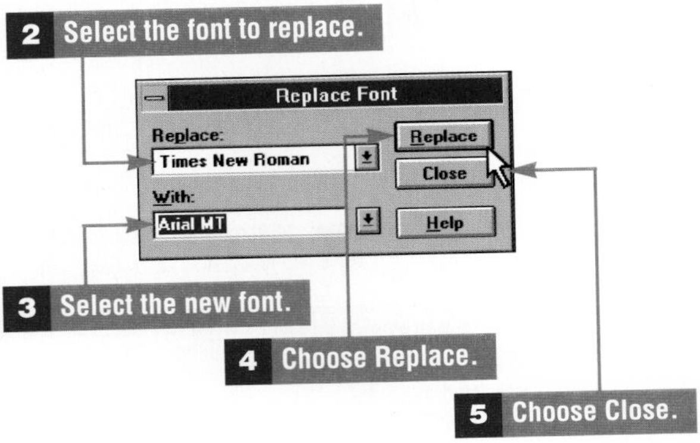

Changing Paragraph Alignment

You can change the alignment, or justification, of selected text in the presentation.

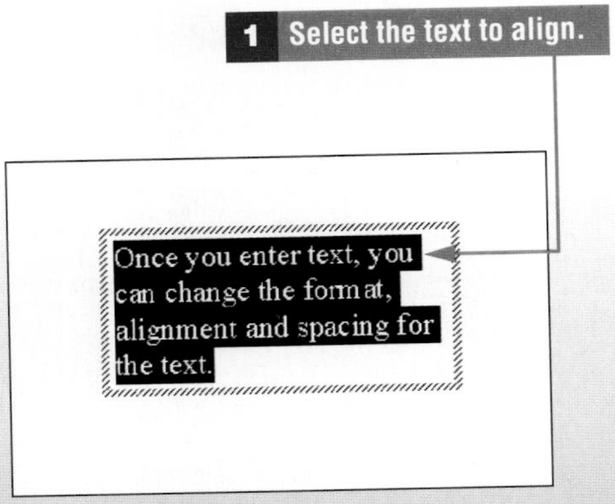

1 Select the text to align.
Once you enter text, you can change the format, alignment and spacing for the text.

2 Choose Format, Alignment.

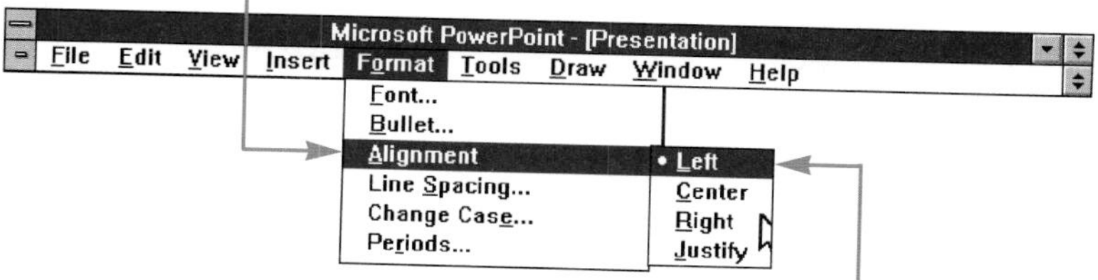

3 Choose the desired alignment for the text.

Changing Spacing

You can change the spacing between lines and paragraphs within selected text.

1 Select the text in which to change spacing.

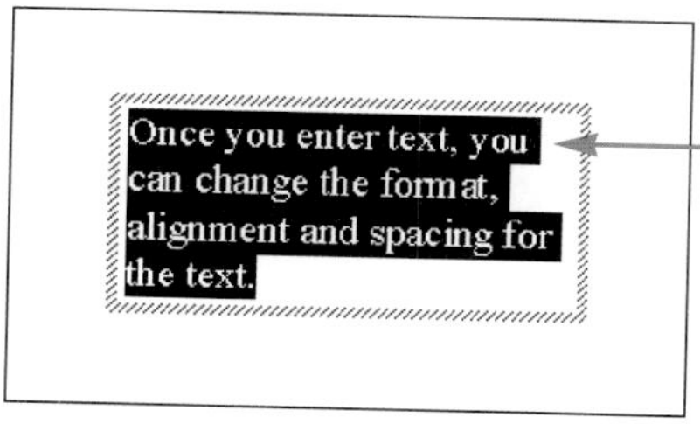

2 Choose Format, Line Spacing.

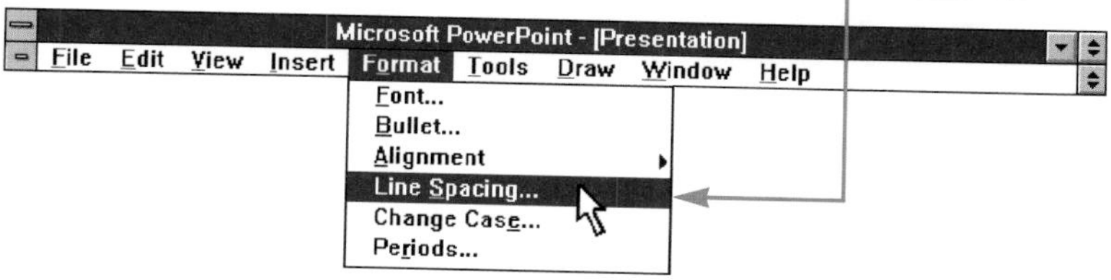

3 Select the desired line spacing for within a paragraph.

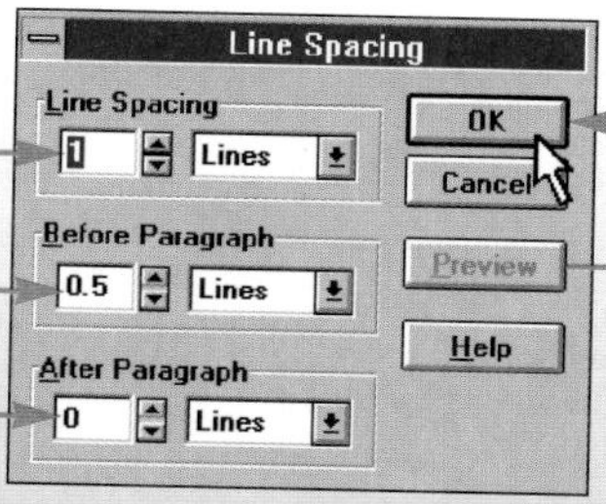

Use Preview to see the selected text with the new spacing.

4 Select the desired spacing for before and after a paragraph.

5 Choose OK.

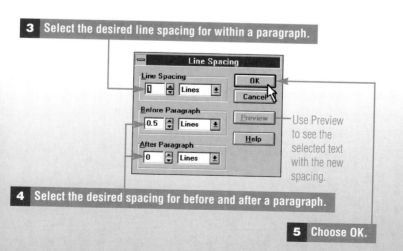

Editing Paragraph Bullets

You can add or delete bullets from selected text in your presentation. You also can choose from among various types of bullets and adjust their size and color.

1 Select the text in which to add, delete, or edit the bullets.

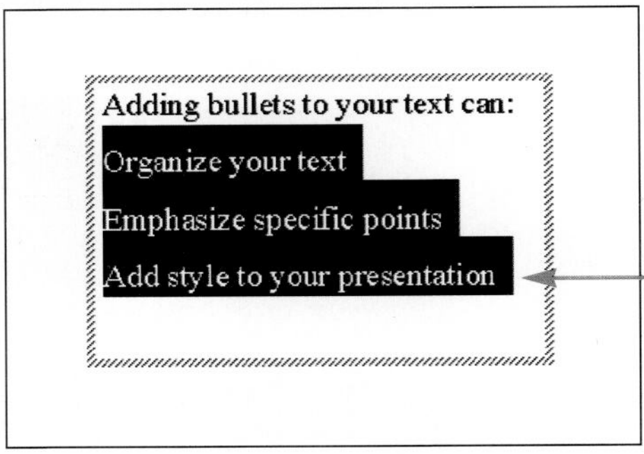

2 Choose Format, Bullet.

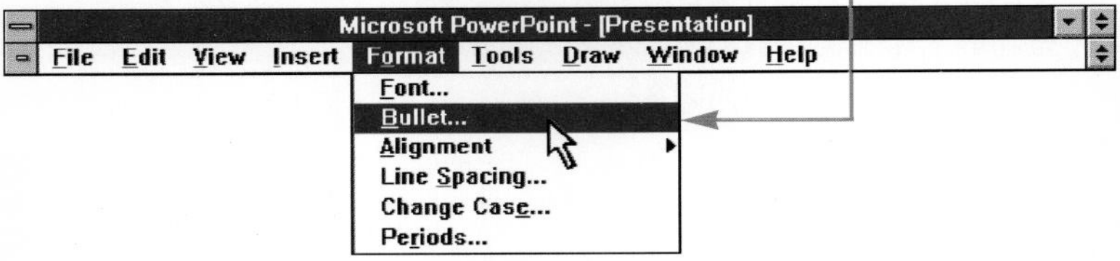

3 Select Use a Bullet.

4 Select the list of bullets to display.

Use Special Color to select the color of the bullet.

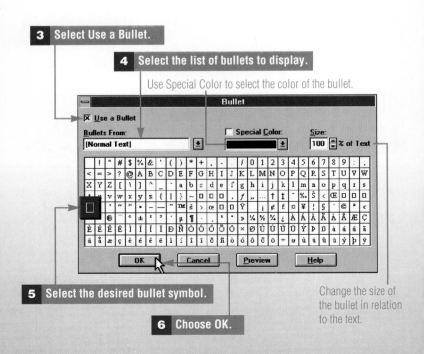

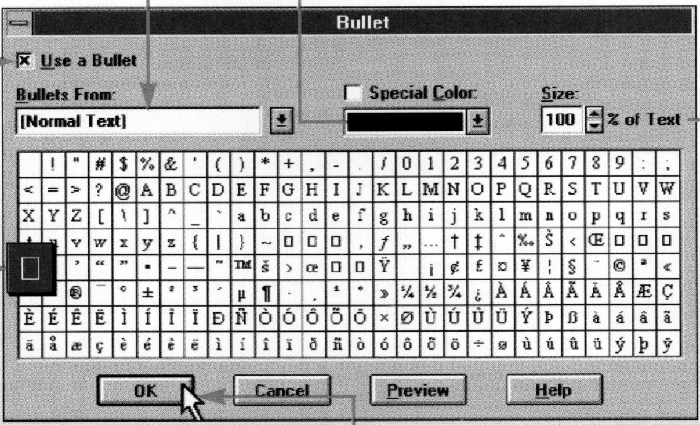

5 Select the desired bullet symbol.

Change the size of the bullet in relation to the text.

6 Choose OK.

Finding and Replacing Text

You can locate specific text quickly using the Find feature. You enter the text to find, and PowerPoint locates each occurrence of that text for you. You also can substitute new text for the located text by using the Replace feature.

To find text

1 Choose Edit, Find.

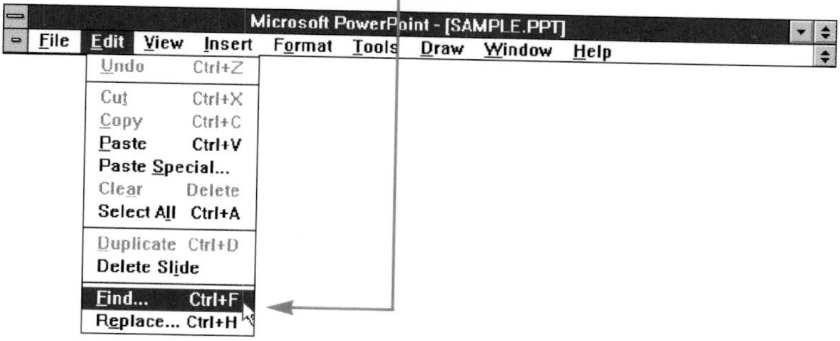

2 Type the text to locate.

3 Choose Find Next.

PowerPoint locates and selects the first occurrence of the text.

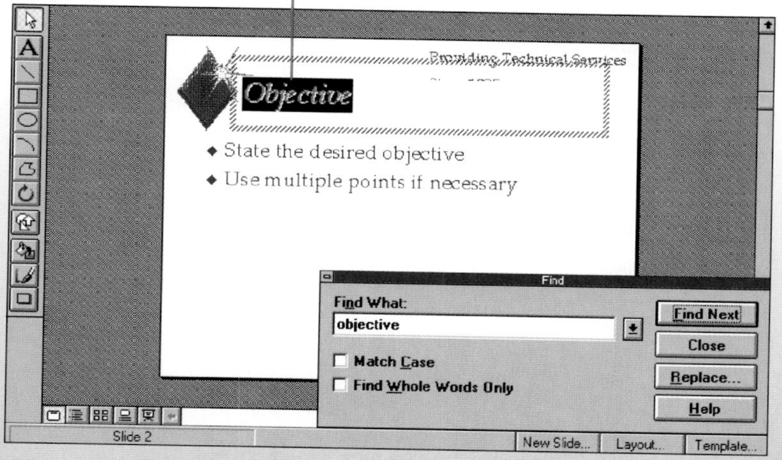

To replace text

1 Choose Edit, Replace.

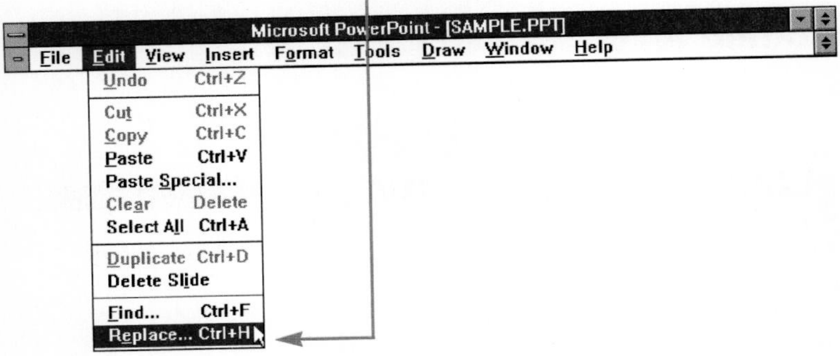

2 Type the text to find.

3 Type the replacement text.

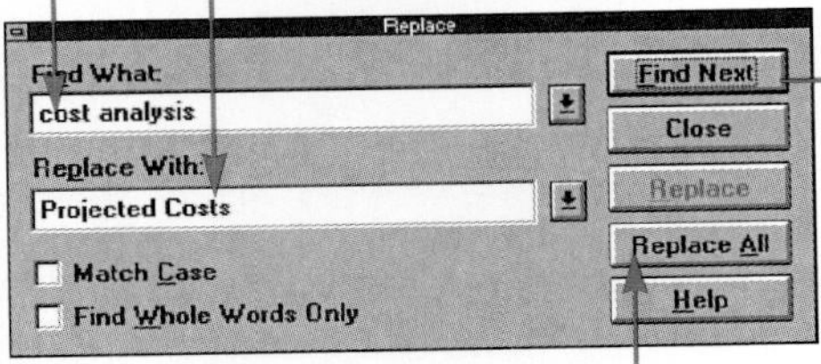

4 Choose Replace All to replace all occurrences of the text.

To find and replace text selectively, one occurrence at a time, use Find Next and Replace.

Index

D

G

H

I-K

L

M

N

O

P

Q-R

S

P. ELIADES

U-V

W-Z